A New
Housing Policy
for America

RECAPTURING THE AMERICAN DREAM

published in association with the
NATIONAL CENTER FOR POLICY ALTERNATIVES (NCPA)

NCPA is a non-profit center on progressive policy for state and local government. Since 1975, NCPA has provided policy models, direct technical assistance, and a broad publications program for the public and public officials. Its current program focuses on economic development, election law reform, environmental hazards, financial institutions reform, and women's economic justice and worker adjustment/job creation. For information write NCPA at 2000 Florida Ave., N.W., Suite 400, Washington, D.C. 20009.

A New Housing Policy for America

RECAPTURING THE AMERICAN DREAM

David C. Schwartz
Richard C. Ferlauto
Daniel N. Hoffman

with a Foreword by U.S. Senator Bill Bradley

TEMPLE UNIVERSITY PRESS
Philadelphia

Temple University Press, Philadelphia 19122
Copyright © 1988 by Temple University. All rights reserved
Published 1988
Printed in the United States of America by the Maple-Vail Book
Manufacturing Group Inc.

The paper used in this publication meets the minimum
requirements of American National Standard for Information
Sciences—Permanence of Paper for Printed Library Materials,
ANSI Z39.48-1984

LIBRARY OF CONGRESS
Library of Congress Cataloging-in-Publication Data

Schwartz, David C.
    A new housing policy for America : recapturing the American dream
    David C. Schwartz, Richard C. Ferlauto, Daniel N. Hoffman.
        p.   cm.
    Includes index.
    ISBN 0-87722-567-2.   ISBN 0-87722-568-0 (pbk.)
    1. Housing policy—United States.   I. Ferlauto, Richard C.
II. Hoffman, Daniel N.   III. Title.
HD7293.S92   1988
363.5'8'0973—dc19   88-1121
                                                             CIP

This book is dedicated, in love and gratitude,
to the memory of Milton Schwartz and Henrienne Rubowitz,
to Ethel Boomstein,
to Sandra, Todd, and Meredith Schwartz,
to Edward and Rochelle Ferlauto,
and to Rosalyn and Allan Hoffman

Contents

vii

Tables and Figures

TABLES

Foreword

THE HONORABLE BILL BRADLEY
United States Senator

As America prepares to enter the 1990s, our nation and its federal government confront both persistent problems and dramatic new opportunities. Our present trade and budget deficits must be reduced. Our economy must adjust to technologies and international relationships that are rapidly changing. As we protect the environment, upgrade our educational systems, and revitalize our cities we will be helping to renew our national economy. I note that each of these goals is important, is interrelated with other major goals, and that each will require new vision and new policy to be attained.

So it is with housing, the subject of David Schwartz's important book. A decent home in a suitable living environment for all Americans remains our national goal; homeownership remains the American dream. The declining rates of homeownership and explosive increase in homelessness that America experienced in the 1980s are a persistent problem and an unacceptable condition. Improving the state of American housing would greatly enhance the country's economy—adding millions of new jobs and tens of billions of dollars in federal tax revenues in the coming decade, if done correctly. It will require new policies, some of them identified in this book, to solve the housing problems we face.

As a United States Senator from New Jersey, I have observed firsthand some of the successful housing policies that the authors of

xi

this book have drafted and helped enact into law in my home state. Their landmark state legislation has helped expand homeownership opportunities, provide affordable rental apartments, and prevent homelessness for tens of thousands of New Jerseyans. Their legislation and policy ideas have been adopted as models, and won honors and awards from national and international bodies, bringing them much deserved recognition. Their proposed new housing policy for America should be studied by all who care about national public policy.

The authors properly identify many of the housing problems that have come upon us in the 1980s and that will develop in the 1990s. They document the decline in homeownership rates of the 1980s in America, showing that the percentage of families able to buy a home of their own has declined in our time, especially among young families and first-time home buyers. The authors detail, too, severe national problems in homelessness, in the decline of affordability and quality of rental apartments, and describe vividly the housing crisis confronting poor people in both urban and rural settings. We must all be concerned when a majority of America's 30 million tenants now live in dwelling units that our federal government acknowledges to be inadequate or overcrowded or cost-burdened. New policies must focus on the 10 million American families who are consigned to overcrowded or dilapidated homes and the 14 million more who pay much more of their incomes than they can afford for shelter.

But the authors go further. They document the housing problems we will confront in the 1990s. Huge demographic increases in frail elderly Americans, in single persons living alone, in single-parent households, in urban-located families of low and moderate income, all present needs for housing that simply doesn't exist and won't be provided by the costly, mostly suburban housing now being produced.

I believe the authors are correct not only in identifying some of the problems but in identifying some of the solutions. They advance a largely self-financing 10-point plan, one based upon successful initiatives developed at state and local levels here and in Western Europe and Japan. To expand homeownership opportunities, the authors propose, first, lease/purchase home-buying plans and policies designed to encourage employer-assisted housing programs, efforts that seem to me to be highly promising and cost-effective. They propose, too, policies aimed at encouraging shared equity or co-investment mortgages, federal downpayment assistance loans, and a countercyclical mortgage interest-rate buydown fund—proposals that are endorsed by major national housing organizations. These are proposals that are worthy of very serious consideration. To enhance needed rental unit production, a pay-as-you-go construction subsidy program is proposed that has worked well in a number of states. The authors also advocate innovative programs to help older and disabled Americans meet their housing needs.

One of the most important of the authors' proposals is for a Federal Prevention of Homelessness Law, a targeted crisis intervention program to aid those facing imminent eviction or foreclosure due to temporary loss of income beyond their control. This effort is modeled on the successful New Jersey Prevention of Homelessness Law, which has helped 15,000 persons remain in their own homes at a cost two to three times lower than shelters and 10 to 30 times lower than welfare motels, over the past three years.

I view these proposals as an excellent starting point for the debate and formulation of a new housing policy. They are pragmatic, targeted to needs, and cost-effective. They also recognize the diverse housing needs of this very diverse country of ours.

Finally, this book reminds us that shelter is so essential to the well being of all individuals, so fundamental to the functioning of all societies, that governments all over the world have come to accept one or more affirmative roles in helping people meet their needs. From the Homestead Acts of the nineteenth century to the present, our national government has played a major role in housing. This book challenges us to rededicate ourselves and our government to thinking and acting anew, in order to help all of the American people attain a decent home in a suitable living environment. Our nation, our government, and all of us as individuals can be energized by that challenge and informed by this book.

In sum, I think the book offers a clear, innovative and important vision of a better housing future for the American people—and suggests ways in which that better future can be achieved.

Authors' Preface

In 1987, as this book was being written, the sale of existing homes and new housing starts both declined, falling toward their lowest point in five years, while homeownership remained below 1980 levels. The percentage of families able to buy a home, which had fallen in every year of this decade and in every region of the country, remained unacceptably low—especially among young families and first-time home buyers. The explosive increase in homelessness that our nation has experienced throughout the 1980s also continued, indeed worsened, while we wrote: at year's end, many cities were reporting double-digit increases in homelessness, with people being turned away from full shelters and a dramatic expansion in families and working people being forced onto the streets. Some states reported that a majority of the homeless were children. The year 1987 witnessed, too, continuation of the country-wide shortage of decent rental apartments affordable by low- and moderate-income American families.

National housing policy, in 1987, continued to be unresponsive to these negative trends. Federal housing assistance was cut, once again, continuing the decade-long pattern of huge, unprecedented curtailments in federal housing involvement. Presidential proposals to increase already skyrocketing homeownership costs by imposing new fees and restrictions in federal mortgage programs continued to be debated actively. A new federal law was passed to aid the already homeless, followed by congressional action to cut more funds than the new law provided from existing federal programs, resulting in a net reduction in assistance (and a probable future increase in home-lessness). And, once again, no program was enacted to facilitate homeownership, to enhance rental unit construction, to prevent homelessness, or to prepare our housing stock for the great demo-graphic changes that our nation will experience in the 1990s.

For the past five years, we have traveled, lived, and worked in communities across America—seeking to help those communities, and their state governments, to meet the real and pressing housing needs of their people in a cost-effective manner and to do so in the face of the near-total federal abandonment of an affirmative national housing policy. For five years, we have been prompted to seek ac-tion by the manifest problems identified above, we have been prompted to seek community- and state-level action by what has seemed to us to be a federal housing policy largely unresponsive, irrelevant, or counterproductive. In that time, we have met, spoken, conferred, or corresponded with more than 1,000 other Americans, similarly engaged. This book, and its expansive but largely self-fi-nancing plan to meet America's housing needs in the 1990s, derives largely from our practical experiences and the lessons that other practitioners have taught us. This preface briefly outlines some of those experiences and acknowledges some of our debt to others.

Some Background

That we would come to write a book on national housing policy was not apparent to us five years ago, in January 1982. At that time, David—a legislator and political scientist—had just been named Chairman of the newly created state Assembly Housing and Urban and Policy Committee. Dan, after studying public policy and admin-istering Indian housing programs in Minnesota, had returned to New Jersey to manage community development programs for the city of Plainfield, and to provide legislative research assistance to David. Rich was working in urban neighborhoods in Connecticut organiz-ing low-income people around affordable housing issues. And, in 1982, despite 10 years of fair housing and zoning litigation, known collectively as the "Mt. Laurel" process, New Jersey's executive and legislative branches had done little to support low- and moderate-income housing programs. But in 1982 that situation changed. It changed because a man froze to death on a heat grate in Newark and New Jersey's homelessness problem became a public scandal overnight.

In the months that followed, we helped put together a legislative coalition of housing activists, housing industry leaders, and the religious community in what we refer to as the "All Everybody Coalition." The coalition's support allowed the passage of a Prevention of Homelessness bill, the merger of the state's housing and mortgage finance agencies into a single agency with expanded authority, a state housing trust fund to provide permanent financial support for low- and moderate-income housing development, and a series of bills to encourage tenant ownership and management programs, the conversion of abandoned housing and commercial properties to housing, and municipal participation in low- and moderate-income housing projects. Some of the programs initiated by the legislature have been adopted in other states; a number have won national and/or international recognition.

But, at the same time that New Jerseyans were doing more for those in need of housing, the impact of a federal government's doing dramatically less for those in need of shelter created a crisis. We began to explore other questions: what else should states be doing to encourage low- and moderate-income housing production and what should federal housing policy look like in the post-Reagan years? To begin answering these questions, we established the American Affordable Housing Conference at Rutgers University. The purpose of the Conference is to underatke applied research in areas concerning the financing and production of affordable housing. Its first activity was a conference held in 1986, "Towards a New Housing Policy for America," that attracted over 350 national participants. This book is a direct result of the ideas that were discussed at the Conference.

Working with the Housing Task Force of the National Conference of State Legislatures and with the American Affordable Housing Conference, we have traveled throughout the country listening to housing advocates and professionals, and have attended numerous conferences, meetings, and hearings. We have learned much. We found that the federal call to state and local governments, non-profits, and the religious community to be creative and innovative in solving the nation's housing needs has been heeded by immensely able and dedicated people. We were continually impressed by the ability and creativity of the non-profits and local and state governments, but we were equally distressed by the fact that these housing providers can produce only a tiny fraction of the needed units each year. Despite the efforts of many states, localities, and non-profits, the nation's need for low- and moderate-income housing has increased dramatically every year during the decade of the 1980s.

Wherever we have traveled, we have found a deep concern on the part of legislators, non-profits, and housing professionals about the negative impact of the current federal policies upon future generations of Americans. More troubling, we found that even after seven years of Reaganomics and a 70 percent cut in federal housing assistance in the name of budget austerity, too few in positions of national leadership are willing to admit that federal housing programs neither caused nor can solve the federal budget crisis, and that a national development strategy of building housing is good for those in need of housing, those in need of jobs, and a government in need of tax revenue.

We are also distressed by much of what passes for a national debate on housing. Too many who would protect the poor from draconian housing budget cuts have isolated the poor in a political wasteland where their needs could be ignored and then forgotten by neglecting what we believe are the legitimate dreams of working people for homeownership or a decent, affordable apartment, dreams that are within the capacity of our nation to make a reality. We are convinced that only by linking the aspirations of the middle class, particularly young families, directly with the needs of the poor and the homeless will the needs of either be politically addressed.

From a programmatic standpoint, we believe that a housing debate focusing on fixing 20-year-old programs, or lobbying for "back to the future" budgets, contending that if HUD appropriations were returned to their 1978 levels the nation's housing needs would be resolved, is not credible. No one could be excited about such a debate. (Only a small number of poor and even fewer middle-class families are direct beneficiaries of federal housing programs.)

To be credible, a new housing policy for low- and moderate-income families must rely on some new and better programs with clearly defined costs and beneficiaries. With this in mind, we sought out and attempted to develop effective programs that are linked politically to important electoral coalitions and fiscally to tax revenues that an energized housing industry would generate. Many of the programs discussed in this book have been implemented by state or local governments, or by the governments of other nations. These programs have a record of utility and efficiency. We believe that these programs can be the model for a new national housing policy. The excuse that the federal government cannot implement a national program is simply untrue and unacceptable. We have met hundreds of dedicated housing advocates and professionals throughout the nation who each day create new standards in efficiency and compassion. There is a wealth of talent throughout this land that can implement the programs that we advocate, if there is a government commitment to enacting them.

ACKNOWLEDGMENTS

Many people deserve special acknowledgment for so generously sharing their knowledge, experience, wisdom, and patience with us. Those who helped directly with the writing and research include Bill Berlin, John Glascock, Susan Gittelman, Greg Sofer, Frances Disori. Data and/or intellectual perspectives of the following persons proved invaluable: John Sidor and his staff at the Council of State Community Affairs Agencies, Warren Lasko and his staff at the Mortgage Bankers Association of America, Alice Shabacoff, Peter Dreier, Woody Wildrow, John Atlas, Allan Fishbein, Michael Carliner, Forest Paffenberg, David Rosen, John Lee, Jim Logue and his staff, Joe Belden, Mary Nenno, Bud Kanitz, Paul Grogin, Christine Minnehan, David Rosen, Helen Seitz, Lawrence O. Houstoun, and U.S. Senator Frank Lautenberg and his staff. We deeply appreciate the careful, selfless office help of Joyce Fishberg, Vicki D'Andrea, and Renee Herman, and the editorial assistance of Bob Stumberg, Doris Braendel, and Susan Lawrence. The financial and intellectual resources of Rutgers, The State University of New Jersey, was crucial to us at many points in the research and writing. Many of the national organizations involved with housing issues, upon which we relied for material and data included in this book, are listed in the Appendix.

Finally, the encouragement provided to us by the continuing interest and support of Bill Bradley, U.S. Senator from New Jersey, merits special acknowledgment.

A New
Housing Policy
for America

RECAPTURING THE AMERICAN DREAM

1
The Need for a New National Housing Policy

In the 1980s, the United States experienced five broad housing trends, each of which evidenced a downturn in the living conditions of millions of American families—middle-class, working-class, and poor. First, there was a decline in homeownership, national in scope; following 35 years of steady increase, the percentage of Americans able to buy a home of their own decreased every year from 1980 to 1987, a trend particularly marked among young families and first-time home buyers.[1] Second, a dramatic, explosive increase in homelessness took place, leaving millions of people to live, and die, in the streets and alleyways of America.[2] Third, the affordability, availability, and quality of the nation's rental housing stock decreased, to the point where a majority of America's 30 million tenants now live in dwelling units that the government considers to be inadequate, overcrowded, or cost-burdened.[3] Fourth, the shortage of housing affordable by the poor reached crisis proportions as more poor people, with less money, sought fewer available apartments, of declining quality, at sharply rising rents.[4] Finally, a pattern of stagnation and decline in the quality of the existing housing stock emerged, consigning 10 million families to inadequate or overcrowded dwelling units and 24 million families to units that the government classified as having "a housing problem."[5]

At the same time that these trends were developing, the federal government sharply cut aid to housing in a number of areas. Sup-

3

port for the construction of new housing by the private sector was cut back, as were expenditures for the production and rehabilitation of public housing and funds to local governments to provide home-ownership opportunities for low- and moderate-income families. Assistance to low- and moderate-income tenants and the number of low- and moderate-income tenants eligible to receive housing aid were also cut. In addition, the government reduced tax incentives to the private sector for the production of rental housing, and decreased federal loans to low- and moderate-income homeowners for the rehabilitation of substandard units. It also reduced housing assistance to elderly and handicapped persons, American Indians, and farmers, groups more likely than many others to need such assistance.[6]

For the 1990s, most analysts agree that at least four demographic trends are likely to pose challenges to our housing policies. First, there will be a huge increase (about 90 percent) in the proportion of Americans who are "old elderly" (i.e., over 75 years of age), a significant number of whom will need new or substantially rehabilitated housing suited to the needs of frail, elderly persons.[7] Second, we can expect a sharp upturn (almost 75 percent) in the number of single persons living alone and a large augmentation in the number of single-parent, female-headed households—population sectors that tend to have lower incomes and smaller family sizes.[8] Third, a major increase is expected in the population of young families in prime first-home-buying years (30–45),[9] families of increasingly smaller size with incomes below the national median. Finally, the concentration of poor families in cities is likely to intensify.[10]

These trends pose real problems for housing policy because, in each case, the gaps and mismatches between available housing and the needs of these growing population sectors are expanding as a function of market forces. For example, tomorrow's smaller young families will need smaller starter homes available at prices, down-payment requirements, and mortgage rates they can afford. But the housing construction trend of the 1980s has been to larger homes[11] at higher prices,[12] while home financing trends in the 1980s have been toward higher downpayment requirements and higher interest rates.[13] Similarly, the trends toward larger homes and fewer available lower-rent apartments are inconsistent with the needs of single persons and the pocketbooks of single-parent, female-headed households. Another example of a widening gap is the increasing concentration of poor families in cities while the vast bulk of new housing starts is suburban[14] and the apartment stock of cities is shrinking because of gentrification and abandonment.[15] What makes these probable trends of the 1990s particularly challenging is that, since each of the fastest-growing population sectors tends to have lower-than-average incomes and savings, unaided market forces are less likely to adapt large numbers of dwelling units to their needs.

National housing policy in the 1980s has not prepared us for the emerging trends of the 1990s. Cuts have been made in programs that could have been used to rehabilitate the homes of the frail elderly. Cuts have also been made in funding programs under which the conversion of older, larger homes into smaller units for singles and single-parents households could have been accomplished. Both direct assistance and tax incentives for the construction of affordable urban apartments have also been reduced.[16] In addition, national housing policy has not included any program to aid young families attain homeownership.

In important ways, then, it seems that the United States has been receding, the federal government retreating, from the great goal of decent, affordable housing for all Americans. Across the spectrum of national housing concerns—on issues of homeownership, homelessness, the affordability and quality of rental stock, and planning for future housing needs—recent federal policies would appear to be largely irrelevant, inadequate, or counterproductive.

America needs a new housing policy.

In order to determine what that policy should be, however, we must look more closely at the problems it must address. The next section, "Housing Problems in the 1980s," presents a detailed consideration of the decline in homeownership, the increase in homelessness, the diminution in affordability, availability, and quality of rental housing units (especially for the poor), and the stagnation and decline in the physical condition of the nation's housing stock. The following section, "Housing Problems and Needs in the 1990s," explores the dimensions, and housing implications, of those major demographic trends identified above: projected substantial increases in the population share represented by the "old elderly," by singles and single-parent, female-headed households, by younger, smaller families, and by the urban poor. Then, in the section on "The Benefits of Meeting Our Housing Needs," a specific and conservative estimate is made of the number of jobs, the quantum of economic activity, and the amount of tax revenues that would accrue from specific levels of housing activity targeted to the problems and trends identified in this chapter. Our section on the "Recent and Current Federal Housing Policies" identifies the basic thrust of U.S. public policies toward housing in the 1980s as an almost unilinear movement to withdraw the federal government from involvement in the provision of shelter. A detailed analysis of federal budgetary and tax actions for the 1980–1987 period is juxtaposed to the housing needs and problems identified earlier.

That juxtaposition reveals a nearly diametric opposition between national housing requirements and national housing policies. For the 1980s, we find that national policies are apt to produce more homelessness and less homeownership, more deterioration and less improvement in the affordability, availability, and quality of housing. For the 1990s, we conclude that continuation of recent and current policy will not produce more housing, better targeted to the life needs of our increasingly diverse population; in fact, current policy is likely to yield less housing, increasingly ill-suited to the family sizes, job locations, and physical needs of our most rapidly growing population groups. And we find, too, that continuation of recent and present policy will tend not to engender the jobs, economic activity, and tax revenues that a more proactive policy might achieve.

Housing Problems in the 1980s

Declining Rates of Homeownership

For most families, owning a home is a basic part of the American dream, a goal for which they save and sacrifice, a symbol of family security, stability, and success. The housing preferences of the American people have been surveyed repeatedly in the last 40 years and each survey confirms a fundamental and nearly universal aspiration to homeownership.[17] Despite great variability in the methods, the population studied, and the era in which the study was done, an overwhelming percentage of Americans (often 90 percent or higher) report themselves as wanting to own a home. A 1984 study by the Roper organization is illustrative: 9 out of 10 adult Americans under 35 regarded homeownership as their highest personal priority.[18]

Between 1940 and 1980, the dream of homeownership came true for an ever larger number and percentage of Americans. In that period, American homeownership levels grew from 44 percent to 65

Table 1
Percentage of U.S. Homeownership, by Age of Householder, 1981–1987

Age	1981	1982	1983	1984	1985	1986	1987*
Total	65.4	64.8	64.6	64.5	64.1	63.8	63.8
Less than 25	20.7	19.3	18.8	17.9	17.4	17.2	16.7
25–29	41.7	38.6	38.3	38.6	37.7	36.7	35.5
30–34	59.3	57.1	55.4	54.8	54.7	53.6	53.3
35–39	68.9	67.6	66.5	66.1	65.7	64.8	64.0
40–44	73.7	73.0	72.8	72.3	71.8	70.5	70.8
45–49	76.2	76.0	75.2	74.6	74.9	74.1	74.5
50–54	78.3	78.8	78.8	78.4	77.4	78.1	77.5
55–59	80.0	80.0	80.1	80.1	79.1	80.0	80.1
60–64	80.0	80.1	79.7	79.9	79.6	79.8	80.9
65–69	77.6	78.0	78.7	79.3	79.4	79.8	79.1
70–74	75.4	75.2	75.3	75.5	76.7	77.2	76.1
75 or more	69.8	71.0	71.9	71.5	70.4	70.0	71.1

*First quarter.
Source: H. James Brown and John Yinger, *Home Ownership and Housing Affordability in the United States, 1963–1985* (Cambridge, Mass.: Joint Center for Housing Studies of MIT and Harvard, 1986), p. 7.

percent. Since 1980, however, homeownership rates have declined. In 1980, for the first time in 35 years, the percentage of citizens able to buy a home declined, and has declined every year since then. Table 1 shows the overall drop in homeownership from 65.6 percent in 1980 to 63.8 percent in 1986 and the steep fall in homeownership among young families (which is discussed in detail later in this chapter). This overall drop in the homeownership rate means that more than 1.6 million American families who would have been able to own a home at the 1980 rate were denied that chance in the 1980–1986 period.[19]

The problem is national in scope. Table 2 reveals considerable regional variation in the shrinking homeownership rate, but the direction is the same—down—in every part of the country. All across America, millions of citizens are finding that the door to homeownership is shut.

Part of the reason for the decline in homeownership in the 1980s is, of course, the skyrocketing cost of buying and maintaining a home.[20] While the median income of America's families was relatively unchanged from 1977 to 1986, expressed in constant dollars, and personal savings rates fell sharply, the median price of both

Table 2
Homeownership Rate, by Region, 1981–1985

Year	Total	Northeast	Midwest	South	West
1981	65.4	61.3	70.2	67.4	59.8
1982	64.8	61.1	69.4	66.7	59.4
1983	64.7	60.4	69.1	67.4	59.0
1984	64.6	61.1	68.6	66.8	59.4
1985	64.1	60.9	67.3	66.7	59.2
Changes					
1980–1985	−1.3	−.4	−2.9	−.7	−.6

Source: H. James Brown and John Yinger, *Home Ownership and Housing Affordability in the United States, 1963–1985* (Cambridge, Mass.: Joint Center for Housing Studies of MIT and Harvard, 1986), p. 7.

new and existing homes just about doubled (see Table 3). Home-ownership costs in 1985 were three times higher than they were, on average, in the 1970s. Between 1970 and 1986, housing prices and mortgage interest rates in the United States rose four to five times faster than did real household incomes. In fact, the real costs of homeownership in 1981–1985 increased even faster than the sharply growing real costs of renting (which went up far faster than infla-tion)—a fact that also discouraged would-be home buyers.

Homeownership has also suffered from the dramatic increase in

Table 3
Median Price of New and Existing Homes, 1977–1986

Year	New	Existing
1977	48,000	42,900
1978	55,700	48,700
1979	62,900	55,700
1980	64,600	62,200
1981	68,900	66,400
1982	69,300	67,800
1983	75,300	70,300
1984	79,900	72,400
1985	84,300	75,500
1986	92,000	80,300

Source: Information supplied by National Association of Home Builders, Research Office, Wash-ington, D.C.

Table 4
Average Annual Mortgage Interest Rates, 1977–1986

Year	Conventional	VA
1977	8.82	8.2
1978	9.37	8.8
1979	10.59	9.7
1980	12.46	11.5
1981	14.39	13.7
1982	14.73	14.9
1983	12.26	12.1
1984	11.99	12.8
1985	11.24	12.0
1986	9.87	10.4

Source: Information supplied by Mortgage Bankers Association of America and U.S. Veterans Administration.

mortgage interest rates that the American housing economy endured throughout the 1980s. Table 4 depicts the extreme fluctuations in mortgage interest rates that took place during the eighties. These fluctuations, which were destabilizing to American housing production and purchasing decisions in themselves, reveal a sharp upward trend. Leading housing economists now posit that a 1 percent increase in current conventional interest rates tends to force at least 10 percent of potential home buyers (400,000 families) out of the market,[21] and a 1 percent increase (based on 1986 home-buying levels) in Veterans Administration (VA) mortgage interest rates tends to drive 1.5 million home buyers out of the housing market. (The larger impact of VA loan cost increases results from the far larger pool of potential borrowers at the lower VA rates.) Table 4 also reveals a 10-year pattern of increase in conventional interest rates in excess of 1 percent and a similar pattern above 2 percent for VA rates. These data, coupled with the low rate of income growth and declining rates of personal savings, help explain America's lost homeownership opportunities in the past decade.

The impact of high mortgage interest rates on homeownership levels was especially pronounced in the 1980–1981 period, when the percentage of American families who could afford the median-priced new home fell from above 50 percent to below 25 percent. Mortgage interest rates, of course, have moderated from the astronomical levels of the early 1980s, but they are still historically high relative to inflation. Mortgage rates foreseeable for the rest of the 1980s, if unchecked, will continue to deny homeownership to millions of Americans.

Another major factor pushing homeownership rates lower in the 1980s has been large and expanding downpayment requirements. In 1978, the typical home purchaser had to make a downpayment of about 33 percent of his or her yearly income to obtain a mortgage; by 1985, that had risen to 50 percent. Between 1984 and 1987, the percentage of lenders willing to make home mortgage loans for more than 90 percent of value (i.e., at less than 10 percent down) declined significantly. This came, in part, as a result of changed underwriting requirements in the secondary mortgage market (which buys mortgage loans from financial institutions that originate mortgages) and has had the effect of sharply increasing income requirements and raising mortgage rates. A 1987 U.S. government survey of major lenders found only 8 percent willing to make conventional loans at less than 10 percent down. Three years earlier, 25 percent of U.S. mortgage loans were made for more than 90 percent of sale price.[22]

Many lenders are demanding 15 percent, 20 percent, or more down, percentages creating a large new class of Americans—discouraged home buyers. These are people—mostly young families and first-time home buyers—whose income approximates or exceeds the national median and who would have the earning capacity of afford monthly mortgage payments on the median-priced American home if only they could accrue the demanded downpayment.

A 20 percent downpayment on the average home sold in 1985 was $15,000—a figure far above what most families have in liquid assets. Since loans with less than 20 percent down typically require mortgage insurance, many Americans are caught between downpayment requirements they cannot meet and paying additional insurance costs. Even at 10 percent down, the average American cannot afford the average American home. In fact, the average American hasn't been able to afford the average American home since 1975.[23]

Today, despite all the increase in two-income families, an affordability gap of about $10,000 a year separates the average family, earning $28,000 a year, from the median-priced home. In 1975, a family needed an income of only $15,775 to purchase the average new single-family home; by 1985, it needed an annual income of $37,657. This represents a 132 percent increase in income needed to buy the average new home, in a decade in which American median family income actually rose by less than 2 percent.[24]

The rate of decline in homeownership has been steepest for young

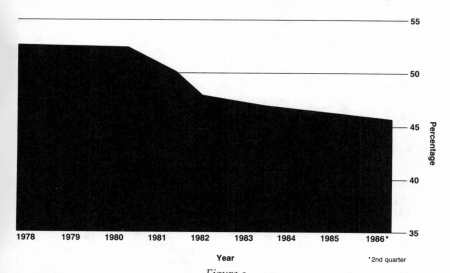

Figure 1
Declining Homeowner Rates for Households Aged 30 to 34 Years, 1978–1986
Source: National Association of Home Builders, National Association of Realtors, and Mortgage Bankers Association of America, *Toward a National Housing Policy* (Washington, D.C.: The Associations, 1987), p. 3.

families (i.e., those headed by persons 25–35 years old) and first-time home buyers. Among families headed by 25–29-year-olds, homeownership levels nose-dived from 41.7 percent to 35.5 percent between 1981 and 1987; among families headed by 30–34-year-olds, the rate skidded from 59.3 percent to 53.3 percent, falling each year from 1981 to 1987. In fact, homeownership opportunities for families in every age bracket below age 50 fell from 1981 to 1987 (see Table 1 and Figure 1). If the rate of homeownership among 25–34-year-olds were today what it was in 1978, there would be an additional 1.6 to 2.6 million homeowners in that age grouping alone.[25]

The waning of homeownership among young families, like that among the population as a whole, reflects a problem that is national in scale and scope. Figure 2 shows that the drop-off in homeownership among younger families between 1978 and 1985 occurred in every region, with variation only in degree of the downward trend. America's younger families were disappointed and disadvantaged in their hope of becoming homeowners in every part of this country during the 1980s.

It was not always thus. Today's young families confront barriers

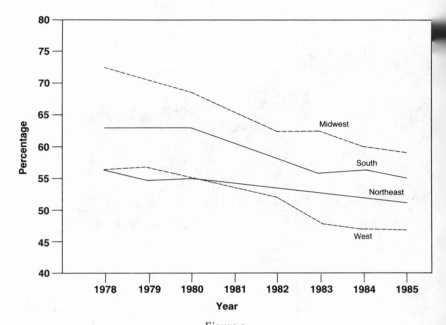

Figure 2
Homeownership for Households Aged 30 to 34 Years, by Region, 1978–1985
Source: National Governors' Association, *Decent and Affordable Housing for All* (Washington, D.C.:
The Association, 1986), p. 4.

to homeownership that previous generations simply did not have to
face. Figures from the Urban Institute and other national sources
make this point graphically:

- In 1959, a typical 30-year-old had his or her real income increase 49 percent over the next 10 years, and paid 16 percent
  of income for the average home.
- In 1973, an average 30-year-old saw income decline slightly over
  the next 10 years and paid 21 percent of his or her income for
  the average home.
- In 1983, a 30-year-old not only earned less than the typical 30-
  year-old in 1973 (in constant dollars), but paid 40 percent of
  income in mortgage payments. Today, according to some analysts, that 30-year-old would be paying 44 percent of income
  for housing.[26]

These unprecedented obstacles to homeownership among our young families were put into context by Anthony Downs, in a recent Brookings Institution publication: "The percentage of all potential first-time home buyers who can actually afford to purchase homes at today's interest rates and prices is much lower than it was in the 1950's, 1960's and 1970's."[27]

Little wonder, then, that a 1986 report by the MIT-Harvard Joint Center for Housing Studies warned that "young households feel thwarted by the high cost of homeownership and alarmed about their prospects of ever being able to buy."[28] The MIT-Harvard study also found that an increasing percentage of discouraged young home buyers were limited by the downpayment requirement, not just by mortgage requirement totals.

Young families are thwarted, too, by the absence of new starter homes in many of America's regional housing economies. Mass production of small homes aimed at the first-time home buyer, once a staple of the home-building industry, is now largely a thing of the past. More than half of the country's active home builders are now aiming their product at the trade-up market (where demand is strong) rather than at first-time home buyers. By 1990, some 80 percent of America's new homes are expected to be customized for the trade-up market.[29]

The contraction of homeownership in the general population and among young families derives largely from housing economics, from a gap between costs and income. It is mostly cost, not choice, that has driven down American homeownership rates. An MIT-Harvard Joint Housing Center study put it aptly: "Changes in living arrangements, lifestyles and labor force configurations have been gradual and cannot explain the dramatic decline in homeownership."[30] Given today's cost factors in housing, it is not surprising that the United States is also experiencing a diminution of homeownership among lower-income families and a concentration of homeownership among upper-income Americans.[31] Figure 3 shows that homeownership, in the 1980s, is twice as prevalent among the highest income grouping of Americans as it is in the poorest grouping. More significantly, Figure 3 shows that, since 1973, homeownership has been declining for the lower-income 40 percent of American society, has been relatively stagnant for the middle 40 percent of our population, and has been rising only among the wealthiest 20 percent.[32]

To some extent these trends represent changes in the demo-

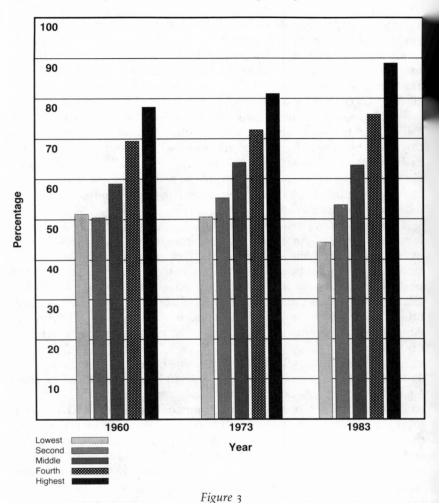

Figure 3
Homeownership Rate, by Income Quintile, All Households, 1960, 1973, and 1983
Source: National Association of Home Builders, *Low- and Moderate-Income Housing: Progress, Problems, and Prospects* (Washington, D.C.: The Association, January 1986), p. 23.

graphic composition of the different income groupings. The lower-income 40 percent now disproportionately contains single mothers and people living alone, subpopulations that have lower purchasing predispositions at all income levels. But even if only married low-income households are considered, the 1973–1983 period witnessed a disproportionate shift toward homeownership by the relatively rich and a decline in homeownership among the relatively poor.[33]

Low-income homeownership is disproportionately concentrated among older people. This has at least three possible interpretations. First, it may be that some lower-income families had higher incomes earlier in life, and so could afford homeownership. Second, some lower-income families may have been forced to postpone homeownership until after what are ordinarily the prime home-buying years. Or, third, a substantial and disproportionate number (and percentage) of young low-income families may have been priced out of the home-buying market. It is probable that all three interpretations have some validity.[34]

The concentration of homeownership among wealthier people, while less well-off citizens are finding it harder and harder to enter the home-buying market, gives rise to reasonable fears that the United States is becoming two separate and distinct societies when it comes to housing. "We seem to be drifting toward a division in American housing between the 'haves' and the 'have nots,' " the President of the Federal National Mortgage Association said in February of 1987, explaining that those who had been able to buy houses in the 1970s, or earlier now had the equity to buy new, larger homes in the trade-up market while young, first-time buyers were having a difficult time affording any sort of dwelling. The President of the Mortgage Bankers Association of America put it more bluntly, saying: "The opportunity for low-income families and first-time buyers to afford a home is vanishing."[35]

Certainly the American housing economy is experiencing a simultaneous feast and famine in the late 1980s. Wealthier Americans are buying larger and larger houses. The average size of new homes is now at an all-time high, as is the number of Americans adding to, renovating, and repairing their homes and the dollar outlays spent on these additions and renovations.[36] Rising home equity reserves for those who bought a home earlier are leading to a strong rise in housing starts in the lucrative, growing trade-up market.[37] And all this is occurring while millions of hard-working American families just can't get started in a home of their own.

Borrowing from the labor economics concept of the "discouraged workers" (one who has given up looking for work and is no longer counted in the ranks of the unemployed workforce), we can term some of these families who cannot get started in a home of their own "discouraged home buyers." To get some idea of the usefulness of this concept we participated in a July 1987 national survey of 20 large mortgage companies with branches in every state.[38] Executives in these companies were asked to estimate the home-purchasing consequences of past, recent, and projected mortgage interest-rate increases and then to estimate the percentages of would-be home buyers who would be able to qualify for mortgages if an interest rate buydown plan (of about 2 percentage points) or a downpayment assistance (second mortgage deferred payment) program were available. Survey results indicated that recent and antic-ipatable interest rate increases into the double-digits range tend, or will tend, to drive about 10 percent of mortgage applicants out of the housing market altogether, and force about 45 percent into non-fixed-rate-financing instruments (e.g., adjustable rate mortgages, balloon payments, etc.). On the current base of approximately 4 million mortgage applications annually, this suggests the possible dis-appointment of about 400,000 discouraged home buyers annually (which is consistent with the number of current mortgage applicants denied credit) and an annual pool of more than 1 million would-be potential home purchasers requiring new forms of home financing. Asked what percentage of mortgage applicants who fail to qualify at double-digit rates would achieve credit worthiness if mortgage inter-est rates were brought down by, say, 2 percentage points, the sur-vey respondents estimated that about 40 percent would be aided by such a program. Computed on a base of 400,000 previously non-qualifying applicants, a buydown program would help more than 150,000 American families to afford homeownership. A similar, and obviously somewhat overlapping, number of families were esti-mated as likely to be helped by a downpayment assistance program.

Beyond discouraged home buyers, we must also take note of the large and growing problem of mortgage default and delinquency in the America of the eighties. In 1985, default rose to almost 1 percent of all extent mortgages, the highest default rate in more than a de-cade. The foreclosure rate has almost doubled since 1980. The vol-ume of payments made by private mortgage insurance companies to cover mortgage default has increased 10 times since 1980.[39]

Housing problems in the 1980s? Millions of Americans cannot buy a home and too many cannot keep the one they've got. When millions of young Americans who want to buy homes can't, and hundreds of thousands who own their homes can't pay their mort-gages, the number of renters is increased—and that drives up rents. An already severe shortage of rental units in some housing markets is made worse. The housing consequences of declining homeownership rates are thus radiated throughout the nation, impacting on the availability and affordability of apartments. Let us examine, then, housing conditions of the more than 30 million American tenants.

Rental Housing: Problems and Crises

As homeownership has declined since 1980, the number and proportion of renter families has grown, reaching 35 percent of all American households in 1985. The MIT-Harvard Joint Center for Housing Studies attributes much of this growth in renting to high and expanding costs of homeownership and notes that the number of renters increased in all income classes and age groups from 1980 to 1985. And as the number and proportion of apartment dwellers grew, so did their housing problems.[40] Between 1975 and 1983, the percentage of tenants living in overcrowded conditions increased by 3.4 percent, while overcrowded homeowner units declined by 35 percent. Cost-burdened tenant households jumped by 59 percent. The percentage of renter families in housing units that the U.S. Department of Housing and Urban Development (HUD) recognized as inadequate, crowded, or cost-burdened grew by 31 percent, up to 15 million households. By 1983 a majority of America's tenant households were officially classified by HUD as having "a housing problem."

The affordability of, and living conditions in, the nation's rental housing stock has been declining for more than a decade. From 1975 to 1984, real gross rents (including utilities and adjusted for inflation) rose by 18 percent nationwide (outstripping inflation substantially), while the median income of renters fell by about 12 percent.[41] Since 1980, real rents have risen between 6 and 25 percent in various regional housing markets, while tenant income had been relatively flat or has declined. Median rents increased from about 20 percent of income in 1970 to 29 percent in 1983. They are substantially higher now, in relation to income, and are expected to rise by 20 to 25 percent, above inflation, in the next few years.[42]

Figure 4 graphically illustrates the escalating rent burdens that tenants have borne since 1974. In sum, the percentage of families with rent burdens above one-quarter of their income increased from 40 percent in 1974 to 60 percent in 1983. The share of households

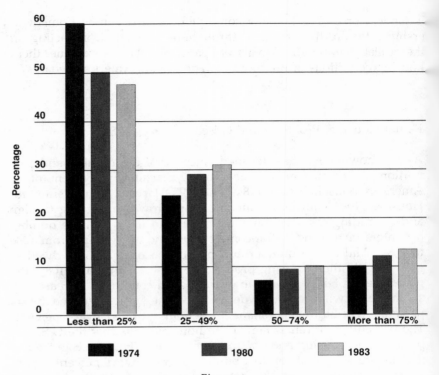

Figure 4
Escalating Rent Burdens: Percentage Distribution of Rent Burdens, All Renter
Households, 1974 and 1983
Source: H. James Brown and John Yinger, *Home Ownership and Housing Affordability in the United
States, 1963–1985* (Cambridge, Mass.: Joint Center for Housing Studies of MIT and Harvard,
1986), p. 15.

with rent burdens above 75 percent of income rose from 8 percent
to 13 percent.

Regrettably, these rent increases did not buy better housing. HUD
data show that the percentage of rental units with no heating equipment increased between 1974 and 1983.[43] A Ford Foundation study
asserts the number of renters living in inadequate units grew by
200,000 between 1978 and 1981.[44] The MIT-Harvard Joint Center on
Housing Studies designed "an index of structural inadequacy" and
found the "number of renter households in inadequate housing actually rose by nearly 7% in the 1974 to 1983 period from 3.60 million
to 3.85 million." The Joint Center reports that the increase in struc-

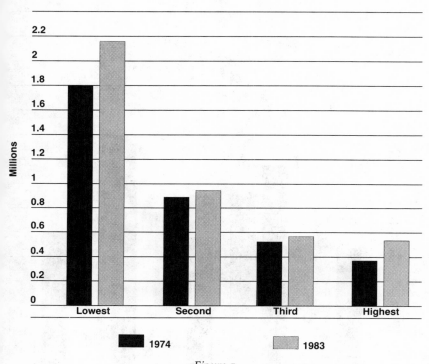

Figure 5
Renters with Inadequate Housing, by Income Class, 1974 and 1983
Source: H. James Brown and John Yinger, *Home Ownership and Housing Affordability in the United States, 1963–1985* (Cambridge, Mass.: Joint Center for Housing Studies of MIT and Harvard, 1986), p. 15.

tural inadequacy occurred even though many substandard units were removed from the housing stock between 1974 and 1983. Indeed, these results imply that for every 100 inadequate units taken off the market during this period, 107 additional units slipped into the inadequate category due to a lack of maintenance and upkeep.[45]

William Apgar of MIT, writing in 1987, notes a continued deterioration of the affordable rental housing inventory in America's cities. Apgar observes that, from 1974 to 1981, 679,000 inadequate city units were withdrawn from the housing inventory, only to be replaced by 757,000 newly deteriorated units.[46]

Figures 5 and 6 show the increase in renters living in inadequate units from 1974 to 1983, a deterioration of living conditions for all income classes, for almost all demographic groups, and for all age

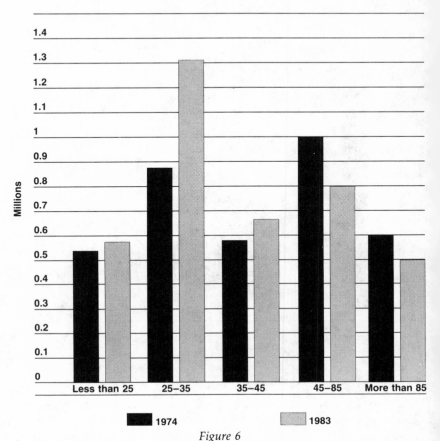

Figure 6
Renters with Inadequate Housing, by Age Bracket, 1974 and 1983
Source: H. James Brown and John Yinger, *Home Ownership and Housing Affordability in the United States, 1963–1985* (Cambridge, Mass.: Joint Center for Housing Studies of MIT and Harvard, 1986), p. 14.

groups under 45. Single parents, younger families, and low-income tenants, however, fared worst.

Not all indicators of housing quality in rental units show a decline, of course. HUD continues to collect data on pre-World War II housing problems (lack of indoor plumbing, no private bathrooms in apartments, etc.). On these indicators, the incidence of deficiencies has been dropping for decades, and improvement continued to be shown during the 1980s.[47]

The issues of affordability and living conditions categorized above as "housing problems" for most tenants have become desperate—truly critical—for the tens of millions of Americans who are low-income renters. As a class, they tend to face crushing rent burdens in a shrinking supply of dilapidated, deteriorating apartments. America's tenant population is disproportionately made up of low- and moderate-income families.[48] In 1984, the median income of all renters was about $15,000—roughly half the national average. Forty percent of all renter households are in the bottom income class; 27 percent of all renters are below the government's poverty line. More than half of all tenants are between 25 and 44, and more than half are single or single parents, categories that tend to have the lowest incomes.

HUD generally categorizes a family as having a "very low income" if the annual dollar value of its earnings and benefits does not exceed 50 percent of the local area median. By these standards, 27 percent of all U.S. households (about 23 million families) have "very low income." These families, overwhelmingly, are tenants: they occupy half of all inadequate housing units, 56 percent of all severely inadequate units, and 72 percent of all cost-burdened units. Between 1974 and 1983, very-low-income families increased by 20 percent, and the housing conditions under which they live deteriorated on every indicator HUD publishes. Forty percent of chronically poor renter households, 10 million families, lived in structurally unsound, overcrowded units.[49]

The rent burdens poor families are paying in the 1980s are simply crushing. The MIT-Harvard Joint Center, which uses somewhat different income classifications than does HUD, found that the median rent burden for the lowest income groups leaped from 35 percent in 1974 to 40 percent of income in 1983 and that one-fourth of the poor paid more than 75 percent of their annual income for rent (see Figure 7).[50]

Whatever definition of poverty is used, the problem of huge, unconscionable rent burdens is the same. Today, at least 6.5 million poor families pay more than half of their income for rent. Of renters with an annual income under $7,000, more than half pay 60 percent of that meager income for rent. More than one-third of single-parent families pay over 75 percent of their annual income for rent, and two-thirds of all poor families—about 42 million Americans by Ford Foundation standards—pay over one-third of their low incomes for rent (i.e., pay a median of 45 percent of income to cover monthly shelter costs).[51]

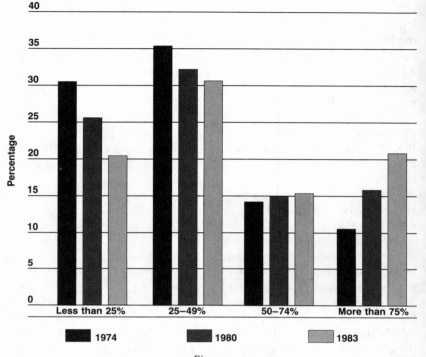

Figure 7
Percentage Distribution of Rent Burdens, Lowest Income Class,
1974, 1980, and 1983
Source: H. James Brown and John Yinger, *Home Ownership and Housing Affordability in the United
States, 1963–1985* (Cambridge, Mass.: Joint Center for Housing Studies of MIT and Harvard,
1986), p. 15.

Part of what is happening is that real income is plummeting
most sharply among the poor, while real rents are climbing most
rapidly in lower-rent units.[52] The lowest income groups in America
lost more real income more quickly in the inflation of the seventies
and the recession of the eighties than did any other population sector. Since 1973, the poorest fifth of the population lost 34 percent of
its real income, compared to a decline of 2 percent for the wealthiest
one-fifth. Between 1970 and 1983, median rents in America rose about
30 percent. In the 1980s, costs in the lower half of the rent distribution rose twice as much as those in the upper half.

The National Governors Association monitored this situation for
families with annual incomes of under $10,000. It reported that, from

1976 to 1986, these families experienced a 4 percent decline in real income and an increase in real rental costs from 48 percent of income to 58 percent.[53] The National Association of Home Builders' study of poor families found a 10 percent increase in real rents from 1974 to 1983, while real rents for families earning over $30,000 per year did not increase.[54]

Paying more rent with less money is obviously hardest on the poor. A major contributing factor to this burden is that the supply of affordable apartments is shrinking, while the number of poor people is expanding.

While analysts may argue about the exact amount, there can be no disagreement that we are losing a substantial number of affordable units each year to abandonment, arson, demolition, condominium conversion, gentrification, and so on. Barry Zigas, President of the National Low Income Housing Coalition, asserts that the stock of low-income housing has fallen by about 1 million units per year in the last decade.[55] Kim Hopper, a Revson Fellow at Columbia University, puts the number at 500,000.[56] William Apgar of MIT estimates that some 200,000 units per year from 1974 to 1983 were lost.[57] The lowest published estimate we have seen puts the number at about 100,000 non-subsidized low-income apartments per year.[58]

Another assessment of the situation was made by James Brown of the MIT-Harvard Joint Center, who estimates that recent years saw a 50 percent growth in apartments renting for $400 a month or more but a 20 percent decrease in the number of units renting below $250 a month.[59] On a related matter, the Government Accounting Office (GAO) reported a loss of 1.1 million single-room-occupancy units between 1970 and 1982.[60]

These analyses differ in detail but not in consequence. The supply of low-income housing in America has been vanishing in the 1980s. And the widening gap between supply and demand will soon be exacerbated by the loss of federally subsidized apartments from the affordable housing pool. There are presently about 1.9 million units of privately owned, federally assisted housing. These are almost all apartment projects built or modernized with HUD-subsidized loans or under contract with HUD to accept tenants receiving federal rent subsidies. Owners of this housing agreed to rent the units to low- and moderate-income tenants for 20 years. After 20 years, owners can opt out and either charge market-rate rent or convert to condominium ownership. The 20-year restrictions have already begun to expire and will continue expiring through 2005. A major portion of the rent-subsidy contracts begin to expire in 1990; by the year 2000 most of the 1.9 million units will be at risk. More than 1 million families who cannot afford to pay market-rate rents are in danger of displacement—many of them into homelessness.

Many of these projects were built in suburban communities or in city neighborhoods now undergoing gentrification. If well maintained or upgraded, the units may be attractive to renters or buyers who can pay for more than federally assisted tenants. The greater profitability potential of market-rent complexes, then, would motivate some owners to prepay their mortgages, displace existing tenants, and convert their properties to market-rate units.

The overwhelming majority of federally assisted projects are owned by partnerships controlled by a general partner who manages the financial dealings of the project on behalf of investors. These general partners have a legal obligation, as fiduciaries for their investors, to obtain the highest rate of return, whether or not the general partner might otherwise wish (for ideological or management reasons) to keep the project as a low–moderate-income complex. That legal obligation, it is asserted, "forces" general partners to raise rents, convert to condominiums, or sell the property to others who will do so. Presumably, the profit opportunities mentioned above will also reduce the number of owners willing to renew subsidized rent contracts—even if the huge sums of money needed to provide the subsidy were to be appropriated by Congress and spent by the President.

The year 2005 may seem distant but the threat that hundreds of thousands of low-income people will be displaced is imminent because the process has already begun. HUD considers the short-term danger to be at least between 470,000 and 577,000 units by 1996. The GAO predicts up to 900,000 units lost by that time.

While the low-income housing stock has been decreasing, the number of poor people who need that housing has been increasing. In 1974, about 8.5 million American families had annual incomes of under $10,000 a year; by 1983 there were about 12 million; and there are more now. About one-third of these families are headed by senior citizens, about half are headed by women, and about one-fourth are black or hispanic families.[61]

With more poor people and fewer low-income apartments, the inevitable result is a "housing affordability gap." The gap—the difference between the number of poor households and the number of units affordable to them—has grown wider every year for the past

20 years. The Ford Foundation estimated the gap at more than 14 million units in 1983.[62] The National Low Income Housing Information Service analyzed the affordability gap using 1980 census data and a 1985 trend update.[63] It found that 40 of the 50 states had a shortage of affordable apartments in 1980 but that, by 1985, all the states had a shortage and every state had a worse shortage than it had in 1980. The national scope of the problem was also observed in a 1982 study by the National League of Cities, which perceived low-income renters to be suffering severe problems in cities all across America.[64] Similarly, a recent U.S. Conference of Mayors study found the need for assisted housing by low-income families up an average of 40 percent in 88 percent of the surveyed cities throughout the country.[65]

What then is the housing crisis for low-income tenants in America? It is that there are now many more poor people but many fewer affordable apartments; it is that the poor now have a lot less with which to pay a lot more to rent apartments that are, on average, declining in quality. And the low-income housing gap is likely to get worse. The Urban Institute warns that the number of very-low-income Americans is expected to increase by almost 6 million people in the 1990s.[66] At current levels of assistance, the number of American families living in substandard or cost-burdened housing will grow by 1 to 3 million. Some experts fear that, by the year 2000, one-third of all Americans and 70 percent of the poor will confront problems of housing adequacy or affordability or both. A recent study of the Neighborhood Reinvestment Corporation predicted that 18 million poor families will be homeless by the year 2003 unless there are dramatic changes in American economic conditions or housing policies.[67]

Homelessness

Nothing so clearly demonstrates the need for a new housing policy than the crisis of homelessness that afflicts this country, the national shame that millions of Americans are living—and dying—in the streets and alleyways of America, sleeping in bus stations and abandoned cars and in chicken coops and on heat grates. It is a condition that rots our cities and is growing in our suburbs and rural areas. The fact of expanding—indeed, exploding—homelessness in America mocks our claim to be a prosperous and humane society.

America in the 1980s has witnessed striking growth and change in the size and diversity of its homeless population. In 1983, HUD undertook a study to estimate the number of persons homeless on any given night. That study, utilizing four sampling methodologies, produced estimates centering on 250,000–350,000.[68] These estimates differed dramatically from those then in use by the federal Department of Health and Human Services (1–3 million), the National Housing Law Project (2.5 million), the National Housing Conference (2.5 million), and the Center for Creative Non-Violence (2–3 million).[69] HUD's methodologies were strongly criticized by scholars and housing advocates and HUD's estimates were ultimately termed "discredited" by many, including the Federal Emergency Management Administration.[70]

Since 1983, there have been few efforts to estimate the size of the homeless population. Analysts, policymakers, and advocates have focused instead on the changing demographic composition of the homeless, and on concrete actions to provide emergency shelter. Nonetheless, it might be useful to explore alternative means of estimating the present size of the homeless population, to get some sense of the magnitude of the problem. To that end, first, we asked the Council of State Community Affairs Agencies to undertake a national survey of their member agencies to seek a "working number of homeless persons" used, in 1987, by those state agencies charged with primary responsibility for a number of programs designed to aid the homeless.[71] Second, we analyzed the 1987 statements of need that each state submitted to HUD in order to receive federal assistance for the homeless.

Of course, these efforts do not resolve the very great methodological difficulties in counting the homeless that HUD encountered. If anything, our attempt to estimate the size of the homeless population compounds methodological problems (because it accepts, as comparable, the different estimation techniques of the several states). Yet our analysis of the reports of 31 states that responded to the Council and 42 states that responded to HUD suggests that the number of Americans who are without shelter on any given night can be conservatively estimated at between 655,000 and 1 million.

Whatever the "real size" of the homeless population, there can be no doubt that it is growing rapidly to crisis or epidemic proportions. Estimates of annual growth in homelessness published in 1984 and 1985 were quite divergent, ranging from 10 percent to 38 percent per year (the lower figures being HUD estimates, the higher figures reported by the U.S. Conference of Mayors).[72] For the winter of 1986–1987, however, data on the homeless were more convergent and consistent. The U.S. Conference of Mayors found shelter needs up 20 percent in all but 1 of 25 surveyed cities.[73] The Partnership for the Homeless of New York undertook a national survey in 47 cities to assess the number of homeless. It found an increase averaging 25 percent in each of the surveyed cities.[74] A National League of Cities survey[75] in the winter of 1986–1987 reported that homeless persons were perceived to be experiencing "severe problems" in 58 percent of surveyed communities across the land. These studies confirm earlier, more qualitative judgments by the National Governors Association[76] and several congressional committees that homelessness *is* a growing national crisis.[77]

Part of the critical nature of the problem is the fact that the number of homeless persons immensely dwarfs that of available shelter beds. In 1985, the House Committee on Government Operations judged the gap between the need and the capacity to provide even the most basic shelter to be "enormous"—and rapidly increasing.[78] Since then, the Conference of Mayors has placed the unmet need at 24 percent, noting that homeless persons were turned away from shelters in more than 70 percent of surveyed cities.[79] The Partnership for the Homeless survey for the winter of 1986–1987 found that there was a shelter gap in 98 percent of surveyed cities, up 14 percent over the previous year, and that 91 percent of the cities responding had to turn away homeless persons from their shelters.[80]

Who are the homeless? Unlike the old stereotype of the Bowery bum, the lone drifter, the mentally unbalanced, today's homeless are, substantially, functioning adults and families with children—a cross-section of the poor.

Perhaps the most dramatic change in the last 10 years has been the sharp increase in the number of homeless families. In 1984, HUD reported that 21 percent of the homeless were families;[81] in 1986, the U.S. Conference of Mayors found the number of families seeking shelter had increased 31 percent over two years in 80 percent of the surveyed cities (to 28 percent overall).[82] In 1987 the Partnership study found a majority of cities (54 percent) reporting that over 30 percent were families with children.[83] The nation's capital experienced a 500 percent increase in homeless families.[84]

On other dimensions, HUD found that 44 percent of the homeless were minorities; single women constituted only 13 percent of the homeless; the median age of homeless persons was about 34.

Later national studies found that about one-third were veterans and only about one-third had a history of mental or emotional imbalance.[85] A number of studies have shown the homeless problem not only to be national in scope but also to have spread out to smaller cities, suburbs, and rural areas.[86]

What makes all these different kinds of people homeless? It is virtually undisputed that the dearth of affordable housing is probably *the* major cause of homelessness in America; witness the House Committee on Government Operations (1985), the National Governors' Association Task Force (1983), the U.S. Conference of Mayors (1984), and the Partnership for the Homeless (1987).[87] These studies put it simply: "Homelessness remains substantially an affordable housing crisis," and, again, "The clear leader as a cause of homelessness this winter, as well as in our survey last year, is the unavailability of affordable housing for low income households."[88]

Peter Kerr of the *New York Times* saw these linkages clearly. In the winter of 1985, he wrote: "the same economic forces that make it impossible for middle class families to buy their first homes prevent some of the poor—those who have been evicted, burned out, or forced out—from finding any shelter at all."[89]

The National Governor's Association Task Force (1983) drew the same conclusion: "Over the grim statistics on homelessness looms the shadow of a housing crisis which may well be unexampled in this century. . . . When one realizes that the major victims of mass displacement are the poor, those with fewest resources to absorb new hardship or to recover in its wake, it is no mystery that the ranks of the homeless continue to swell."[90]

Given this linkage between housing unaffordability and homelessness, and that shelter is so basic a human need, it stands to reason that families will double up and triple up as long as they can, will stay with friends and relatives, and will even live apart if they must, rather than, or before, they submit to homelessness. These families are America's hidden homeless. They are the "housing vulnerable," one layoff, one domestic argument, away from being on the streets. The New York Partnership for the Homeless estimates there are 10 million doubled-up families nationally; other estimates vary from 4 to 14 million.[91] And their number is growing. Every one of the 29 cities surveyed by the U.S. Conference of Mayors in May of 1987 reported that the number of families "temporarily" living with friends or relatives had increased over the previous year.[92]

Stagnation and Decline in Improving America's Housing

The quality of America's housing stock improved vastly from 1945 to 1975.[93] Millions of new housing units were constructed in those three decades. Amenities that were luxuries at the end of World War II—garages, second bathrooms, air conditioning—became commonplace in American homes. The number of primitive housing units lacking basic modern facilities such as kitchens, bathrooms, electricity, and indoor plumbing declined appreciably. Smaller family sizes and larger homes drove down the percentage of Americans living in overcrowded conditions from 10 percent in 1945 to about 4 percent in 1975.

Since 1975, however, there has been more stagnation and decline than improvement on the indicators of housing conditions in America.[94] Conditions actually deteriorated on seven of nine modern indicators of maintenance and upkeep. Table 5 summarizes the number of housing units with structural defects in 1974 and 1981. The mechanical subsystems considered in Table 5 are, of course,

Table 5
Number of Occupied Dwelling Units with Structural Defects, 1974 and 1981
(in thousands)

Defect	1974	1981	% Change
Maintenance and upkeep			
Some or all wiring exposed	2,375	2,375	0.0
Lacking working outlets in some rooms	3,078	2,728	−12.8
Breakdown in water supply	1,549	1,850	19.4
Breakdown in sewer/septic cesspool	833	923	10.8
Inadequate heat	2,890	2,937	1.6
Cracks in holes in walls or ceilings	4,024	4,647	15.5
Holes in interior floors	1,308	1,561	19.4
Roof leaks	4,737	4,928	4.0
Signs of rats or mice	6,676	10,499	57.3
Mechanical subsystems			
Shared or not complete kitchen	1,582	1,330	−15.9
Shared or no bathroom	2,633	2,120	−19.5
Lacking some or all plumbing	2,076	1,626	−21.7
No heating equipment	329	447	35.9

Source: National Association of Home Builders, *Low- and Moderate-Income Housing: Progress, Problems, and Prospects* (Washington, D.C.: The Association, 1986), p. 9.

Table 6
Housing Problems in the United States, 1975–1983 (in thousands)

Occupied Units	1975 No.	1975 %	1977 No.	1977 %	1981 No.	1981 %	1983 No.	1983 %
Total								
All units	72,553		75,399		83,203		84,842	
Inadequate	7,704	10.6	7,641	10.1	7,695	9.3	7,561	8.9
(Severely inadequate)	(3,123)	(4.3)	(2,949)	(3.9)	(2,985)	(3.6)	(2,876)	(3.4)
Crowded*	2,742	3.8	2,455	3.3	2,489	3.0	2,230	2.6
Cost-burdened†	8,752	12.1	10,101	13.4	12,899	15.5	14,425	17.0
Total with problems	19,198	26.5	20,197	26.8	23,083	27.8	24,216	28.6
41–80% median family income	13,506		14,581		14,966		15,455	
Inadequate	1,616	12.0	1,527	10.5	1,612	10.8	1,551	10.0
(Severely inadequate)	(576)	(4.3)	(479)	(3.3)	(556)	(3.8)	(520)	(3.4)
Crowded*	749	5.6	670	4.6	611	4.1	503	3.3
Cost-burdened†	1,373	10.2	1,574	10.8	2,631	17.6	2,769	17.9
Total with problems	3,738	27.7	3,771	25.9	4,854	32.4	4,823	31.2
50% & below median family income	19,117		20,966		21,818		22,943	
Inadequate	3,918	20.5	4,025	19.2	3,899	17.9	3,805	16.6
(Severely inadequate)	(1,876)	(9.8)	(1,826)	(8.7)	(1,866)	(8.6)	(1,633)	(7.1)
Crowded*	856	4.5	867	4.1	928	4.3	926	4.0
Cost-burdened†	7,049	36.9	8,138	38.8	9,192	42.1	10,368	45.2
Total with problems	11,823	61.9	13,030	62.2	14,019	64.3	15,099	65.8
Owners								
All units	46,920		48,964		54,361		54,890	
Inadequate	3,507	7.5	3,478	7.1	3,445	6.2	3,420	6.2
(Severely inadequate)	(1,203)	(2.6)	(1,095)	(2.2)	(1,197)	(2.2)	(1,178)	(2.2)
Crowded*	1,585	3.4	1,350	2.8	1,234	2.3	1,034	1.9
Cost-burdened†	2,552	5.4	3,064	6.3	4,197	7.7	4,581	8.4
Total with problems	7,644	16.3	7,862	16.1	8,876	16.3	9,035	16.5
41–80% median family income	7,902		8,591		8,577		8,953	
Inadequate	760	9.6	718	8.4	717	8.4	705	7.9
(Severely inadequate)	(221)	(2.8)	(196)	(2.3)	(218)	(2.6)	(227)	(2.5)
Crowded*	431	5.5	394	4.6	311	3.6	259	2.9
Cost-burdened†	311	3.9	381	4.4	653	7.6	744	8.3
Total with problems	1,502	19.0	1,493	17.4	1,681	19.6	1,708	19.1

Table 6 (cont.)

Occupied Units	1975 No.	%	1977 No.	%	1981 No.	%	1983 No.	%
50% & below median								
family income	9,000		9,716		10,007		10,073	
Inadequate	1,521	16.9	1,535	15.8	1,514	15.1	1,410	14.0
(Severely inadequate)	(665)	(7.4)	(610)	(6.3)	(736)	(7.4)	(559)	(5.6)
Crowded*	303	3.4	253	2.6	259	2.6	234	2.3
Cost-burdened†	2,146	23.9	2,497	25.7	3,046	30.4	3,219	32.0
Total with problems	3,970	44.1	4,285	44.1	4,819	48.1	4,863	48.3
Renters								
All units	25,633		26,535		28,842		29,952	
Inadequate	4,197	16.4	4,193	15.4	4,250	14.7	4,141	13.8
(Severely inadequate)	(1,920)	(7.5)	(1,854)	(7.0)	(1,788)	(6.2)	(1,689)	(5.7)
Crowded*	1,157	4.5	1,105	4.2	1,255	4.4	1,196	4.0
Cost-burdened†	6,200	24.2	7,037	26.5	8,702	30.2	9,844	32.9
Total with problems	11,554	45.1	12,335	46.5	14,207	49.3	15,181	50.7
41–80% median family								
income	5,604		5,990		6,389		6,502	
Inadequate	856	15.3	809	13.5	895	14.0	846	13.0
(Severely inadequate)	(355)	(5.3)	(283)	(4.7)	(338)	(5.3)	(293)	(4.5)
Crowded*	318	5.7	276	4.6	300	4.7	244	3.8
Cost-burdened†	1,062	19.0	1,193	19.9	1,978	31.0	2,025	31.2
Total with problems	2,236	39.9	2,278	38.0	3,173	49.7	3,115	47.9
50% & below median								
family income	10,117		11,250		11,811		12,870	
Inadequate	2,397	23.7	2,490	22.1	2,385	20.2	2,395	18.6
(Severely inadequate)	(1,211)	(12.0)	(1,216)	(10.8)	(1,130)	(9.6)	(1,074)	(8.4)
Crowded*	533	4.4	614	5.5	669	5.7	692	5.4
Cost-burdened†	4,903	48.5	5,641	50.2	6,146	52.0	7,149	55.6
Total with problems	7,853	77.6	8,745	77.7	9,200	77.9	19,236	79.5

*Crowded households are only those in physically adequate units.
†Cost-burdened households are only those in adequate units and not crowded.
Source: Iredia Irby, "Attaining the Housing Goal?" unpublished paper, Division of Housing and Demographic Analysis, U.S. Department of Housing and Urban Development, Washington, D.C., July 1986, p. 16.

outmoded indicators from pre-World War II days when units were built lacking kitchens, bathrooms, or full indoor plumbing and heating equipment. Even on these indicators, however, conditions improved only modestly, and actually deteriorated on the number of units with no heating equipment.

HUD's 1983 *Annual Housing Survey*, moreover, revealed a dramatic increase in what the government calls "occupied units with housing problems." The survey found that 24.2 million American families lived in inadequate, overcrowded, or excessively costly housing (29 percent of all housing units), up from 19.1 million in 1975. These statistics reflect a manifest downturn in American living conditions.

The 1983 survey (summarized in Table 6) indicates that more than 7.5 million families occupied units deemed "inadequate" by HUD and almost 2.25 million households were overcrowded (the latter, a very conservative estimate because HUD excluded structurally inadequate units from its analysis of overcrowding). These figures were down very marginally from the 1975–1977 and 1981 survey numbers (Table 6), although the number of overcrowded families with very low incomes actually rose from 1975 to 1983. Almost 10 million American families were living in substandard, overcrowded conditions.

But the biggest change in American housing conditions revealed in Table 6 is the dramatic downturn in housing affordability. The number of cost-burdened housing units rose in each surveyed year, from 8.75 million in 1975 to 14.42 million in 1983. Not surprisingly, the cost-burden data is worst for poor families. The number of low-income, cost-burdened units more than doubled from 1975 to 1983.

It is also useful to review HUD's data on specific subpopulations. Table 7 represents a comparison of 1975 and 1983 HUD survey findings on the quality and affordability of housing units occupied by city residents, female-headed households, the elderly, the poor, blacks, and hispanics. Table 7 shows that the number and percentage of families in each of these groups experienced a substantial deterioration in cost-burden and housing conditions. For each of these subpopulations, the number and percentage of cost-burdened families increased, as did the number and percentage of families with housing problems. For city residents, hispanics, and female-headed households, the number (but not the percentage) of families living in structurally inadequate dwellings also increased. Among the poor

Table 7
Housing Problems in the United States, by Type of Household, 1975 and 1983
(in thousands)

Type of Household	1975 No.	1975 %	1983 No.	1983 %
Metropolitan residents				
Total with housing problems	12,926	26	17,015	29.3
Cost-burdened units	6,896	13	11,204	19.3
Inadequate units	4,118	8.3	4,241	7.3
Female-headed				
Total with housing problems	7,489	43.5	10,255	43.8
Cost-burdened units	4,713	27.4	7,088	30.3
Inadequate units	2,396	13.9	2,722	11.6
Hispanic				
Total with housing problems	1,551	49.8	2,381	51.5
Cost-burdened units	485	15.6	1,032	22.3
Inadequate units	630	20.2	813	17.6
Low-income				
Total with housing problems	3,738	27.7	4,823	31.2
Cost-burdened units	1,373	10.2	2,769	17.9
Inadequate units	1,616	12	1,551	10
Black				
Total with housing problems	3,905	51.8	4,712	51.4
Cost-burdened units	1,254	16.6	2,196	24.0
Inadequate units	2,084	27.6	2,053	22.4
Elderly				
Total with housing problems	4,646	32.3	4,940	27.7
Cost-burdened units	2,558	17.8	3,157	17.7
Inadequate units	2,016	14	1,730	9.7

Source: Iredia Irby, "Attaining the Housing Goal?" unpublished paper, Division of Housing and Demographic Analysis, U.S. Department of Housing and Urban Development, Washington, D.C., July 1986, p. 19.

and among blacks, the number of families living in inadequate units remained about the same.

The problem of housing quality is not about to be solved without new government policies and actions. Table 5 shows a deterioration of America's housing stock on most modern indicators of upkeep and maintenance. Table 6 shows so marginal an improvement in the housing inventory, on premodern indicators of housing quality, that it might take decades for the structurally defective units to be replaced. Table 7 shows the number of disadvantaged people living in dilapidated units to be about the same or higher over a decade of supposed progress.

In 1982, the President's Commission on Housing declared, "Americans today are the best-housed people in history."[95] Since then, homeownership rates have declined, the quality and affordability of apartments has declined, a crisis of homelessness has exploded, and 24 million families live in "problem" housing. With almost 10 million families in unsound or overcrowded homes, and 14 million more paying more than they should for shelter, we may be the best-housed people in history, but our progress has largely been stopped. We are now regressing.

HOUSING PROBLEMS AND NEEDS IN THE 1990S

Projections of future problems are by nature inexact. Yet there are a number of problems that are quite clearly about to come upon us; some things have begun to happen, or are about to happen, that housing experts and demographers are agreed upon as problems (if not at all agreed upon as to solutions). We think it important to describe some of these coming changes because the new housing policy America needs is one that not only meets our present and continuing needs but that anticipates our emerging requirements.

Emerging Housing Needs of the 1990s That Are Unlikely to be Met Via Unaided Market Adaptations

As we saw earlier, the 1990s are likely to be years in which there are substantial mismatches and gaps between the diverse housing needs of our rapidly changing population and the character of the American housing stock available to meet these needs. Major demographic trends, relevant to housing, will almost certainly include: an increase in the population share of young families in prime first-time buying years (a 6 percent rise in the 30–34 bracket, 75 percent growth in the 33–44 cohort); a huge increase (91 percent) in the proportion of Americans who are over 75 (the so-called "old elderly"); a sharp

Table 8
Distribution of Households, by Age of Householder, 1980–2000

Households	18–24	25–29	30–34	35–44	45–54	55–64	65–74	75+	Total
1980 (N = 84,842)									
Married couples									
Children	1.8	4.6	6.5	10.7	5.8	1.7	0.3	0.1	31.5
No children	1.7	2.2	1.3	1.7	5.3	8.7	6.2	2.6	29.5
Other families									
Children	0.9	1.3	1.5	2.3	1.1	0.4	0.1	0.1	7.6
No children	0.3	0.2	0.1	0.5	1.0	1.3	1.0	0.8	5.1
Single individuals	2.1	2.4	1.8	1.9	2.1	3.5	4.7	4.2	22.6
Non-family groups	1.3	0.8	0.4	0.4	0.2	0.2	0.2	0.1	3.6
Total	8.0	11.4	11.6	17.4	15.6	15.8	12.5	7.7	100.0
2000 (N = 106,006)									
Married couples									
Children	0.8	2.1	4.4	11.8	5.8	1.4	0.4	0.1	26.8
No children	0.5	0.7	0.7	2.2	6.4	6.6	5.0	3.2	25.4
Other families									
Children	0.7	1.0	1.4	3.2	1.6	0.4	0.2	0.1	8.5
No children	0.1	0.2	0.2	0.8	1.7	1.2	0.9	1.1	6.1
Single individuals	1.2	2.2	2.2	4.3	4.5	4.0	4.8	6.6	29.7
Non-family groups	0.6	0.7	0.5	0.8	0.5	0.2	0.1	0.1	3.6
Total	3.9	6.8	9.3	23.1	20.5	13.8	11.4	11.2	100.0
Percent Change, 1980–2000									
Married couples									
Children	−39.9	−40.3	−11.1	45.8	32.7	4.9	45.6	163.4	12.2
No children	−59.6	−54.9	−22.8	73.0	58.6	.02	6.7	63.1	13.3
Other families									
Children	−4.7	4.0	20.8	82.9	88.0	48.4	57.6	84.2	46.2
No children	−40.9	2.3	48.7	130.0	117.0	27.3	28.2	78.3	58.2
Single individuals	−21.7	19.2	62.3	199.2	179.9	47.9	35.4	110.6	73.6
Non-family groups	−37.9	5.2	50.3	199.3	194.2	40.8	2.2	47.4	29.5

Source: Margery Austin Turner, *Housing Needs to the Year 2000* (Washington, D.C.: National Association of Housing and Redevelopment Officials, 1986), p. 13.

upturn (almost 75 percent) in the number of single persons; the continued and heightened concentration of the poor in central cities; and a large augmentation in the number of single-parent families. Table 8 summarizes some of these likely trends.

The American housing market has historically adapted well, and reasonably quickly, to the needs of relatively affluent families. Unaided, the market responds far less completely and less quickly to the non-affluent. Therefore, each of the trends noted above creates a housing supply or housing finance problem. Young families, the "old elderly," single-parent families, and the poor all fall in the non-affluent category. Let us consider each of these groups and trends briefly.

Homeownership for Young Families

Because of the housing finance obstacles young families have faced in the 1980s, the 1990s will witness a strong pent-up demand for homeownership among families headed by householders aged 25 to 44. More than 1 million Americans aged 18–34 who ordinarily would have formed new households have stayed and/or will stay at home with their parents in the 1980s. At least 400,000 of them would ordinarily have achieved homeownership. Also contributing to pent-up demand are the more than 1 million families headed by people under 34 who did form households but failed to achieve homeownership in the 1980s and who would have been able to do so at pre-1980 homeownership rates.[96] An additional million or more young families will enter their prime home-buying years in the 1990s but won't be able to achieve homeownership unless home-purchasing rates return to 1980 levels.

Based on current trends, the housing market these young families will enter is not likely to be building very many homes at a size or price they can afford. As noted earlier, 80 percent of the home builders will be aiming their product at the trade-up market; the size of the average new home (now at an all-time high) will be well beyond the needs of the young family with fewer children (see Table 10) then ever before. The "average house" will also be much more expensive than younger families can afford, as land and construction costs are expected to rise. Trends in median income[97] and personal savings[98] have been mixed or declining for the average American throughout the 1980s, especially for younger families—giving little hope that such families in the 1990s will be much better able to come up with the larger downpayments or pay the still high interest rates predicted for the 1990s.

Homeownership has always been the cornerstone of American housing policy, because homeownership has been—and remains—the American dream. To achieve that dream in the 1990s, young American families may need a new downpayment assistance loan fund, a lease/purchase homeownership plan, or a governmentally encouraged employee homeownership program or may want to coventure their home-buying purchase in partnership with a National Housing Investment Corporation. Initiatives like these are essential if the American government is to remain faithful to the dream.

Independent Living for Senior Citizens

The growth of the elderly population will confront our housing policy with important challenges. Households headed by persons 65 or older have been growing throughout the 1980s, reaching 17 million in 1987 and projected to be 21.4 million by 1995. The number of "old elderly" is expected to grow from an estimated 7 million in 1987 to 11.9 million by the year 2000.[99]

Most older Americans will continue to live healthy, fruitful, independent lives in the 1990s. They will already have met their basic housing needs: a majority of senior citizens own their homes, have paid their mortgage, enjoy substantial equity as a result of appreciation in the value of their home, and want to remain living there as long as possible.

The incidence of housing problems among elderly householders in the 1980s has been lower than for the population as a whole. The households of the elderly have been less frequently cost-burdened, less frequently crowded, and only marginally more likely to live in structurally inadequate units than has the American population at large. In addition, a declining proportion of elderly householders fall into the low-income category.[100] All these trends are likely to continue into and through the 1990s.

But some senior citizens will need housing help in the 1990s to avoid needless institutionalization. National studies on the needs of older Americans estimate that about 15 percent (or about 3.5 million senior citizens in the 1990s) need support services, dwelling unit modifications, or new housing specially designed to accommodate their level of physical functioning. The 3.5 million figure is low because it does not count the roughly 300,000 elderly people who, at any given time, live in nursing homes but could be discharged if suitable units were available.[101] Gerontologists and housing policy analysts estimate a 1990s need of about 1.7 million new or substantially rehabilitated units specially designed for the frail elderly and about 2 million more units with support services but not major structural modifications.

The private housing market is beginning to adapt to the needs of upper-income frail elderly persons—albeit more slowly than the demand is growing. But the growing proportion of senior citizens who are of low and moderate income will probably need some governmental help in order to live in appropriate units with appropriate services. American policy in the area of senior citizen housing should pursue two broad goals not now adequately addressed at the federal level: (1) helping the well elderly stay in their own homes and (2) providing needed services to the frail elderly to prevent needless institutionalization while maintaining dignified living.

Although three-quarters of older people own their homes, 80 percent of which are mortgage-free, many are "house rich and cash poor." They lack the income to maintain their homes and pay for property taxes, insurance, and major repairs. For these senior citizens, finding a way to use their equity reserve without having to sell the homes would be an important solution to their housing and income needs. At least five state governments have adopted home equity conversion programs, some of them based on reverse annuity mortgage instruments.[102] Federal housing legislation contemplates limited study and experimentation in this area,[103] but federal housing policy in the 1990s certainly should include a major program to help millions of senior citizens live where, and as, they want to live. If the federal program ultimately adopted includes a limited, reverse equity feature, as it should, the National Housing Investment Corporation advocated in Chapter 3 could be a useful mechanism to achieve this goal. Helping senior citizens stay in their own homes via home repair programs and property tax relief programs is more likely to be a state and local initiative, but there may well need to be federal encouragement given to these other levels of government.

For the frail elderly, the problem is more difficult and the need for federal help more acute. Many ways to combine housing with support services for elderly residents exist. The housing varies in terms of its size, physical design, service arrangements, manner in which residents pay for services, and types of management. But there is a common theme of providing assistance with daily living tasks and a supportive environment to help elderly people maintain independence as long as possible. This fills the gap between totally independent living and institutionalization, without reliance on costly nursing home care.[104]

Since the services become an integral part of the housing, the financing, development, and management of these facilities are more complex. Among the options for service-related housing are congre-

gate housing complexes, shared group homes, continuing care retirement communities, and the addition of services to existing senior
citizen apartment complexes. The demand for federal support of these
service programs can only grow.

Rental Units for Low- and Moderate-Income Groups

In the 1980s, more poor people lived in America than ever before,
poor people with less money, seeking fewer available apartments of
inferior quality, paying higher rents. In the 1990s, these problems
will worsen unless a new construction program begins to expand
the supply of units appropriate to the size and job locations of renter
households.

That conclusion may seem obvious, but to some it is not. In fact,
recent years have witnessed a major debate about the adequacy of
the supply of rental units. HUD and a number of housing economists, while acknowledging that certain local housing markets have
too few vacancies, have argued that most parts of the country have
an adequate supply of rental units to accommodate poor people
presently living in inadequate units if only a rent subsidy were available to those families. Others, including the National Association of
Homebuilders, the National Association of Housing and Redevelopment Officials, leading planners, and some university researchers, have contended that a new construction program will be necessary in the majority of urban markets because most of the vacant
apartments that do exist are not well matched to the size, location,
and budgets of poor families.[105]

The debate is far from academic. Notwithstanding the substantial numbers of poor families who receive rent subsidy certificates
but fail to find acceptable housing and must forego benefits, the
President and Congress have sharply curtailed newly federally subsidized construction efforts and concentrated almost exclusively on
a rent-subsidy program (vouchers). Beyond cutting new construction to almost no new units, recent federal tax policy changes are
expected to reduce private apartment production by 40 percent in
the late 1980s, which would result in a 20–28 percent increase in
rents in the long run.[106]

A major study of this supply versus subsidy issue, undertaken
by the Congressional Research Service and published in January 1987,
casts much-needed light on the subject. CRS used a computer sim-

ulation of 48 American housing markets utilizing the latest available data from HUD's *Annual Housing Surveys*. It identified the size and income of families living in inadequate or overcrowded units, compared the housing needs of those families (number of bedrooms needed etc.) to the array of vacant units in each area, and assessed the subsidy needed to relocate the ill-housed poor families in structurally adequate housing at 30 percent of their income. The findings:

> When family and unit sizes are taken into account . . . there is no area in which the supply of standard quality vacant units is sufficient to permit all unsatisfactorily-housed families to move to units in which they would not be overcrowded. Moreover, the vacancy rate in the area is not an acceptable prediction of the proportion of families which cannot be rehoused. . . . In central cities, from one-tenth to nine-tenths cannot be rehoused. In suburban areas, the range is from fewer than 50 households (a rounded 1 percent) to two-thirds; in the Standard Metropolitan Statistical Area as a unified market, from one-tenth to three-quarters. The median proportion of those who cannot be rehoused are 39 (central), 25 (suburban), and 33 percent (SMSA), respectively.
>
> In both city and suburban areas, families of five or more persons constitute two-thirds or more of those not rehoused. Regarding the SMSA as a whole as one market area does not materially change this result.[107]

The study reveals much about using vacancy rates as a guide to whether or not poor people can find apartments:

> *It is apparent from the figures [in the study] that there is no clear relation between the rental vacancy rate in any city and the proportion of its inadequately housed population which can be rehoused. . . .* This indicates that when rent-paying ability is not a factor, the vacancy rate explains between one-sixth (16 percent) and somewhat under one-third (30 percent) of the variance in the proportion of inadequately housed families able to be rehoused in the currently existing standard quality stock in any particular geographic area. That is, although not totally without relevance, *the crude vacancy rate alone is an unsatisfactory guide to determining the most appropriate housing policy to follow in order to end families' living in inadequate housing.* (Emphasis added.)[108]

The congressional study suggests that a minimum of $2.9 billion in additional certificates or vouchers would be needed annually just to rehouse the poor now living in inadequate rental units.[109]

Given the existing housing needs of poor American families, the expected increase in the number of lower-income families, and the continuing loss of low-income housing stock to abandonment and gentrification, a need exists for at least 350,000 new and substantially rehabilitated low-income rental housing units each year for the rest of this century. In Chapter 3, we suggest several new ways in which the building of these units might be encouraged by federal policies. The policies we recommend provide better targeting of federal dollars and greater cost-effectiveness than previous construction subsidy programs. The programs we advocate to help young families acquire homeownership and to build housing units designed for the frail elderly will also be of some help to low- and moderate-income families, because these programs will free up a substantial number of apartments (vacated by the young families and frail elderly), some of which will filter for use by lower-income renters.

Housing for Single-Parent Households

The number and percentage of female-headed households has grown tremendously in the past 40 years, from about 3.5 million in 1950 (9 percent) to over 9 million in 1980 (15.3 percent), of which about two-thirds are single-parent households. This growth has taken place in every decade since 1950, but exploded by 65 percent in the 1970–1980 period. And the number of female-headed single-parent families is expected to grow by almost one-half in the 1990s.[110]

Single-parent, female-headed households live, disproportionately, in inferior housing with extremely limited financial resources to improve their housing (either by rehabilitation or moving). These households, as represented in HUD's 1981 *Annual Housing Survey*, had a substantially greater probability of living in inadequate, crowded, or cost-burdened dwelling units than did the population as a whole (see Table 9). They also had extremely low median incomes ($9,210) to cope with these housing problems. Nationally, only 40 percent of female-headed single-parent families owned their own homes in the 1980s (compared to 60 percent for the general population). These families tended to be renters and were concentrated in urban areas, especially in central cities.[111]

There are a wide variety of cost-effective housing policies and programs that will be needed, in the 1990s, to assist these families, these women and children, to live in more decent, safe, sanitary housing at affordable costs. We consider these, at length, in Chapter 7. Here, we merely note that the demographic trends our society faces in the 1990s include a strong continuation of the increase in

Table 9
Housing Problems of U.S. Population and Female-Headed, Single-Parent
Households, 1981

Occupied Units	All Households		Female-Headed, Single-Parent Households	
	No.	%	No.	%
All units	83,203		5,856	
Total with problems	23,083	27.8	3,162	53.9
Inadequate	7,695	9.3	861	14.7
Crowded	2,489	3	365	6.2
Cost-burdened	12,899	15.5	1,936	33.1

Source: Eugenie Ladner Birch, ed., The Unsheltered Woman (New Brunswick, N.J.: Center for Urban Policy Research of Rutgers, 1985).

economically vulnerable, poorly housed women and children American public policy needs to be modified so that they can be housed, as our national housing goal puts it, "in a decent home in a suitable living environment."

More Housing, Better Targeting

The America of the 1990s will need, then, more housing, better targeted to the life needs of our increasingly diverse population.

We will need more housing to meet the pent-up demands of young families (whose family formation and homeownership rates fell in the 1980s) and to meet the new demands of a still-growing population. At the start of the 1980s, the housing industry and housing advocates agreed that we required about 2 million units year to match expected family formation in a decade (the 1980s) in which 40-plus million Americans would turn 30 years old. The recession of 1981–1983 and the high cost of housing slowed family formation and we fell millions of units short of the expected expansion in housing stock. In the 1990s, the number of Americans turning 30 will again exceed 40 million, but consensual estimates put the expected housing unit growth at only 1.5 million units per year. That level of building will not meet the needs of the American people nor reduce their cost burdens.

America should seek to target housing better to the places where and to the people for whom it is needed. More than 80 percent of the expected household growth in the 1990s will occur in metropolitan areas, placing severe stress on the housing stock of the central cities.[112] Yet America's housing market is still aiming too greatly at suburban and exurban areas, creating more sprawl.[113] Much of the growth in the U.S. population in the 1990s will be in the "old elderly," single-parent families, and lower-income groups, but too little of the extant housing market is oriented to the real needs of everyday life for these Americans.

More housing, better targeted to the life needs of our increasingly diverse people. Let us consider, then, some of the economic and governmental benefits we might derive from pursuing these goals.

THE BENEFITS OF MEETING OUR HOUSING NEEDS

A policy that allowed the United States to achieve its major housing goals in the 1990s would also generate, during that decade, millions of new jobs and billions of dollars for the federal treasury in corporate and personal income tax revenues, and would engender about $.5 trillion in economic activity. It is appropriate to be specific and conservative in estimating the jobs, economic development, and governmental benefits likely to derive from meeting our housing goals. Accordingly, let us consider a housing policy that is targeted on only three housing problems that emerged in the 1980s, that will grow more pressing in the 1990s, and that warrant governmental response because they concern large numbers of people whose needs are unlikely to be met by the unaided market: the housing requirements of young families, the frail elderly, and the poor. These groups did not have their housing needs adequately met in the 1980s; their numbers and their likely housing difficulties will grow in the 1990s; their below-average incomes suggest that the housing market is likely to be less responsive to their claims. To house each of these population sectors adequately, it may well be necessary to adopt governmental policies encouraging the construction of new housing units and/or to assist families, through loans or grants, so they can afford existing dwelling units.

Based on demographic trends discussed above, there would seem to be a need in the 1990s to encourage the supply or affordability of starter homes for about 3.3 million young families, of new or substantially rehabilitated units suited to the life needs of 1.7 million frail elderly people, and of 3.4 million new or substantially rehabilitated units for low- and moderate-income families. Of this need for 8.4 million new, rehabilitated, or affordability-enhanced units in the decade of the 1990s, at least 6.8 million will have to be newly constructed or substantially rehabilitated. More specifically, as described below in Chapter 3, the national need in the 1990s will be to facilitate 1.7 million newly constructed starter homes for young families (i.e., about 170,000 per year), 1.7 million new or moderately rehabilitated units for the frail elderly (about 170,000 per year), and 3.4 million new units for the poor (almost 340,000 per year).

To assess the jobs, economic development, and governmental benefits of meeting our housing goals, in a specific and conservative manner, let us consider only these 6.8 million housing units as the decade-long target of new federal governmental activity. For the purpose of this analysis, let us hypothesize a housing policy that aims at encouraging the supply and/or affordability of these specific 680,000 units each year for 10 years.

A 1980–1981 study by the Bureau of Labor Statistics, cited in the December 1981 *Monthly Labor Review*,[114] found that, for each billion dollars of multi-family construction contract expenditures, 25,400 jobs were created. Similarly, for each billion dollars of single-family construction activity, 22,000 jobs were created. Using BLS formulas, and assuming a construction cost of $60,000 for each rental unit to be produced by our hypothesized housing policy, a cost of $90,000 for each homeownership unit, and a cost of $15,000 for each unit rehabilitated for the frail elderly, some 920,000 new jobs would be created each year, or 9.2 million for the decade.

A correction factor deriving from a 1984 University of Maryland study[115] on the economic multiplier effect of housing construction, applied to the target numbers in our hypothesized housing policy, suggests an additional 276,000 jobs would be generated by multiplier effects. Adding multiplier-effect jobs to the previous "basic jobs generated" total yields an estimate of 11.96 million jobs created over the decade of the 1990s. Using BLS formulas and the Maryland multiplier yields a very conservative estimate of $3.3 billion in individual federal income and wage tax revenues annually, or $33 billion for the decade.

If housing equals new jobs, it also equals new economic activity—that is, the wages, profits, and commerce directly associated

with the construction of new dwelling units, plus the additional indirect impact of spending the dollars resulting from housing construction in other areas of the economy. In 1979 the National Association of Home Builders (NAHB)[116] provided an exceedingly
conservative estimate of this economic activity. Excluding all the spin-
off purchases encouraged by new construction (furniture, draperies,
garden supplies, etc.), the Association gauged the overall economic
impact of 1,000 new, single-family homes at $110 million and the
economic activity generated by 1,000 new multi-family units at more
than $50 million.

Using these conservative estimates, the hypothetical level of
housing activity considered in this chapter would result in economic
activity worth about $440 billion in the decade. Utilizing an updating
correction factor (derived largely from computing wage differentials
in housing construction from the 1979 NAHB data to the 1987 BLS
indices) yields a conservative estimate of economic activity for the
decade-long period of about $600 billion (unadjusted upward for in-
flation).

The foregoing analysis suggests that the opportunity costs in-
curred by the United States in not investing in housing are tremendous. But, of course, the cost-benefit ratios of federal investment in
housing have been the subject of debate in recent years. While most
analysts have recognized the substantial contribution of housing to
the American economy, there are capital allocation analyses that
purport to show that America has overinvested in housing.[117] Compared to other nations, this is untrue. In almost every other indus-
trialized country, housing represents a higher proportion of gross
national product than it does in the United States. Domestically, the
amount of mortgage credit has remained roughly constant for the
past 40 years, relative to this nation's total credit volume.

In 1987, one proponent of the view that housing has received
too generous a share of America's capital described in detail the
probable consequences to the national economy if housing had received the lower quantum of dollars he advocates: housing stock
would be reduced by 25 percent and housing prices would be 28
percent higher while wages would be up only 13 percent, the real
interest rate would decline by only 1 percent, and GNP would increase by 10 percent.[118] Readers will decide for themselves, of course,
if this is the economy they would want for their future and that of
their children—one in which a much smaller and far more costly

housing stock yields widespread overcrowding, diminished home-ownership, and increased homelessness, in exchange for marginally lower interest rates and rapid GNP acceleration.

Those who would argue that America has overinvested in housing note that a major component of that investment level is the federal tax deduction for mortgage interest payments. To produce a slightly lower interest rate for corporate borrowers producing non-housing goods, these analysts would have to advocate the elimination of this incentive to homeownership. Because this deduction is responsible for the affordability of homeownership for millions of American families—at this point, for most American home-owning families—the consequences to our economy and society of efforts to diminish housing credit must be stated clearly: more cars but fewer driveways, lower interest rates but higher shelter costs, fewer homes and fewer homeowners. Interestingly, no major national corporation that might be presumed to benefit from lower interest rates has publicly joined in the call to diminish, further, homeownership in America.

We have said that a national housing policy targeted on the major specific needs of large and growing population sectors who need help, if that policy were successfully pursued in the 1990s, would provide not just housing but jobs for millions of Americans and would contribute significantly to our economic growth and federal treasury. Can our recent and current national housing policy meet these targeted needs? Is our recent and current national housing policy adequate to the requirements of the 1980s and the challenges ahead in the 1990s? If so, it ought to be continued. If not, we need a new housing policy for America—one that will accomplish these important national goals.

RECENT AND CURRENT FEDERAL HOUSING POLICIES

The basic thrust of federal housing policy in the 1980s has been to diminish sharply the national government's involvement in virtually every aspect of the provision of shelter. The President and Congress have cut:

- support for the construction of new housing by the private sector and governmental expenditures for the production and rehabilitation of public housing;

- funds granted to local governments to provide homeownership opportunities for low- and moderate-income families;
- direct governmental assistance to low- and moderate-income
  tenants;
- the number of low- and moderate-income tenants eligible to
  receive the reduced amounts of appropriated new housing aid;
- federal tax incentives to the private sector for the production
  of rental housing;
- federal loans to low- and moderate-income homeowners for
  the rehabilitation of substandard units;
- housing assistance to elderly and handicapped persons, American Indians, and farmers.

Recent presidential proposals would terminate almost every major program of federal housing help for the American people. They
would dramatically curtail federal involvement in promoting homeownership by increasing downpayment requirements, insurance fees,
and closing costs for government-insured mortgages; seeking ways
to sell or transfer the basic assets of the Federal Housing Administration (FHA) to private investors; and withdrawing government
backing for federal home mortgage loans to veterans and others.

Cuts in Direct Federal Housing Assistance Expenditures[119]

Expenditures on housing have been cut more deeply in the 1980s
than have expenditures on any other federal activity. Total budget
authority for the Department of Housing and Urban Development
diminished by 57 percent from 1980 to 1987, from $35.7 billion to
$15.2 billion. The HUD budget has declined from 7 percent of the
federal budget in 1978 to about 1 percent in 1987 (see Figure 8).

These profound cuts have affected HUD's most basic programs.
For example, new budget authority for assisted housing (primarily
rental assistance to elderly and handicapped persons, low- and
moderate-income families, and public housing construction and
modernization) was slashed by more than 70 percent in the 1980s,
from $26.7 billion in 1981 to $7.5 billion in 1987 (see Table 10). Con-
sequently, the number of new units to be covered by such assistance
fell from more than 204,000 in 1981 to 76,406 in 1987, a 62 percent
reduction (see Table 11). In fact, the number of new HUD-assisted
units, which averaged about 300,000 a year in the late 1970s, aver-

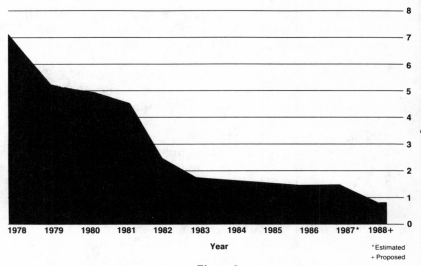

Figure 8
Budget Authority of HUD, as a Percentage of the Total Federal Budget,
1978–1988
Source: National Association of Home Builders, National Association of Realtors, and Mortgage
Bankers Association of America, *Toward a National Housing Policy* (Washington, D.C.: The Associ-
ations, 1987), p. 4.

Table 10
New Budget Authority for Assisted Housing, HUD, FY 1977–FY 1987
(in billions of dollars)

Fiscal Year	New Budget Authority
1977	28.0
1978	31.5
1979	24.4
1980	26.7
1981	19.8
1982	13.3
1983	8.7
1984	9.9
1985	10.8
1986	10.0
1987	7.5

Source: U.S. Department of Housing and Urban Development, *Annual budget, 1977–1987* (Washington, D.C.: The Department, 1977–1987).

Table 11

Total HUD-Assisted Housing: New Incremental Units, FY 1981–FY 1988

Program	FY 1981	FY 1982	FY 1983	FY 1984	FY 1985	FY 1986	FY 1987 (proposed)	FY 1988 (proposed)
Public housing (regular)	33,242	8,944		5,212	5,448	3,994		
Public housing (Indian)	3,128	3,192	2,500	2,762	2,178	2,078	2,459	1,000
Section 202 Elderly/Handicapped (Section 8 Support)	15,166	16,038	14,308	14,277	12,639	11,515	10,274	2,000
Section 8 (New Construction)	42,942	10,080						
Section 8 (Existing)	90,354	23,418	36,147	53,835	36,513	29,853	9,649	
Section 8 (Mod Rehab)	19,916	6,799	14,917	7,074	4,902	9,413	5,075	
Housing vouchers			14,104	38,364	35,002	48,949	79,000	82,000
Total units	204,748	68,471	67,872	97,264	100,044	91,854	76,406	
% new construction	46%	56%	25%	23%	20%	19%	17%	4%
% housing vouchers					39%	38%	64%	96%

Source: U.S. Department of Housing and Urban Development, *Annual Budget, 1981–1988* (Washington, D.C.: The Department, 1981–1988), as issued in press packet by National Association of Housing and Redevelopment Officials.

49

Table 12

Trend in Funding of Major HUD Programs, FY 1981, FY 1987 (Proposed), and
FY 1988 (Proposed) (in millions of dollars)*

Program	FY 1981	FY 1986 (estimates)	FY 1987 (proposed)	FY 1988 (proposed)
CDBG	3,695	2,990	2,625	2,625
UDAG	675	316	20	
Section 312	130	40	85	
HODAG		72		
Assisted housing†	26,689	9,970	7,362	3,920
Public housing modernization	1,699	1,441	1,000	1,000

*Initial appropriation of Budget Authority.
†Includes Public Housing, New Construction and Modernization, Section 8, Section 202 Elderly
Handicapped, and Housing Vouchers.
Source: U.S. Department of Housing and Urban Development, Annual Budget, 1981, 1986–198
(Washington, D.C.: The Department, 1981, 1986–1988).

aged about 100,000 a year in the 1980s, while both the number o
poor people and the depth of their poverty increased.

The decline in assisted housing is shown in Table 12, where
major reductions in two programs of assistance to homeowners are
also observable. Section 312 loans to aid homeowners in rehabilitat
ing their properties and Community Development Block Grant
(CDBG), which have been used to promote homeownership for low
and moderate-income families (and a plethora of other housing-re
lated efforts) have suffered cuts of 69 percent and 19 percent respec
tively (see Table 12).

The most extreme cut in federal involvement has been in hous
ing supply investments: the government has virtually withdrawn
support of housing construction. In fiscal 1980, HUD was involvec
in 129,400 new rental housing starts; by fiscal 1986 HUD-related renta
starts approximated only 19,000, or about 6 percent, of national renta
unit production. And most of these minimal construction activitie
were based on pre-1981 commitments. By honoring pre-1981 com
mitments the overall number of federally assisted units increasec
from 1981 to 1987, but at a rate slower than the loss of low-income
apartments or the growth in poverty and homelessness.

During the 1980s, the national government also raised rent bur
dens on currently assisted households from 25 percent to 30 percen
of income, reduced eligibility of new assistance recipients to only

those households in the most extreme poverty, and cut rural housing programs sharply, even as the farm economy in much of America deteriorated.

All the cuts reported above were agreed upon by the President
and Congress, although Congress generally acted to accept major
reductions in housing expenditure reductions less severe than those
requested by the Administration. Congress has also typically refused to approve Administration plans to spend even less than the
cut-back figures appropriated by the House and the Senate. Table 13
shows the Administration's effort to avoid spending these dimin-

Table 13
Rescissions and Shifts in HUD Budget Authority, FY 1987 and FY 1988
(in millions of dollars)

Program	Authority	Note
*Proposed FY 1987 Rescissions**		
Housing Development Action Grants	$ 99.6	Entire appropriation
Section 8 Moderate Rehabilitation	238.8	Reduction of 2,500 units
Rental Rehabilitation Grants	125.0	Will leave a 1987 round of $95 million
Housing Counseling Services	3.5	Termination
Urban Development Action Grants	205.4	January 1987 round canceled
Community Development Block Grants	375.2	Reduces FY 1987 level
Salaries and Expenses	19.0	
Total	$1,066.5	
Shift of Fund Availability, FY 1987–FY 1988†		
Public Housing Modernization	$436.9	Leaves $1 billion level in FY 1987 and FY 1988
Public Housing Operating Subsidies	85.3	Balance in FY 1987 funds
Section 202–Housing for the Elderly or Hand-icapped:		
Section 8 Authority	267.2	2,000 units shifted to FY 1988
Direct Loan Authority	90.7‡	
Total	$880.1	

*Subject to approval of the Congress within 45 days.
†Subject to congressional approval.
‡Technically shown as a decrease in 1987 authority and an increase in 1988 authority.
Source: U.S. Department of Housing and Urban Development, *Annual Budget, 1981–1988* (Wash-
ington, D.C.: The Department, 1981–1988), as issued in press packet by National Association of
Housing and Redevelopment Officials.

ished dollars in fiscal 1987 and 1988. Not shown in Table 13 are Administration proposals to rescind, in fiscal year 1988, 75 percent of the Farmers Home Administration's (FmHA) 1987 rural housing program. These recissions, if approved, would have reduced home-ownership, rental, and mortgage insurance programs for rural America by $2 billion.

Beyond the deep and pervasive cuts in direct federal expenditure discussed above, the President and Congress have agreed on three other policies that are likely further to curtail federal involvement in housing in the 1980s and 1990s. These are the reduction of tax incentives to the private sector for the production of rental housing, the sale of public housing to present tenants with limited resale controls (so that the stock is less likely to be retained for low-income families), and the substitution, on a demonstration basis, of less generous housing vouchers for previously existing Section 8 rent-subsidy certificates.

Tax Reform

The Tax Reform Act of 1986[120] reduced or eliminated five previous federal incentives for the production of rental housing and created one new incentive. Capital gains are taxed at a higher rate than heretofore, depreciation schedules are lengthened, thereby reducing the early year attractiveness of investment in rental units. Losses on real estate no longer offset other taxable income for most of the class of investors traditionally interested in rental housing. A stringent limitation is imposed on the amount of tax-free bonds that states can issue. And housing bonds are restrictively regulated and lumped in with all other tax-free bonds, forcing state officials to choose between housing activities and roads, schools, water projects, and so on. The major new tax incentive is a tax credit program described below.

Most housing industry spokespersons, university researchers, and public officials' study groups who have written on the subject expect rents to increase and rental unit production to decrease as a result of these tax changes. The National Association of Home Builders predicted a 28 percent rise in local rents above inflation, and the National Apartment Association has estimated a probable production decline of 225,000 to 300,000 units over the next few years and a 15–25 percent increase in rent above inflation.[121] Writing in *Com-*

mon Cause magazine, one housing expert put probable rent increases at "20% or more."[122] University researchers have described the expected production fall (after a period of time in which "in-pipeline" projects covered by the old tax rules are constructed) as "substantial," projecting a rise in rents as well."[123]

The new tax incentive for rental unit production created by the tax reform is a three-year tax credit program, expiring in 1989. Under this program, each state will be permitted to allocate a limited amount of tax credits (calculated at $1.25 per citizen) providing a maximum 9 percent annual tax credit for 10 years for the construction or rehabilitation of low-income housing units not federally subsidized for up to 80 percent of the value of the unit, a maximum 4 percent annual tax credit for 10 years for the acquisition of low-income housing units without any rehabilitation, or for units that receive other government subsidies including tax-exempt bonds. However, expenditures must exceed $2,000 per unit for an owner to claim either the 9 percent or the 4 percent tax credit. Although tax credits are extended over 10 years, the set-aside for low-income units must be maintained for a "compliance period" of 15 years.

Ten percent of each state's allocation must be set aside for nonprofit organizations that have as one of their corporate purposes the fostering of low-income housing. However, there is no rural/urban breakdown for the distribution of funds. If not utilized, the nonprofit set-aside will be neither repooled nor carried over to the ensuing year. Tax credits for historic rehabilitation will fall from 25 percent to 20 percent for buildings placed in service starting in 1988. Rehabilitation of pre-1936 structures that are not certified as historic will qualify for 10 percent tax credits.

It is too early to assess the chances for this program to encourage the construction of low-income housing. On the one hand, the state agencies designated to allocate and administer the program are trying hard to make it work, successful national intermediaries are trying to find investors for a pool of tax credits, and dedicated housing advocates, including the National Low Income Housing Coalition, are working to make the program successful. On the other hand, the state agencies are reporting that they expect to be able to allocate only a rather small fraction of the credits, and national surveys of housing developers show that only a handful of builders believe they can make the tax credits work.[124]

Almost all knowledgeable persons agree on one thing about the new tax credit program: it will require state or local subsidy appropriations on top of the tax credits to develop affordable units for low-income tenants.[125] In consequence, if not in intent, the tax credit program will devolve some responsibility previously assumed by the federal government to state and local governments. In practice, therefore, the tax credits must be seen as part of the decrease of federal involvement in housing.

The Sale of Public Housing[126]

On October 23, 1984, HUD announced plans for a Public Housing Homeownership Demonstration Program, maintaining that a 1974 amendment to the 1937 Housing Act permits sales of public housing units to low-income tenants subject only to HUD approval. In 1985, the demonstration program was launched in an effort to sell at least 1,600 public housing units owned by 18 participating local housing authorities. If the program is deemed successful, HUD's announced goal is to expand the sales program and "privatize" a substantial portion of the nation's public housing stock.

The first sale occurred in 1986, received national publicity, and started an ongoing debate over the appropriateness and feasibility of privatization. Proponents of the program, including the conservative Heritage Foundation, which championed the effort, base much of their advocacy on a British policy under which the Thatcher government sold about 800,000 units of public housing to tenants in the early 1980s. Britain's "Right to Buy" program allows public housing tenants to purchase their units at a discount of up to 60 percent of market value. It has been very popular and is credited with a marked improvement in the physical appearance of both housing units and neighborhoods. American supporters of the HUD effort see the program as a means of extending homeownership to the poor.

Opponents of the sale of public housing stress that the demographics and history of British public housing are very different from those of the United States. Public housing in Britain is much more common; about one-third of all housing there is publicly owned rental housing, with the mean income of families in British public housing not far below that of owner-occupied housing and actually higher than that of families in private rental units. In the United States, on the other hand, only 1.5 percent of all housing is publicly owned, consisting mostly of elderly and single-parent househoulds with very low incomes.

The typical public housing project in Britain is a duplex, garden apartment, or four-unit walk-up, not the multiple-unit high rise that is common in American cities. Only 4 percent of the units sold in Britain were in high-rise apartment buildings; the rest were town homes, duplexes, or detached houses. Moreover, British public housing is much newer and in better physical condition than the private housing stock. In the United States, public housing is older and many are buildings in poor physical condition.

Opponents also argue that HUD's demonstration program will leave the worst units, housing the poorest tenants, in the public housing inventory while selling off the best units to wealthier tenants at highly subsidized prices, mortgage rates, and downpayments.

Most of all, opponents contend that the privatization program will reduce the number of apartments available to the poor. The program has limited resale controls because, after five years, a tenant-owner can sell the unit at market prices. Accordingly, critics believe that better units will be removed from the low-income stock, few public housing tenants will be able to afford to buy even at HUD's subsidized prices, and there may be a wave of foreclosures in a few years, at least in those units that need major repairs.

Peter Dreier, Director of Housing of the Boston Redevelopment Authority, suggests a middle course. Writing in the *New Republic* in 1986, Dreier argued:

If some public housing is to be sold, it should be transformed into resident-owned limited-equity cooperatives. This is a midpoint between renting and owning. It gives occupants greater control over their homes, and by restricting the resale prices it keeps them affordable over the long run. But to make it work, the government would have to provide residents with substantial subsidies. These would include help to repair the long neglected projects, funds to help residents pay the monthly costs of ownership and maintenance, and adequate training to give owner-residents the tools to manage the co-ops. Any way you approach it, government support is needed to house the poor, to fill the gap between what it costs to build housing and what low-income renters and owners can afford to pay.[127]

That is not HUD's present plan, of course. Nor is there any government intention to build a new low-income apartment for each public housing unit that is ultimately sold to middle-class or wealthier families.

Let us put the sale of public housing units into appropriate context. There is now a waiting list of 800,000 American families for the
nation's 1.3 million existing public housing units. In some cities, the
waiting list is so huge that it takes 10–20 years for a new applicant
to receive an apartment. Yet the Administration has continually proposed, and Congress approved, cuts in new construction of public
housing. In the first year in which public housing units began to be
sold off, new public housing units authorized were cut from 3,993
(fiscal 1986) to 2,500 (fiscal 1987). All the while, housing economists
and advocates agree that the current need for new construction exceeds 20,000 new units per year.

The cost of rehabilitating substandard public housing units was
found to be $23 billion in a 1986 national study.[128] Despite this, pub-
lic housing improvement funds were cut again in 1986–1987. This
policy of underfunding the rehabilitation and maintenance of public
housing seems particularly shortsighted since the current value of
all public housing units is $70 billion and replacement costs would be
much higher.

Some analysts have also been skeptical of HUD's motives regarding the proposed sale of public housing units. Most of the 3.5
million residents of public housing are very poor, with incomes averaging $5,000–$6,000 per year. Noting that HUD knowingly imposed higher rent burdens, these analysts have questioned HUD's
real interest and concern for public housing tenants.

It is consequences, not motivation, that concern us. In 1987, on
the fiftieth anniversary of the historic Housing Act of 1937, which
authorized the creation of federally supported public housing, the
national government was cutting back on the construction and
maintenance of public housing and beginning to sell it off with only
limited plans to keep or replace sold units for low-income use. It
seems incontrovertible that the planned sale of public housing constitutes another example of the decrease of federal involvement in
housing.

Vouchers for Rental Assistance[129]

In 1983, Congress authorized HUD to introduce a new form of rental
assistance, housing vouchers, on a demonstration basis. As with the
previous form of federal rental assistance, "Section 8 Certificates,"
vouchers subsidize tenants in existing units chosen by the tenant

that meet standards of physical adequacy. The voucher program differs from Section 8 in four major ways.

- The voucher program relies exclusively on existing housing stock. There is no contemplated use of vouchers to encourage needed new construction of rental housing.
- Voucher recipients are free to rent, at their own expense, a more expensive unit than is permitted by Section 8.
- The amount of the voucher is based on a "standard rent" in each locality, not on the rent actually paid by the tenant.
- Vouchers represent a 5-year federal commitment rather than the 15-year commitment behind each Section 8 Certificate.

In most recent years, HUD has proposed replacing the Section 8 effort with an all-voucher system. Congress has continued the Section 8 system at a reduced level, permitting an expansion of the voucher program.

There is no question that vouchers are less generous to tenants, that the vouchers are intended to reduce federal expenditures on low-income housing, that the program explicitly rejects any federal responsibility for stimulating new construction, or that the truncated time frame of federal commitment (15 years to 5) makes vouchers a short-term palliative.

There is substantial disagreement, however, over several other matters. One issue concerns the workability of the program in areas with low vacancies. In late 1986 and early 1987, both Boston and New York City found that 62 percent of voucher recipients could not find housing. HUD publications acknowledge the problem for places like New York, but suggest that, nationally, only about 25 percent of vouchers and certificates go unused and that vouchers are working comparatively well in such low-vacancy areas as Montgomery County, Maryland, and New Haven, Connecticut.

Another issue relates to the freedom vouchers offer tenants to pay more than 30 percent of income for rent and the fact that HUD pays the difference between 30 percent of income and standard, not actual, rents. Opponents of the voucher program contend that these features of the program will only result in higher rents and more tenants paying a disproportionate share of income for shelter. Early statistics on the voucher program suggest that almost half of all voucher recipients are in fact paying over 30 percent of income for rent. HUD counters by stating that this is a basic plus for the program because paying more for housing *as a matter of choice* is a critical tenet of the voucher effort. HUD believes that studies will ultimately show those paying more are getting better housing and not being overcharged; the voucher system enables tenants to stay in units with rapidly escalating rents, if they choose to do so.

A third point of contention is the cost of subsidy. Surprisingly voucher subsidy costs have been somewhat higher than those for Section 8 Certificates. This seems to be happening because the family, not the government, gets the savings when they pay less than the fair market or standard rent level, and vouchers are less sensitive than certificates to state welfare grants. HUD expects voucher subsidy costs to decline, however, because vouchers will recognize no more than two rent increases over a five-year period. Of course this feature of the vouchers will increase rent burdens on many assisted tenant families. HUD publications accept that fact because it means that more families will be able to be served within the total available pool of subsidy dollars.

At present, HUD seems to want more poor families to get fewer dollars for a shorter period of time. In most respects, then, vouchers would appear to be still another example of the cut-back of federal involvement in housing.

In 1983, the Administration sought and Congress supported two limited new programs that, purportedly, would have enhanced federal involvement in housing activities. These efforts, Housing Development Grants (HODAGs) and Rental Rehabilitation grants, have produced some, but relatively little, housing in their early years. They were scheduled for elimination (HODAG) or severe reductions (Rental Rehabilitation) in the Administration's 1988 budget.

Housing Policy in 1987–1988

Throughout the 1980s, Congress has legislated—often reluctantly— deep and pervasive cuts in federal housing involvement.

The President's proposed 1988 budget[130] recommended virtual dismantling of the federal system of housing assistance and a massive, destabilizing withdrawal of federal involvement in the U.S. homeownership financing system. On the housing assistance side, the Administration proposed to terminate 16 important housing programs entirely, to cut HUD budget authority by another 50 percent, to decrease incremental housing units to a figure 68 percent below 1981 levels, to encourage the construction of a minuscule 3,000 units of new housing (down from the 204,000 of 1981, almost half of which were for newly constructed units). The following program terminations related to housing are included in the Administration's budget for fiscal year 1988:

- HUD Urban Development Action Grants (UDAGs);
- HUD Housing Development Grants (HODAGs);
- HUD Solar Energy and Conservation Bank;
- HUD Section 202 Elderly/Handicapped Housing Program;
- HUD Section 8 Moderate Rehabilitation;
- HUD Section 8 Existing Certificates;
- HUD Public Housing Program;
- HUD Section 312 Rehabilitation Loan Program;
- HUD Section 108 Loan Guarantee Program;
- FHA Mortgage Insurance for Investor Loans;
- FHA Mortgage Insurance for Second Homes;
- EPA Sewage Treatment Grants;
- FmHA Section 502 Homeownership Program;
- FmHA Section 515 Rental Housing Program;
- FmHA Rental Assistance Program;
- FmHA Water and Waste Disposal Loan and Grant Programs.

These program terminations would end virtually all federal efforts to assist homeownership-oriented construction, all homeowner loans for rehabilitation of substandard dwellings, all rural construction programs (both homeowner and rental), and all public housing construction and would replace the entire existing structure of rental assistance with the voucher program.

With reference to the federal homeownership financing system, the Administration proposed higher downpayments, higher insurance premiums, higher cash closing costs, reduced eligibility for government-backed mortgages, and the sale of hundreds of millions of dollars in Federal Housing Authority assets.

These proposals, if adopted, would reduce homeownership opportunities for hundreds of thousands of American families. The reduced eligibility and asset sales, it is generally agreed, could disrupt the American national mortgage finance system by restricting needed loan volume in the Federal National Mortgage Association (FNMA) and Federal Home Loan Mortgage Corporation (FHLMC) and by eliminating the necessary asset base for Federal Housing Administration insurance, essentially eliminating FHA.

In acting on housing authorization and appropriation bills, Congress has accepted almost none of the President's recommendations. The Administration seems committed to attaining some further cutbacks in federal housing activity by executive action. It seems likely that the Reagan Administration will end by having achieved a profound truncation, but not elimination, of federal housing involvement. But, though Congress appears unwilling to exact further cuts from HUD, it also seems unable to do very much in the way of new initiatives. Housing legislation that moved through both houses of Congress in 1987 accepted, for the most part, scaled-back federal activity and proposed very little by way of a new housing policy for America.

The Impact of Federal Policies on America's Housing

Bringing decent housing within the reach of the people has been a basic priority of American government—one with deep historic roots. From the Homestead Act in the nineteenth century to the creation of the Federal Housing Administration, the Farmers Home and Veterans Administrations' home mortgage programs, and on through the creation of a smoothly functioning federal secondary mortgage credit market, the national government again and again has provided essential tools to make homeownership an attainable goal for a majority of Americans. From 1959 to 1977, five presidents—Republicans and Democrats alike—signed into law 10 separate housing acts strengthening the home mortgage financing system and creating a network of programs to increase the supply and affordability of rental housing.

Since 1980, however, the basic thrust of national housing policy has been to withdraw the federal government from housing activity. It has been a policy of cuts in direct housing assistance, cuts in indirect (tax) incentives for housing supply, cuts and proposed cuts in federal support for housing credit. Let us examine the impact of these policies.

In the 1980s, as noted above, America experienced a downturn in homeownership rates, especially among young families. Downpayment requirements, interest rates, and home prices increased faster than real incomes and savings. Homeownership became more concentrated among the wealthiest 20 percent of Americans amid a rising tide of mortgage default and delinquency.

National housing policies have exacerbated some of these problems and been irrelevant to others. Some federal credit agencies acted to increase downpayment requirements in the 1980s. Federal credit policy obviously failed to smooth out the interest rate rollercoaster ride that has inhibited homeownership. Federal housing policies included no tax incentive for downpayment savings plans, no direct, cost-effective downpayment assistance program, no emergency mortgage default assistance plan. If, today, many Americans are finding that the door to homeownership is closed to them, U.S. housing policy has varied between ignoring their knocking and hiding the keys.

In the 1980s, too, we observed that a majority of America's tenants live in cost-burdened, overcrowded, or dilapidated dwelling units. Increasing the supply of rental housing might have helped reduce both crowding and cost burdens, but national housing policy was to cut, to all but abandon, both direct assistance and tax incentives for new construction. To the decline in the quality of rental stock, national policy responded by providing less rehabilitation funding. To the crisis in rental housing for the poor, the national government answered by cutting rental assistance and by making it harder to get rental assistance.

The 1980s witnessed a scandalous explosion in homelessness. Federal cutbacks in housing supply and rental assistance for the poor tended to increase this tragic phenomenon. Surely the President's announced view that most homeless people are on the streets by choice bespoke not even the kind of recognition of the facts from which decent policy might flow. National housing policy in the 1980s, a policy of knowing neglect of our public housing inventory and manifest unconcern about the stagnation and decline in the quality of our housing stock, is more apt to produce homelessness than homeownership.

In the 1990s America will require more housing, better targeted to the life needs of an increasingly diverse population. We will require more housing: to provide shelter for a still growing population; to accommodate the pent up demand of people who delayed household formation in the 1980s; and to meet the homeownership goals of an increasing number of young families. We will need better targeting of our housing production, rehabilitation and conversion in order to shelter the record number of frail elderly, single-parent families, and lower-income Americans we expect in the population of the 1990s.

It is hard to envision how any of this country's future housing needs will be met by continuing our current and recent policies. We are likely to need more housing, but recent and current housing policy has been to withdraw both direct assistance and indirect incentives for housing production. We will probably need to substantially rehabilitate a million or more existing units for use by the frail elderly, but funding that could be used for this purpose has already been cut. We may want to facilitate the conversion of older, larger homes for use by the smaller families of the future or to increase affordability to single-parent families or to accommodate the all-time high number of single persons we expect; again, recent and current policy withdraws assistance and incentives for these purposes.

Recent and current national housing policies, if pursued into the future, give little promise that the government will help with the supply of decent affordable shelter in the 1990s. These policies simply do not adequately address the coming gaps and mismatches between America's people and America's housing stock. Continuation of our present policies will not expand homeownership or expand shelter in the America of the 1990s. The failed housing policies of the 1980s are unlikely to prove more appropriate or more successful in the decade ahead.

Of course, it can be argued that recent and current housing policies never were intended to provide a direct cure for America's housing ills. Rather, it might be contended, they were designed to reduce federal spending and, in that very indirect way, to contribute to a better overall economy in which more people could afford their own homes or apartments without dependence on federal assistance and incentives. If that is the rationale, the policies fail on those grounds, too. During the period during which these policies were being adopted and implemented, federal spending did not decrease and the budget deficit was not significantly reduced. The only effect of all the housing cuts was to hurt those in need of housing.

Certainly these cuts have been part of the shift in federal spending priorities away from domestic needs and into military procurement. Continuation of this trend seems to us to be morally questionable and politically unwise. From an ethical perspective, it appears unjustifiable that housing help for the poor be cut to avoid a tax increase for the relatively rich in order to pay for the common defense. Whatever America's defense needs are, or will be, they ought not be financed in this way at this price. America's national security seems more likely to be diminished than enhanced by homelessness and the concentration of an increasingly emiserated poor in declining urban neighborhoods.

Separate and apart from considerations of deficit reduction and military spending, we need a new housing policy for America because recent and current policies have not, will not, and cannot meet the nation's housing needs or solve its emergent housing problems.

BEYOND CURRENT NATIONAL HOUSING POLICIES

American housing trends and national housing policies have covaried together, both going the wrong way, for almost a decade. The trends—mounting unmet needs, declining affordability, increasing homelessness, gaps and mismatches between the housing stock and the life conditions of the American people—are likely to continue into the 1990s unless national policies are improved.

The policies can be improved. They can be substantially improved rather easily and at relatively low cost.

All through the long night of federal abdication of responsibility, good new housing policies and programs have been invented, tried out, and evaluated at the state and local levels. Throughout the 1980s, state governments, municipal governments, community groups, non-profit corporations, private charitable foundations, religious institutions, labor unions, business leaders, and lots of concerned citizens—all across America—refused to give up on helping people achieve decent, affordable housing just because the federal government was doing so.

At the state and local level, then, housing activity has been expanded, not cut. Beyond the federal government, housing efforts in the 1980s have been encouraged by new ideas, new energies, new monies, new methods, new partnerships.

Unfortunately these efforts cannot meet the housing needs of the American people because the magnitude of the problem requires federal resources to do that. But some state and local efforts are good models from which improved federal policy can be derived; and the many new state and local programs constitute a new reality to which improved federal policy must relate. Most important of all, there are now literally thousands more people in America involved in housing issues than there used to be—state legislators and administrators, local elected officials, community leaders, clergy, labor union people, business people, foundation officers, and interested citizens. These people are, at once, the talent pool and constituency needed to develop a new housing policy for America.

For these reasons, we now turn to state and local housing policies in the 1980s.

2
State Programs and National Policy

In the 1980s, state governments increasingly turned their attention to the affordable housing problem, responding with a diverse array of innovative and effective programs. At least 39 states enacted or adopted one or more major new housing programs during the 1980–1987 period.[1] These new state programs, more than 230 in all,[2] seek to meet a broad range of housing needs, utilizing a wide variety of new financing methods. They involve an extensive set of new partners, bringing to bear a substantial number of new funding sources.

In this chapter, we analyze the growth and character of state-level housing programs in the 1980s. This analysis yields three conclusions. First, some state-level programs deserve consideration as models for a new national housing policy; that is, the federal government should probably adopt them as national programs. Second, some of these programs should remain largely the province of the states but need support from the federal level. Third, none of these programs, nor all the states together, can meet America's housing goals without a substantial enhancement in federal involvement. The new state programs of the 1980s provide a solid base, but cannot substitute, for a new national housing policy.

STATE-FUNDED HOUSING PROGRAMS, 1980–1987

Expansion in the number, diversity, and sophistication of state housing programs has been dramatic. Before 1980, most of the states had only one basic program: they sold tax-free bonds (typically a federally authorized mortgage revenue bond) to bond buyers, who accepted interest levels below those borne by taxable investment vehicles, and then loaned the bond proceeds to qualified builders and income-eligible home buyers at interest rates somewhat below those prevalent in the conventional market. For multi-family projects, affordability of rents was sought (beyond the interest-rate subsidy derived from the tax-free bond mechanism) by providing federal rent-subsidy guarantees to the project sponsors.

Tax-free bond programs remain important to the states, and are discussed later in this chapter. But, since 1980, the states have sought new and different housing capital and have done so in an aggressive and imaginative fashion. States have used, for example, general fund revenues, general obligation bonds, taxes on real property title transfers, offshore oil revenues, casino tax revenues, lawsuit settlement proceeds, pension fund investments, taxable bond funds, repayments of indebtedness, new types of housing securities, state-held unclaimed properties, and much more.[3]

In marked contrast to the federal cut-backs, states have spent far more of their tax-derived revenues on housing in the 1980s than ever before—at least $3 billion, collectively, in the first six years of the decade. Seventeen of the states have adopted housing trust funds since 1980—dedicating a permanent, stable, annually renewable revenue source in order to meet housing needs.[4]

Finding the national government to be an increasingly unwilling partner, the states have sought new coventurers in affordable housing efforts. In the 1980s, states have jointly financed housing projects with municipalities, counties, foundations, churches, hospitals, universities, non-profit housing corporations, banks, developers, self-help owner-builders, public housing authorities, corporations, rural homesteaders, city-wide builder–bank–non-profit coalitions (urban housing partnerships), national housing intermediary entities (Local Initiatives Support Corporation, Enterprise Foundation), area redevelopment agencies, urban homesteaders, and others.[5]

With new monies and new partners, the American states found new financial methods by which to make housing affordable. Among these are interest-rate buydowns, deferred payment loans, lease purchase contracts, shared appreciation and shared equity mortgages, sale and lease back arrangements, loan closing cost buy-downs, up-front capital grants as a form of subsidy for rental projects, joint purchase/rehabilitation loans, and special mortgage insurance programs (extending protection to borrower types and housing stock not covered by federal or private insurance).[6] Of course, the states also widely employed more typical kinds of housing assistance: direct low-interest loans, second mortgages, loan guarantees, rent-payment guarantees, and direct subsidies.

Beyond new financing methods, a few states used their regulatory powers to achieve housing affordability (e.g., via the adoption of more flexible codes) and urged, induced, or required their local governments to do the same (e.g., by inclusionary or anti-snob zoning and bonus density zoning). In some instances, states have donated surplus land and requested or required local governments to do likewise.[7]

Some states have addressed new housing needs as well as old, including those of single parents, female-headed households, single persons living alone, and the frail elderly. But mostly the states have dealt with the basics: they have tried to expand homeownership opportunities, to stimulate needed rental units, to facilitate rehabilitation of substandard units, and to aid local groups with the costs of land acquisition, predevelopment, and construction so as to increase the number of affordable housing units for low- and moderate-income families.[8]

In the 1980s, then, the states—collectively—came of age in the area of housing. More than two-thirds of all housing programs now operated by the states (beyond traditional bond-financed ones) were begun in the last seven years. These new programs have new staff to run them and new state-wide pro-housing coalitions behind them; they represent new thinking and new energies.

In many ways, the states are now well ahead of the national government in the things they are trying to do to build affordable housing. The states now seem ready to be full partners with the federal government. America is ready, it would appear, for a robust federalism on housing policy.

Let us consider in greater detail what the states have been doing. Unless otherwise indicated, all the programs described here are funded by means other than mortgage revenue bonds and were begun in or after 1980.

New Homeownership Programs

Since 1980, at least 11 states have adopted 24 separate programs to stimulate new construction of affordable homes for low- and moderate-income families. Twenty-two of the states have initiated more than 30 homeownership efforts that concentrate not on new construction but on making the purchase of existing homes more affordable.[9] The construction-related programs usually provide lower-rate financing to builders, but some states have gone further—offering builders deferred payment loans, direct grants, mortgage insurance, no-cost infrastructure improvements, or incentives to enter into lease/purchase contracts with low- or moderate-income buyers. The states have invested or earmarked at least $600 million for construction-related programs in recent years. Because many of these programs are very new, and available data on them sketchy, it is difficult to estimate precisely the total number of dwelling units that they will produce. We know that at least 25,000 units have already come on line but that is a small fraction of the ultimate number.

State-level homeownership programs that can, but need not, be used to stimulate new construction are more numerous and varied. Most of these programs offer reduced-interest, first-mortgage loans to low- and moderate-income families, using state revenue to buy down the interest rate, usually from an already lower than conventional rate achieved via tax-free bonding. A few state programs make second mortgages available, sometimes with very low or no interest or deferred payback. At least three states use their funds this way as a kind of homelessness prevention program, to forestall mortgage foreclosures against temporarily out-of-work homeowners. A number of states target their homeownership programs not just to low- or moderate-income families but to first-time home buyers, which tends to help younger families. Many of the states target geographic areas especially in need of affordable housing (urban centers, rural communities, high housing-cost counties, areas hit by natural disaster, etc.).

The idea of having an interest-rate buydown fund, which is a typical part of the 30-plus state homeownership programs, has merit as a potential national policy. Such a fund could be used countercyclically, when interest rates rise above moderate levels, to maintain affordability for first-time home buyers and to provide anti-recessionary jobs, wages, and profits.

Five state-level homeownership efforts warrant specific mention as models for new national housing programs. These are:

- Connecticut's downpayment assistance program;[10]
- New Jersey's lease/purchase plan (also implemented in Colorado);[11]
- Massachusetts' Home Ownership Opportunity Program;[12]
- New York's Nehemiah Plan;[13]
- California's shared equity mortgage program.[14]

Connecticut's Downpayment Assistance Program promotes homeownership for low- and moderate-income families by providing a low-interest (6 percent) second loan that is linked to a Connecticut Housing Finance Authority first mortgage. The downpayment loan can cover up to 25 percent of acquisition costs and may be paid back over a 30-year term (except that the payback period may not exceed that of the first mortgage). The program is limited to income-eligible owner-occupants who have not owned their primary residence during the three years immediately preceding the loan. In practice, this is a program targeted to first-time home buyers or low or moderate income. Begun in the mid-1980s, the program had already helped over 1,400 home buyers by 1986 on total loans of less than $13 million.

New Jersey's lease/purchase project provides affordable housing to low- and moderate-income families by offering low-interest mortgages and an option to save the amount necessary for a downpayment. A potential home buyer rents a unit in the project for two years with an option to purchase it at the end of the lease term. To provide for the downpayment, a portion of each month's rent is placed in an escrow account in the prospective homeowner's name. In practice, lease/purchase involves a multi-party partnership in which a city or other local public body issues bonds for construction financing, a non-profit organization assumes ownership for the initial two-year period, and the state housing agency provides permanent mortgage financing for the renter/buyer.

Lease-purchase works. The program began only in 1986, but already a 72-unit condominium project has been constructed for moderate-income families in Atlantic City, of which 24 units have been set aside for low- and moderate-income tenants at an 8.25 percent mortgage interest rate. In addition, a 108-unit development has been

built in New Brunswick, of which one-third of the units are designated for tenants whose incomes fall within the lower third of eligible participants; the interest rate is 8.25 percent. Thousands more
lease/purchase units are in various stages of development.

Also begun in 1986 is Massachusetts' Homeownership Opportunity Program, which aims to stimulate production of new homes
for purchase by moderate-income buyers at low interest rates with
long-term affordability controls. In this program, Bay State cities and
towns make joint application with profit-oriented or non-profit developers for state funds to subsidize construction and mortgage affordability of homes. Eligible purchasers are moderate-income
households (incomes of $17,000–$43,000) who qualify for mortgages
at 5.5–8.5 percent. All projects must include municipal contributions, such as donated land, reduced taxes, fast project approvals,
or zoning density increases to reduce the costs of the housing produced. The announced program goal was production of 2,500 units.
Within months of initiation, more than 100 cities and towns expressed interest; the first 24 applications were submitted in June of
1986, totaling 1,100 units.

The Massachusetts effort is similar to New York's Affordable
Homeownership Development Program. That effort, initiated in 1985,
enhances homeownership for low- and moderate-income individuals and families. It provides grants or loans, combined with public/
private investment, for one- to four-family units, including owner-
occupied cooperatives and condominiums. The program is funded
by a $25 million appropriation. Eligible applicants (a municipality,
housing development fund company, not-for-profit corporation, or
charitable organization that has as one of its primary purposes the
improvement of housing) apply to the state's Affordable Housing
Corporation for loans relating to the acquisition/rehabilitation or
construction of low- and moderate-income housing. In the first two
years of operation, this program granted funds to about 70 projects,
providing some 3,800 new or rehabilitated units.

A more comprehensive and complex partnership for affordable
housing is New York's Nehemiah Plan, which combines several
sources of funding into an innovative financial configuration to produce modestly priced single-family homes in large numbers. The
program is credited with upgrading one of New York City's most
deteriorated neighborhoods by providing 1,000 new homes to low-
and moderate-income families.

It worked this way. Private-sector leaders provided interest-free construction loans (in New York City, the lenders were a consortium of churches). The State of New York provided below-market permanent financing to every Nehemiah Plan home, allocating over $29 million of mortgage funds. The city donated the land at a cost of one dollar per lot along with a property tax abatement. The city also provided a $10,000, non-amortizing, interest-free second mortgage for each unit. The second mortgage is paid only upon resale of the home; its principal due is gradually reduced to zero over 15 years. In addition, if the home is sold after less than 15 years, the homeowner must share the appreciation with the city. The city's share of appreciation also gradually decreases to zero over 15 years. After 15 years, the second mortgage is completely forgiven, and the homeowner may retain all the appreciation in the value of the home. These features contribute to community stability by encouraging residents to remain in their homes.

By 1986, 693 Nehemiah homes had been completed and occupied, 179 were under construction, and 241 more were planned for 1987. The waiting list for new Nehemiah homes includes over 5,000 families. The success of the program led to plans to expand the Nehemiah program to other neighborhoods.

The federal government could replicate the Nehemiah Plan in other areas of the country by providing funds for the interest-free, non-amortizing second mortgage or the interest-free revolving construction loan fund. These funds could be granted to localities with incentives for state and local governments and private non-profit organizations to provide additional subsidies. Proposals for precisely these federal actions have been included in housing authorization bills in both houses of Congress.

The deferred payback, shared appreciation feature of the Nehemiah Plan is also central to California's Homeownership Assistance Program. That program, begun in 1981, was designed to help income-eligible first-time home buyers purchase manufactured housing or rental units in buildings being converted to condominiums. As described by the Federal Home Loan Mortgage Corporation, the program revolves around two financing components—a primary loan made by a participating lender that conforms to its normal lending criteria, and a second, shared appreciation, loan with deferred interest. The primary loan is eligible for sale in the secondary market. The second trust financing, or "CHAP" loan, is funded by the state.

The second loan funded by the state may cover up to 49 percent of the property's purchase price. These loans accrue contingent payments above principal. That is, the loans do not bear interest in the standard sense. Rather, a borrower is obligated to repay the principal amount of the loan plus, upon resale, a part of the property's appreciation proportional to the original loan-to-value ratio of the CHAP loan. Thus, if a $20,000 CHAP loan is made for the purchase of an $80,000 unit, the state has a 25 percent interest in the property. If the property were subsequently sold for $100,000, the state receives its original loan amount plus 25 percent of the appreciation, or $5,000. The borrower nets $15,000 in appreciation.

Borrowers acquire CHAP loans by applying to participating lenders for the maximum primary loans for which they can qualify. Borrowers must make downpayments of at least 5 percent and must commit 35 percent of gross income to monthly housing costs including utilities. The state then lends borrowers the difference between the purchase price and the total of the downpayment and the primary loan. The state financing is in the form of a wraparound or all-inclusive loan, which enables the lender originating the primary loan to service both loans as one. The borrower's income is recertified by the lender at the end of two years, again after five years, and thereafter every five years. In the event that a borrower's income has increased to the point where housing costs fall below 25 percent of gross income, mortgage payments are increased up to a 35 percent level and the increased payments are applied to reduce the state loan.

The California program has helped 500 or more low- and moderate-income families achieve homeownership.

The state homeownership assistance programs described in this section include several features that are potentially useful for a new federal homeownership effort. First, the states have experimented with interest-rate buydown funds. As indicated above, this could be an important innovation at the federal level, one that could operate countercyclically both to expand homeownership opportunities and to enhance and protect our national economy. Second, at least a few states have had success with deferred payback, shared equity, or shared appreciation arrangements. A national program using these features would be even more actuarially sound than any single state program can be. It would make our national government an equity investor in two of the best assets our country has—our young families and our housing stock. Third, lease/purchase projects seem worthy of consideration—both as a potential national program and as a state program deserving of federal encouragement. Finally, all the successful state programs involve a wider array of partnerships than previously has been involved in affordable housing efforts. This is a principle that will be important to any new housing policy for America. A new national housing policy should provide incentives and flexibility for participation by employers, states, cities, non-profits, and others.

New Rental Housing Programs

Since 1980, at least 15 states have initiated some 33 or more programs designed to increase the supply or affordability of rental housing.[15] The majority of these programs aim at the production of new units by providing low-interest loans (or, in a few cases, by up-front capital grants or loan guarantees); many more offer one-time loans than offer continuing rent subsidies. Indeed, the number of new one-time state loan programs dwarfs the combined total of programs that provide continuing rent or operating subsidies. One-time loan subsidies are simpler and less expensive to administer than are continuing subsidies. At the state level, these one-time loans or grants have tended to be shallower subsidies than the continuing subsidy programs.

The states have also experimented with rent guarantee programs (Maryland), shared equity contracts with builders (operating in Hawaii and authorized in New Jersey), 100 percent loan-to-value mortgages (Connecticut), loans targeted to specific geographic areas (Nevada, Maine, West Virginia, California), loan guarantees (Michigan), and emergency rent payments to prevent homelessness (New Jersey, Pennsylvania, Connecticut, Massachusetts). But, again, most states have adopted rather simple one-time, low-cost loan programs as their primary rental housing program.

A few states have recently entered, or chosen to remain in, the public housing business—providing new publicly owned apartment complexes. In this regard, a New Jersey program—the Housing Assistance Corporation—is interesting because it permits the state itself to act as a developer of rental housing (or to be managing partner, limited partner, or contract builder). In current projects, the Corporation is committed to build but not to manage rental complexes, contracting to turn them over to public housing authorities or non-profits who intend to keep the units in the low-income housing inventory permanently.

This strategy has great advantages over rental production policies that seek to induce private developers to build apartments and lease them at below market rents for a limited term of years. We have already seen, in Chapter 1, the immense costs—in both financial and human terms—that can ensue when the term expires and the private sector desires to obtain higher rates of return by converting whole complexes to market-rate rents.

An improved federal housing policy might well provide support to states that, like New Jersey, agree to develop permanent, public, and community-based supplies of affordable rental housing.

New Rehabilitation Programs

Great variety and innovation has characterized state actions to encourage the rehabilitation of existing housing units. At least 24 states have adopted one or more new housing rehabilitation programs since 1980, accounting for 44 or more new programs in all.[16] The vast majority of these programs aim at helping low- and moderate-income homeowners, or the owners of low-income rental units, to bring their properties up to safe conditions via low-interest loans. About 25 percent of the programs are largely intended to promote energy conservation.

The financial arrangements by which states have sought rehabilitation of housing stock demonstrate much new thinking. The states have tried first, second, and third mortgages (Colorado), deferred payback periods (Maryland, Massachusetts, Colorado), forgivable loans (Minnesota, Georgia), joint city/state loan programs (Washington, Michigan), loan insurance (Minnesota), zero interest loans (Maryland), shared equity loans (Wisconsin), and resale controls (Minnesota).

The states have also targeted their rehab money to the types of rehabilitation efforts and to the geographic areas they perceive to be most in need of assistance. Recognizing the needs of frail elderly or handicapped persons to make structural changes in their homes, Massachusetts, Maryland, New Jersey, Kentucky, Minnesota, and Delaware have adopted programs targeted to these groups. Geographic targeting (mostly to cities, rural communities, and areas impacted by environmental problems) has been successful in Connecticut, Maine, Massachusetts, Michigan, Virginia, and Washington.

As indicated in Chapter 1, America's housing stock has not been improving in quality in the 1980s the way it had been in the 1945–1975 period. While the federal government has cut back on helping low- and moderate-income families to upgrade their homes, the states have increased their efforts to do so. Certainly the states' clear commitment to upgrading the housing stock ought to be part of a new housing policy for America.

One strategy for housing rehabilitation that is being tried with state funds in Massachusetts and New Jersey has the potential for revitalizing whole inner-city neighborhoods and for helping lower-income families remain in neighborhoods undergoing revitalization. This strategy involves the rehabilitation and conversion of factories, office buildings, and warehouses to mixed residential and commercial use. In Massachusetts, it is called the CORE Focus Program. Begun in 1985, this effort is targeted to small Bay State cities that utilize state-administered grants, loans, and rent subsidies to do these mixed-use projects in larger properties within downtown or commercial districts. Within 2 years of start-up, the program had stimulated development of 100 apartments and 15 stores.[17] In New Jersey, the Old Buildings, New Communities Act authorizes similar activities, and an exciting array of urban-oriented projects are now being explored that qualify for state assistance.[18]

Mixed-use projects should enhance the success of housing conversion/rehabilitation efforts by creating jobs and profit centers, which, in turn, minimize the risk on the housing rehabilitation loans. Mixed-use projects also have the potential to enhance housing affordability by utilizing a portion of the generally higher and more rapid appreciation of commercial property to subsidize or offset housing costs. Mixed-use development of this type comes under a number of existing federal programs that have suffered funding cuts in recent years. An improved federal policy, we think, would encourage additional mixed-use housing rehabilitation programs.

Housing Programs for the Elderly

State housing programs for the elderly are considered at length in Chapter 5 of this book. Here, we merely note that the states have been very active and innovative in their housing efforts on behalf of older Americans, trying out a number of housing arrangements and services that are not yet, but probably should be, federally supported. More specifically, about half the states have initiated one or

more programs for seniors (at least 40 programs in all) since 1980.[19]
At least five states have adopted major programs to help asset-rich
but income-poor seniors use the equity in their houses to meet expenses that are hard to manage on fixed incomes. These states have
authorized reverse annuity mortgages or home equity conversion
funding. An even larger number (11) have provided services of a
medical, nursing, or housekeeping nature in existing senior citizen
apartment complexes. States have also experimented with housesharing arrangements, accessory apartments, special rehabilitation
of units for the frail elderly, and much more.

Programs to Meet Non-traditional Housing Needs

At least 19 states have adopted one or more programs to meet non-
traditional housing needs in this decade (more than 35 such programs in all).[20] Shelters for the homeless, group homes with support
services for the handicapped, single-room occupancy facilities for
lower-income persons living alone, apartment complexes with child
care services for single-parent families (allowing the parent to work
and/or attend school), safe temporary housing for battered women, boarding homes for deinstitutionalized mental patients, accessory apartments permitting adult children to welcome aged parents back into the family while respecting the privacy needs of
both nuclear families, clustered but scattered-site apartments associated with area hospitals to serve the handicapped, transitional
housing for the temporarily homeless, house-sharing programs—all
of these have been constructed and operated with state funds in the
1980s.

The vast majority of these programs are concerned either with
the elderly and handicapped or with homeless individuals and families. For these populations, states have learned that they must provide needed services along with housing. The same is true in housing for single-parent families and for a number of other non-traditional
groups. Homeless people need far more than a warm, safe place to
sleep; they tend also to need employment services, health services,
and housing counseling. Frail elderly and handicapped persons typically require some medical, nursing, or housekeeping services. Single parents can't responsibly go to work or school unless child care
arrangements can be made. For non-traditional population groups,
it is almost always housing plus services that is needed.

Federal budget cuts in the 1980s have made it harder and more costly for states to meet these needs. But non-traditional population groups are fast-growing in our nation. A new housing policy for America should include funding for needed services in federally assisted housing complexes.

STATE MORTGAGE REVENUE BOND PROGRAMS

By far the largest number of state housing programs—spending the most money and producing the greatest number of housing units— are those that utilize revenue bonds to subsidize single-family homeownership and to stimulate the production of rental units. As indicated earlier, these are state programs subsidized principally by the federal government in that the interest on these bonds is not liable to federal taxation. Therefore, the federal Treasury foregoes tax revenues that would ordinarily be paid on taxable investment vehicles. State and local governments provide below-market mortgages based on the spread between conventional interest rates and the lower interest rates (yields) that bondholders are willing to accept on tax-free bonds.

Table 14 shows that almost every state in the union now uses revenue bonds to facilitate homeownership for low- and moderate-income families or to stimulate the production of rental units affordable by such families. Figure 9 illustrates the strong growth in state and local use of these bonds for housing purposes from 1976 to 1985. It is estimated that this bonding activity was instrumental in facilitating the production of more than 1.5 million units of low- and moderate-income housing in the course of that decade.

Since the 1960s there has been a debate about the costs and benefits of tax-free housing bonds. Estimates of *direct revenues* foregone by the federal Treasury range from $15 million to $40 million per $1 billion in bonds issued. Estimates of the 1985 total of direct revenues foregone by the Treasury, on $36 billion in bonding activity, range from $540 million to $1.44 billion. Assessment of the *total costs* of state local housing bonds to the federal government in 1985, however, range from zero (by those contending that housing bonds engender such a quantum of taxable economic activities as to totally offset costs) to about $7.5 billion.

In 1986, federal legislation imposed the following stringent limitations on the states.

Table 14
Cumulative State Housing Finance Agency
Homeownership and Rental Programs, 1985: Number of Loans by Type of Construction

State Agency	Cumulative Homeownership				Cumulative Rental		
	New	Existing Rehab	Home Imprs.	Total	New/Sub Rehab	Mod Rehab	Total Units
Alabama	—	—		20,261	—	—	N/A
Alaska	23,437	25,426	1,123	49,986			N/A
Arizona	N/A	N/A	N/A	N/A	3,356		3,356
Arkansas	4,943	7,660	1,395	13,998	12,663	286	12,949
California	15,027	1,660	850	17,537	11,124	857	11,981
Colorado	4,441	7,752		12,193	14,429		14,429
Connecticut	7,927	38,387		46,314	2,710		2,710*
Delaware	2,005	4,623		6,628	2,892	643	3,535
Dist. of Columbia	3	670		673	28,105		28,105
Florida	4,388	3,924		8,312		333	333
Georgia	5,268	5,032		10,300	478		478
Hawaii	1,662	2,452		4,114	2,135		2,135
Idaho	3,023	5,853	918	9,794	27,598	936	28,534
Illinois	2,100	7,500		9,600	883		883
Indiana	3,513	14,051		17,564	5,993		5,993
Iowa	N/A	N/A	N/A	N/A			N/A
Kansas	4,134	19,704		23,838	4,291		4,291
Kentucky	3,599	3,011		6,610	4,139		4,139
Louisiana	877	13,261	565	14,703	5,317	104	5,421
Maine	2,652	7,609	869	11,130	15,889	1,745	17,634
Maryland	1,623	13,345		14,968	58,884	377	59,221
Massachusetts	13,337	7,016	13,287	33,640	34,596		34,596
Michigan	8,057	10,136	50,760	68,953	17,535		17,535
Minnesota	4,713	6,136		10,849	18,254		18,254
Mississippi				10,963			668
Missouri	—			20,234			

78

Nebraska	3,720	16,964		22,152	2,339	1,986	4,325
Nevada	—			7,430	4,370	320	4,370
New Hampshire	4,581	6,342		10,923	3,136		3,456
New Jersey	900	21,408	880	23,188	35,221	1,527	36,748
New Mexico	8,227	5,955		14,182	4,256	2,909	4,256
New York City HDC	N/A	N/A	N/A	N/A	53,723		56,632
New York State HFA	N/A	N/A	N/A	N/A	73,625	1,225	74,850
New York State MLEAC	N/A	N/A	N/A	N/A	31,875		31,875
State of N.Y. MA	—	—		44,500			N/A
North Carolina	8,510	5,457	95	14,062	7,985		7,985
North Dakota	898	2,581		3,479	949		949
Ohio	2,328	18,438	422	21,188	3,125	769	3,894
Oklahoma	5,986	8,818	347	15,151	6,224	60	6,284
Oregon	1,586	8,345		9,931	5,324	133	5,457
Pennsylvania	4,562	12,438		17,000	18,520	323	18,843
Puerto Rico HFC	N/A	N/A	N/A	N/A	N/A	N/A	N/A
Puerto Rico HBFA	—			—	—		N/A
Rhode Island	4,070	26,870		30,940	8,493	56	8,549
South Carolina	4,943	9,014		13,957	5,697		5,697
South Dakota	4,174	17,983		22,157	2,736	44	2,780
Tennessee	7,913	19,862		27,775	3,400		3,400
Texas	6,539	6,036		12,575	8,712		8,712
Utah	9,100	5,925		15,025	2,862		2,862
Vermont	1,651	5,846		7,497	1,967		1,967
Virgin Islands	—				N/A	N/A	N/A
Virginia	20,300	24,300	500	45,100	27,182	1,053	28,235
Washington	2,573	3,068		5,641	12,646		12,646
West Virginia	1,977	9,542		11,519	9,998		9,998
Wisconsin	5,135	13,805	9,080	28,020	14,618*		14,618*
Wyoming	6,246	4,808		11,054	147		147
Total	232,648	459,013	82,559	889,866	621,029	15,686	636,715

N/A = not applicable.

— = information not available.

*Includes only bond-financed units.

Source: Council of State Housing Agencies, Production Activities of State Housing Finance Agencies: 1985 and Cumulative (Washington, D.C.: The Council, 1986), p. 239.

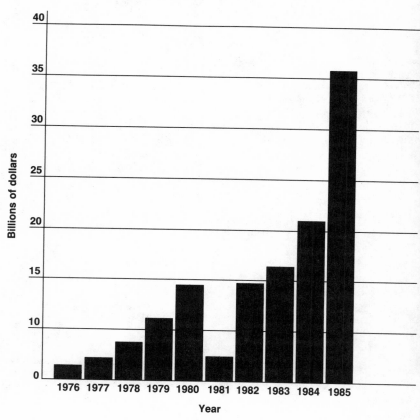

Figure 9
Sale of Long-Term Bonds for Housing: State and Local Government Bonds Sold,
1976–1985
Source: Information supplied by Council of State Housing Finance Agencies.

- The total volume of private activity bonding (of which housing bonds are a component) in which a state may engage is capped at $75 per resident. In effect, this means that housing activities must compete against all other bond-funded activities states do in partnership with the private sector.
- On January 1, 1988, the volume cap dropped to $50 per resident.
- On December 31, 1988, states lose their authority to issue mortgage revenue bonds for single-family homeownership programs.

The volume caps do not constitute a very great problem for the states in periods of moderate interest rates but may well require modification if interest rates rise sharply. An indexing of volume caps to interest rates would probably constitute a modest improvement in public policy.

But the elimination of state authority to aid low- and moderate-income families in their quest to attain homeownership via issuance of mortgage revenue bonds for single-family units is a counterproductive policy because it will clearly reduce homeownership opportunities and levels, will diminish housing construction and forgo tax revenues on housing and related economic activity (which tend significantly to offset, if not outweigh, the federal tax "loss" associated with tax-free housing bonds). It is also inconsistent with major policy choices in the tax reform law. The mortgage interest-rate deductions were retained in that law for both primary residences and second homes—deductions that tend disproportionately to benefit upper-income taxpayers. These deductions were retained, it was said, to encourage homeownership. Eliminating mortgage revenue bonding authority will discourage homeownership for young and low- and moderate-income families while retaining tax breaks for those who need them less.

A new housing policy for America should restore tax-free bonding authority to the states.

State Housing Trust Funds

In response to declining federal support for housing, states in the 1980s began looking to their own resources to finance housing activities. At least 17 states have adopted a state-wide housing trust fund. A trust fund is a source of revenue dedicated to funding a specific program.

States have capitalized these funds in a variety of ways. In 1985 California created a trust fund that raises about $20 million annually by taxing offshore oil production. Maine has created the HOME (Housing Opportunities for Maine) program, dedicating $2.2 million from a real estate transfer tax. The program supports an interest rate buydown program for first-time home buyers and supports shelters for the homeless. The transfer tax is administered by the state housing authority. Delaware, Florida, and New Jersey are among the other states that capitalize housing trust funds from realty transfer taxes or recording fees. The New Jersey trust fund, known as the Urban and Balanced Housing Fund, raises $20 million annually. The program, established within the Department of Community Affairs as part of the Fair Housing Act of 1985, assists municipalities and non-profits with the construction and rehabilitation of low- and moderate-income housing. At least 50 percent of the units must be occupied by low-income families. Resale controls guarantee that these units continue to remain occupied by eligible households.

Other states have developed contributory, non-tax sources of revenue to capitalize trust funds. In 1977, for example, Massachusetts restructured taxation on life insurance companies, negotiating a lower tax in exchange for contributions to the Massachusetts Capital Resource Corporation. More than $100 million has been collected by this fund. A similar approach, not necessarily targeted on insurance companies, might work in other states, where the civic pride of the business community and the desirability of a tax rate reduction could combine to finance a trust fund.

Several states and cities have negotiated successfully to achieve various development objectives with banks that hold public deposits. Negotiated programs now exist in Illinois, Colorado, Ohio, Montana, New York City, and Chicago.

FUTURE DIRECTIONS FOR STATE HOUSING POLICY

Most of the state programs summarized above are direct investment programs. Relatively few states have widely used their powers of taxation and tax abatement or their regulatory powers. And no state has yet moved effectively to encourage major employers to get involved in housing for their workers.

Taxation

One of the things that restricts the ability of young families to save enough money for a downpayment is the taxation of interest income on their savings. Elimination or deferral of taxation on savings, as on Individual Retirement Accounts, clearly constitutes a major incentive for personal savings. To date, however, neither the states nor the federal government have enacted legislation creating an Individual Housing Account—although such legislation has been introduced in state legislatures. Also, neither the states nor the federal government have dedicated any portion of tax revenues deriving from programs assisting housing construction to additional housing activities. Such a tax recapture program could give a strong boost to needed new housing efforts. Individual Housing Accounts and housing tax recaptures seem to warrant the attention of state (and federal) policymakers. Greater attention to these policies can be expected at both state and federal levels in the years ahead.

Regulatory Actions

Housing costs are driven up dramatically by state and local regulatory policies and practices. Zoning, permit-review, and construction-related codes are probably the three most important regulatory domains affecting the cost of housing. Very few states have effectively examined how their regulatory policies increase housing costs—and fewer still have done much about it. Yet exclusionary zoning, endless permit-review processes, and inflexible codes inflexibly administered can make housing prohibitively expensive for the majority of families.

In the future, the states can be expected to begin more rigorous evaluation of their regulatory policies and practices (and those of their subdivisions) with an eye to improving housing affordability. These policy domains historically have been the exclusive domains of the states. Federal efforts to influence the states (e.g., withholding assistance to municipalities with rent control) will be unavailing intrusions, seen as overreaching, and strongly resisted by state and local governments. A new housing policy for America ought not include federal intrusions, as they will weaken—not strengthen—the federal/state partnership we need.

Employer-Assisted Housing

A shortage of affordable housing for workers is hurting businesses, communities, and major regional economies all across America. For employers in high housing-cost areas, the lack of affordable housing means recruiting problems, excessive personnel relocation expenses, the out-migration of negatively impacted businesses, and a slowing of regional economic growth. For communities, housing shortages mean loss of jobs, both actual and potential, and exurban sprawl, as housing is built further and further out from commercial centers in an effort to find cheaper land. The pattern is already clear in New York, New Jersey, Connecticut, Massachusetts, and California; other states will experience it soon.

Large employers are not yet major suppliers of housing capital in the United States, as they are in Western Europe and Japan. No state (or the federal government) has yet enacted an Employer-Assisted Housing Act to provide needed incentives for this to happen—although some policymakers have raised the idea in New Jersey and Massachusetts and in the Congress. An Employer-Assisted Housing Program—whether utilizing matching grants to aid employees in downpayments, or utilizing a tax-advantaged employee homeownership program on the model of employee stock ownership plans—would seem to be a likely new direction for state, and federal, housing policy.

TOWARD A FEDERAL/STATE HOUSING PARTNERSHIP

The states can be laboratories for the development of a new federal housing policy, and they can be full working partners in shaping and implementing that policy, but the states cannot be a substitute for the federal government. State housing programs cannot suffice to meet our housing needs in the absence of a new, better federal housing policy.

The states have often tried out new ideas and new programs, later picked up by the federal government. Many of the New Deal's most important innovations, for example, had their origin in the states, as did some significant federal environmental protection legislation. But the states simply lack the financial resources needed to provide the help that the American people need if they are to meet their housing needs. In the 1980s, with all the new ideas, new programs, new monies, and new partners that the states have developed, we are still falling behind, ever further behind, in achieving our housing goals. We are still observing a decline in homeownership, an increase in homelessness, a shortage of affordable rental housing, and the deterioration or non-improvement of too large a portion of our housing stock.

The adaptations in housing stock required for the 1990s—the "more housing, better targeted to the life needs of our increasingly diverse population," that we seek—won't be, can't be, achieved by state action alone. The states may now be well ahead of most current federal thinking in recognizing the needed changes and in trying to make some of them. Without federal collaboration, however, state programs will not attain the dollar investment levels necessary to achieve these changes.

What, then, is to be done? We think an expansive-but-largely self-financing federal/state housing partnership is called for. In this partnership, the federal government would develop a limited number of new programs that build upon, support, and are supported by those state housing initiatives that have proven most successful and cost-effective. A constructive federal government, a housing partner of the states, would function in the following ways. First, it would adopt as national housing programs two efforts that have worked very well in a number of states but that require national scope to achieve risk reductions and economies of scale. Second, it would cofinance, with the states, programs demonstrably successful at the state level, in order to increase the number and size of these programs to levels that more readily match the need. Third, it would initiate programs that the states can administer but cannot originate themselves because the needed incentives are federal in character; that is, it would supplement and complement state programs and would overcome barriers to the initiation of state-administered programs. Fourth, it would restore to states the authority to run the most successful and popular of the state housing programs. Finally, it would adopt financing techniques that the states have found useful in order to enhance housing funding in a fiscally responsible manner.

There follows a brief outline of what a federal/state housing partnership might look like. This partnership is described in greater detail in Chapter 3.

Federal Adoption of Proven State Programs

A National Housing Investment Corporation

The states have abundantly demonstrated the utility of downpayment assistance programs to help younger families, first-time home buyers, and low- and moderate-income families attain homeownership. Several of these should be cofinanced by a federal/state partnership and are discussed below. One form of downpayment assistance—shared equity and/or shared appreciation loans—should be adopted as a national program, because national scope will provide both needed risk reductions and economies of scale.

A national shared equity or coinvestment fund, a fund that would make loans to eligible would-be home buyers, for a needed portion of the downpayment, and then recapture principal and interest or appreciation in later years when the family has a better income foundation or when the house is sold, would make our federal government a full housing partner of the states. This fund could be located in a National Housing Investment Corporation. It should be national in scope in order to provide a national (i.e., optimally diversified) base of appreciating housing assets (i.e., to achieve major risk reductions). A National Housing Investment Corporation could have an equity interest in a high-quality portfolio of appreciating properties, such that the realized appreciation could be reinvested to produce an even larger number of affordable housing units. It is anticipated that this fund could be so structured as to be entirely self-financing within a few years.

In addition, the National Housing Investment Corporation (or an existing entity in the federal credit system) should be authorized to make a secondary market in shared equity mortgages, much as Government National Mortgage Associations (GNMAs) and Federal National Mortgage Associations (FNMAs) do with other mortgage instruments. This secondary market function, including the assumption of risk, would enable banks to sell their shared equity loans (a large incentive to make such loans) and would attract the interest of non-bank investors in pools of shared equity loans. In this way the power of major private-sector financial entities can be brought to bear to produce and maintain affordable homes. A National Housing Investment Corporation could also coventure multi-family housing with labor unions, community groups, and religiously oriented non-profits—and could do so on a deferred, shared appreciation basis so that the non-profit could acquire complete ownership over time.

Housing Rehabilitation and Services for the Frail Elderly

The states have demonstrated the usefulness of several models and methods to develop housing suited to the needs of frail elderly persons, including some that provide much-needed medical, nursing, and housekeeping services as an integral component of the housing.

These models work; they produce dwelling units appropriate to the special needs of a major and growing portion of our population.

But the states simply lack the financial resources needed to produce enough of these units. In the 1990s, our nation will need so many such units (probably, 1.5 million or more) as to dwarf the fiscal resources of the states. Moreover, if these needs are not met, it is primarily the federal government, not the states, that will pay for the needless institutionalization of the elderly that will result. For these reasons, it would seem that a new federal program to meet the housing needs of the frail elderly ought to be initiated, using some of the successful and cost-effective techniques developed at the state level in the 1980s.

Federal Cofinancing of Proven State Programs

Two forms of downpayment assistance, deferred loans (Alabama, Connecticut, California, and New York) and lease/purchase plans (New Jersey and Colorado), show much promise in helping young families, first-time home buyers, and moderate-income households to achieve homeownership. These innovations will need some federal support if they are to become more widely adopted and/or to grow in the states already using them. Both of these programs can be structured so as to be self-financing after a brief startup period (i.e., after initial loan repayments begin).

Two other state-level programs have substantial promise as stimulants both to homeownership and to the production of rental housing. These are interest-rate buydown funds and housing assistance corporations through which the state can itself act as a developer for public or community-based housing. A national interest-rate buydown fund could be held in reserve until mortgage interest rates rose above a given threshold or until recessionary indices reached predetermined levels. States could be asked to match the buydown fund to further enhance construction activity in their jurisdictions. We recommend that a tax recapture program be instituted (further discussed below) so that the buydown fund would be replenished by revenues accruing from the construction activity generated by the fund.

Similarly, matching grants could be offered to states adopting housing assistance corporation laws, becoming developers of low-income, and mostly rental, housing. This approach appears to be both more economical and more permanent than past federal policies designed to spur rental production and infinitely superior to present policies, which ignore production needs altogether.

New Federal Incentives for Homeownership

The states have worked with an extensive set of new partners in their affordable housing efforts in the 1980s. Major employers, however, have not yet become the partners they could, and we think should, be. This is true largely because the incentives required to bring major employers into programs for workers' housing are federal in character. Favorable tax treatment for Employee Home Ownership Programs (like already-established Employee Stock Ownership Plans) would be most valuable to employers if they operated with reference to the federal, not state, tax code. Authorization to include housing assistance as part of cafeteria-style, or flexible, employee benefit packages would also have to be federal. Part of the effort to encourage employer-assisted housing could be matching federal and state grants to employers (and therefore could be cofinanced), but the federal government would first have to take the quite inexpensive tax-related steps discussed above.

Favorable federal tax treatment would also help young families save for a downpayment. Individual Housing Accounts deserve consideration in that regard. State tax-advantaged savings plans, in the absence of federal action, would be largely unavailing.

Restoring State Tax-Free Bonding Authority

As indicated earlier in this chapter, the largest and most popular state-level housing programs are those associated with the issuance of tax-free bonds, but federal tax reform legislation eliminates the ability of the states to issue such bonds for single-family homes after 1988. We strongly advocate restoration of this authority to the states, who did a good job with these bonds at modest cost to the federal Treasury. America needs more, not fewer, tools to build affordable housing.

New Federal Financing Techniques

A Federal Housing Trust Fund

At least 17 states have adopted housing trust funds since 1980—dedicating a permanent, stable, annually self-replenishing revenue source in order to meet housing needs. The federal government should do likewise. A federal trust fund—such as Social Security, the Highway Trust Fund, or the recently reauthorized Superfund for toxic waste cleanup—is basically a government account capitalized by the dedication of a permanent, annually renewable revenue source. A federal housing trust fund would provide a permanent, stable source of public monies to encourage the construction of low-, moderate-, and middle-income rental units.

A trust fund accomplishes three goals that a simple annual appropriation bill, even with multi-year budget authority, does not. First, a trust fund focuses attention on a problem or need in a special way. Prior to Superfund or the Highway Trust Fund, Congress did appropriate funds for some cleanup programs and highway projects, but when Congress truly became serious about the problem it created a trust fund. After nearly a decade of federal cuts, housing deserves affirmative attention.

Second, although Congress need not appropriate all available trust fund dollars in any given fiscal year, a trust fund provides the sense that there will be a long-term, predictable level of dollars and of housing activity that the states and private sectors can expect. This is particularly useful to the states, to private building and financial sectors, and to potential home buyers.

Third, the trust fund financing mechanism, in combination with a new source of revenue, is in keeping with the fiscally responsible concept of "pay as you go" program financing. A trust fund created in this manner will have no negative impact on the deficit.

A Tax Recapture Program for Affordable Housing

For almost a decade, our federal government has emphasized the cost but not the value of housing programs. We suggest that all or a portion of the federal tax revenues that are directly attributable to that housing construction stimulated by federal/state partnership activities be recaptured (earmarked) for use to provide additional affordable housing.

From Outline to Program

The outline of a federal/state housing partnership presented in this chapter is not a new housing policy for America. Our preferred policy for this country is advanced in Chapters 3 and 4 below. But the ideas and energies expressed in the new state housing programs of the 1980s are central to a new housing policy for this nation—and may properly serve as an introduction to the consideration of federal housing policies that follows.

3

A New Federal/State Housing Partnership

In this chapter we propose a new federal/state housing partnership, describing in some detail a number of major new initiatives that the federal and state governments could cost-effectively coventure with the private sector to meet America's housing needs in the 1990s. More specifically, we advance a 10-point plan, largely self-financing, to expand homeownership opportunities for millions of young families, to provide several million affordable rental units, and to help our nation's large and rapidly growing senior citizen population remain in or adapt their homes to their life needs.

Let us briefly summarize this plan first. To expand homeownership opportunities for about 3.30 million young families and first-time home buyers in the decade of the 1990s—that is, to build or enhance the affordability of starter homes for 3.30 million families over and above those expected to be accommodated by the private market and present governmental programs—we advocate the following new programs that build on successful innovations in the states or in Europe:

1. a federal mortgage interest-rate buydown fund;
2. a joint federal/state downpayment assistance program supported by a federal tax code that allows single-family mortgage revenue bonds and offers private developers other limited incentives;
3. a new National Housing Investment Corporation empowered

91

to make direct coinvestment and shared equity loans to families, and to make a secondary market in shared equity loans;

4. an Employer-Assisted Housing Act encouraging major employers to become substantial providers of housing capital, as they do in much of Western Europe and Japan.

In the 1990s, America will also need at least 3.5 million new or newly affordable apartments for low- and moderate-income families (i.e., 3.5 million units in the decade, beyond those few that can be expected to be built or subsidized under existing federal and state efforts). To meet this need, we recommend:

5. a reinvigorated public housing construction program to help provide shelter for the very poor;
6. a community-based rental supply initiative that links the resources of federal and state governments to those of community non-profit housing development corporations;
7. an employer-assisted rental unit production effort.

The housing needs of America's senior citizens, which have been substantially unaddressed in the 1980s, are conceived here as two-fold: helping the frail elderly who already own homes to remain living there and assisting those frail elderly who have never owned a home to afford new or substantially rehabilitated apartments. In either case, the housing may require adaptation to suit their physical needs. We suggest:

8. an integrated network of programs to achieve these purposes, including a new home equity or reverse mortgage program, to help 1.7 million frail elderly in the 1990s.

Some of these new methods will require new startup monies. To finance these programs on a pay-as-you-go basis, we describe below:

9. a federal housing trust fund;
10. a revolving tax recapture program, spending the tax revenues that would never have come into federal or state treasuries but for the eight new programs suggested above.

Our proposed homeownership, rental, and senior citizens programs, respectively, are described in the first three sections below.

These include the new methods by which a federal/state housing partnership might help to meet the shelter needs the 1990s. The next section contains our recommendations for new ways to fund the new methods.

EXPANDING HOMEOWNERSHIP: NEW METHODS

A Mortgage Interest-Rate Buydown Fund

Recent surveys of leading mortgage banking firms suggest that if mortgage interest rates are modestly reduced or if downpayment costs are lessened, about a quarter of a million additional families each year could purchase a home; that is, they could make the monthly payments at marginally reduced interest rates, or at current rates if they could accrue a larger downpayment. These are families who are actively seeking, but cannot achieve, homeownership without lowered interest rates or downpayment costs. Under our present system of home financing, many of these families will never be able to afford a home.

Recognizing this dilemma, several states have responded with programs to overcome the high interest rate and downpayment cost barriers. The largest of these efforts is the tax-free mortgage revenue bond programs of state housing finance agencies. In 1984, the state housing finance agencies issued $17.3 billion of mortgage revenue bonds for low- and moderate-income housing.[1] But state governments have also recognized that such bonds, alone, do not provide deep enough subsidies. Four states that deal directly with downpayment and interest costs ought to be considered as national models. The Delaware Assisted Loan Program and the Massachusetts Homeownership Opportunity Program are interest-rate buydown models. The Connecticut Downpayment Assistance Program and the New Jersey lease purchase program can serve as downpayment cost-reduction models.

The Delaware Assisted Loan (DEAL) Program buys down the rate on state housing finance agency mortgages. In 1986, the rate reduction was 1 percent (100 basis points), from 9.75 percent down to 8.75 percent.[2] The program, capitalized at $5 million from the sale of mortgage revenue bonds, was targeted to families earning less than $21,600 annually. The program was judged to be a success and, at this writing, Delaware is considering funding the program through the state's housing trust fund.

Massachusetts has a larger, more complex mortgage interest-rate buydown program. This program, called the Massachusetts Home-ownership Opportunity Program (HOP), is a collaboration of the state Housing Finance Agency and the Massachusetts Housing Partnership.[3] Moderate-income HOP home buyers receive a 30-year, fixed-rate, Massachusetts Housing Finance Agency (HFA) mortgage. During the first nine years of the mortgage, payments are structured as if the mortgage were a graduated payment mortgage (GPM), which is an amortizing mortgage structured to allow home buyers to make smaller monthly payments initially with payments increasing during the life of the mortgage. Except that the mortgage is not a GPM, it is a subsidized mortgage. The difference between the payments needed to amortize the HFA mortgage and the reduced payments made on the ersatz GPM are provided by the Massachusetts Housing Partnership, which is a combination of corporate donations and state-appropriated funds. Partnership assistance equals the amount necessary to reduce the interest payments by 3 percent (300 basis points) during the first five years of the mortgage, followed by a 2 percent (200 basis point) reduction during the next two years, followed by a 1 percent (100 basis point) reduction for the next two years. At the beginning of the tenth year the home buyer's monthly principal and interest payment is equal to the full amount needed to amortize the HFA mortgage.

In return for this financial assistance, which is geared to the construction of moderate-cost units, home buyers are obligated to certain resale controls on the home and are liable for the repayment of the financial assistance under certain conditions. As a result of the resale controls, the program adds to the state's permanent stock of affordable housing, while the repayment requirements create a fund for assisting future home buyers.

Delaware and Massachusetts (like the handful of other states that have, or have had, similar programs) have found mortgage buydowns to be an efficient and cost-effective method for meeting low- and moderate-income housing needs. Unfortunately, these programs have scant funding and most states have no buydown program at all. A national mortgage buydown program is needed.

A national buydown program would substantially expand America's home-purchasing power. For example, a rise in interest rates from 9.5 percent to 10.5 percent on an $85,000 mortgage forces 11 percent of all home buyers (based on 1986 home-buying levels, more than 400,000 families) out of the market. The Mortgage Bankers Association of America also estimates that 450,000 families are forced to change their borrowing behavior (either by moving from a fixed-rate mortgage to an adjustable one, or by making a larger downpayment, or by not purchasing a home at all) for each percentage-point rise in interest rates.[4]

In addition to expanding homeownership opportunities for low- and moderate-income families, a national interest-rate buydown program could be an important countercyclical regulator for the economy. By buying down mortgages when interest rates are at their highest, the federal government could guarantee a minimal level of affordable housing starts even when the economy is in recession. This would help keep builders building and workers working and even out fluctuations in the highly cyclical home-building and financing industries. A national buydown program could help prevent the wave of bankruptcies that affected the home-building industry in the early 1980s from occurring again.

As conceived, the national mortgage interest-rate reduction program would be tied to prevailing FHA mortgage interest rates. Buydowns would be 300 basis points less than the FHA mortgage interest rate when interest rates were between 9 and 12 percent. If rates rose above 12.00 percent, the buydown would be sufficient to obtain a 9 percent fixed-rate, 30-year mortgage. The buydown program could be suspended should mortgage interest rates fall below 9.00 percent.

The mortgage interest-rate buydown program would be designed to encourage homeownership for both low- and moderate-income families. Set-asides for each income category would be established by the federal program administrator. The program would be limited to first-time home buyers of moderate cost units. Maximum home sales prices would be limited to 100 percent of each state's median new home sales price. For example, a $90,000 home purchased with a 5 percent downpayment would carry a mortgage of $85,500. If the prevailing mortgage interest rate is 11.75 percent and that rate is brought down to 8.75 percent at a cost of 16 points (16 times $855 equaling $13,680), monthly mortgage payments could be reduced by more than $190.

There are various estimates of the costs of buydown programs. Traditional "rules of thumb" are that the payment of one point (1 percent of the mortgage loan) reduces the mortgage interest rate between $\frac{1}{8}$ percent and $\frac{3}{8}$ percent.[5] Individual case analysis would indicate that the precise value of a point varies somewhat within this range depending upon the mortgage interest rate and the term that the mortgage is actually held.[6] However, the figure of one point equaling a mortgage reduction of 18.75 basis points is a reasonable, but conservative, figure to use for making estimates of what it would cost to implement a national mortgage interest-rate buydown program.

We propose enactment of a national mortgage buydown program that would use new federal tax revenues discussed later in this chapter to provide loans to 1.1 million young families in the decade of the 1990s (about 110,000 annually).

Downpayment Assistance and Lease/Purchase Programs

The mortgage banker survey described above found not only that tens of thousands of families are unable to afford current interest rates but tens of thousands more are denied homeownership because they are unable to accrue a large enough downpayment. These families could afford market-rate carrying costs. In fact, many of these families already pay rent equal to monthly ownership costs, without any of the tax or personal advantages of homeownership.

In 1974, personal savings rates reached a post-World War II high of 9.4 percent. Since that time, savings rates have fallen, reaching a post-war low of 3.9 percent in 1986.[7] Correspondingly, personal family income between 1975 and 1985 rose only 1.5 percent.[8] In sharp contrast, median home prices for new and existing homes climbed an inflation-adjusted 40 percent.[9]

Connecticut has chosen to address the downpayment barrier through creation of the Connecticut Downpayment Assistance Program. The program works exclusively with the Connecticut Housing Finance Authority's (CHFA) mortgage revenue bond program.[10] It targets assistance only to low- and moderate-income families.

Although conceived as a downpayment assistance program, the Connecticut program is in many ways a blended mortgage program combining general obligation and revenue bond borrowing rates. Capitalized by state general obligation bonds, the program provides financing for the difference between what the home buyer can afford as a downpayment, as judged by formula, and the largest CHFA mortgage that the lender can offer. This financing is provided as a second mortgage for 30 years at 6 percent annually. The downpayment assistance can be up to 25 percent of the home's sale price, if by having such a large downpayment or second mortgage, monthly costs will be brought within minimum CHFA first-mortgage underwriting criteria. The monthly second-mortgage cost is a factor in considering CHFA first-mortgage eligibility. The Connecticut program has been in existence since 1984. During this time more than 2,000 low- and moderate-income families (up to 80 percent of area median income) have become homeowners through this program.

A program that helps the home buyer save a downpayment before purchasing a home is the New Jersey lease/purchase program. Lease/purchase homeownership is a process in which prospective home buyers rent a unit that they hope to buy in about two years. During the two-year lease period a portion of the rent is escrowed for a downpayment.

The program is initiated by floating a short-term tax-exempt note. This initial tax-exempt financing is usually provided by a municipality, housing agency, or local development corporation. The note is used to finance construction; permanent financing is deferred until the prospective purchasers are ready to execute a mortgage. Rentals during the lease period are keyed to paying the interest on the notes, taxes, and insurance; in addition, by the end of the lease period at least 5 percent of the purchase price will be available for a downpayment.

At present, this tax-exempt note financing can only be used by non-profit developers. Under the federal Treasury regulations for this type of note, property owners are required to make the units available as rental property for 10 years regardless of the terms of the notes. The exception to this requirement are units developed by state or local governments or non-profits organized for charitable purposes.

Developers have included the Housing and Mortgage Finance Agency (HMFA) through its development subsidiary, the Housing Assistance Corporation, municipalities, and local development corporations. Municipalities have also made land available for projects to enhance affordability further. Lease/purchase projects are also eligible for state housing trust fund assistance.

Key to helping renters become buyers is the HMFA's ability to issue a tentative mortgage commitment at the time the leasee moves into the unit. The agency establishes a pool of mortgage money for a project shortly after construction begins. The prospective purchaser knows the mortgage interest rate on the unit before moving. This allows the project sponsors to select a tenant likely to qualify for a mortgage.

The lease/purchase program is in fact a lease program and a purchase program. Assuming that a tenant can qualify for a mortgage, it is at the tenant's option whether or not to purchase at the end of the rental term. If the tenant does not wish to purchase, he or she must leave the unit at the end of the lease, but may keep all down-payment savings.

In sum, lease/purchase housing enhances affordability because the tenant is paying a lower-than-market rate rent while saving a downpayment. The downpayment premium that tenants pay is in effect a forced savings plan. This has proven to be a helpful budgeting tool for many program participants. As a result of this short-term rent subsidy and the built-in savings program, families in New Jersey are finding that they can achieve homeownership.

Currently implementation of lease/purchase housing is complicated. One needs a municipality, local development agency, or other non-profit organization capable of issuing short-term tax-exempt financing, a local property management entity to manage the property during the two- or three-year construction and lease period, and a supportive state housing finance agency that is legally authorized (not all are) to bond for permanent takeout mortgage financing long before the prospective purchasers are ready to buy the units. Lease/purchase housing should not have to rely on so many actors having to take the right action at just the right time in order for the project to succeed. Three supportive federal tax policies would greatly encourage the undertaking of lease/purchase projects.

First, federal tax regulations regarding project financing should not prohibit private developers from developing lease/purchase housing. Tax law should be modified so that privately developed lease/purchase units can be eligible for tax-exempt financing. Encouraging the private sector to build lease/purchase housing would be good for communities because private-sector builders would bring their vast construction expertise and experience, as well as financial capacities, to a project. Lease/purchase would also be good for builders. Should the construction industry be hit by a building slow-down, lease/purchase housing developed on a large scale by private-sector developers could have important countercyclical economic effects. The tax law changes needed would cost the Treasury nothing. Tax-exempt financing is already subject to federal volume limitations. If states choose to allow developers to use available state tax-exempt authorization, the federal government should not prevent it.

A second tax law change would be to permit two years of straight line depreciation during the lease period without the depreciation's being subjected to recapture. If tax law permitted this type of depreciation, states and localities could syndicate or sell the depreciation rights to a project as part of their tax-exempt financing agreement with a developer. The revenue raised by the sale of tax depreciation could then either be used to lower the unit construction cost or be given to the prospective purchaser to enlarge the size of the down-payment on the unit above what the built-in savings program accumulates.

Third, in order for this short-term tax depreciation to be fully marketable, tax law regarding limitations on passive losses should be relaxed. Although there are other features in the tax code that make investing for tax advantages less desirable, a relaxation of passive loss restrictions would bring many traditional investors back to housing investment. If a passive loss exemption for tax-exempt lease/purchase projects were created, there would not be a wholesale rush for this investment because states are still limited as to the amount of tax-exempt revenue bonds that they can issue, and states would only want to put a fractional amount of tax-exempt bonding authority into this type of housing. As a result of these ceilings, tax loss to the Treasury would be minimized.

With a supportive federal policy we believe that the states and the private sector would create at least 20,000 lease/purchase home-ownership units annually. Further, a supportive federal policy would be inexpensive since the tax code changes needed to expand lease/purchase development would have negligible effects on revenue collected by the federal Treasury.

A National Housing Investment Corporation

A few states have issued general obligation bonds to fund a down-payment assistance program that is used in conjunction with their housing revenue bond program. These states deserve great credit for establishing such programs. However, these programs are limited to those receiving state housing finance agency assistance, who are just a fraction of those who could qualify if greater mortgage and downpayment assistance were available. Furthermore, these programs create a debt for the entire state, but benefit relatively few families.

Unlike these programs, the New Jersey lease/purchase program does not create a state debt, but it has other drawbacks. It is rather complicated, requiring tax-exempt short-term local borrowing, long-term Housing and Mortgage Finance Agency financing, and the participation of a municipal, state, or non-profit entity to manage the development and rental periods. Since the program works best for new construction, and is not geared to scattered-site development, lease/purchase projects tend to be small subdivisions. Although lease/purchase programs have these limitations, a more supportive federal policy towards lease/purchase housing could create new opportunities for many.

The private sector has responded to the need for downpayment assistance too. In the New York–Philadelphia real estate market, firms such as Home Share Equity, Inc., have been established.[11] These firms match prospective home buyers in need of downpayment financing with individuals willing to coinvest in a house. The home buyer and coinvestor agree on equity positions in the housing unit purchased. Both parties make mortgage payments on their respective equity interest. Since few investors could absorb the substantial negative cash flow, the home buyer pays rent to the coinvestor for the latter's interest in the unit. At an agreed-upon date the home buyer must refinance the unit and buy out the coinvestor. If the home buyer is unable or unwilling to buy out the coinvestor by refinancing, the unit is put up for sale and the proceeds are divided between the residing owner and the coinvestor in relation to their respective equity positions. Coinvestment agreements generally last from three to five years.

The three-to-five-year term of coinvestment agreements gives the purchaser time to acquire additional savings to buy out the coinvestor's downpayment, in part by taking advantage of the tax benefits that accrue from homeownership. Additionally, the property appreciation that accrues during the three- to five-year-period can be recaptured in refinancing.

On a small scale this program is effective. But its implementation relies on finding an investor willing to invest in the specific piece of property at the moment the home buyer is seeking to buy a home. This can be problematic. Furthermore, the tax advantage to the coinvestor has diminished as a result of tax reform. What the concept needs to work is a large institutional coinvestor. We propose that Congress create a National Housing Investment Corporation to be this large investor.

The National Housing Investment Corporation (NHIC) would be a government corporation capitalized initially by a federal appropriation. The corporation would serve as an institutional coinvestor for those savings-poor, but otherwise mortgagable, families who wish to purchase a home. The corporation would lend qualifying families 50 percent of their downpayment on a home, but not more than 10 percent of the home's purchase price, nor less than 5 percent. Maximum sales prices on homes would be limited to 100 percent of the state median. Although most units in this price range would be eligible for FHA-insured mortgages, FHA participation would not be required and conventional mortgages could be sought.

NHIC loans would be structured similarly to zero coupon bonds in that no interest or principal would be due on the loan until the date when all principal and interest is due. NHIC loans would be recorded as second mortgages and have a term of six years. No additional debt could be placed on the home until the NHIC loan is satisfied. Interest rates on the NHIC loans would be modest, geared to encourage homeownership, and would not be more costly than federal borrowing. Unlike Home Share Equity, Inc., agreements, NHIC debt would be structured to allow families whose household incomes increased during the six-year loan period to pay off the loan through savings rather than mandatory refinancing with all its related costs. However, should a family's income not permit savings to be used to pay off the NHIC debt, the unit could be conventionally refinanced, taking advantage of equity growth from mortgage payments and from appreciating property values.

In most cases home buyers will want to satisfy the NHIC at the conclusion of the six-year loan term. However, there may well be instances when a family is not able to refinance a unit either because of rising mortgage interest rates, declining income during the initial ownership period, lack of appreciation, or some other reason. In these instances the NHIC will have the option of converting the debt (the other option being to force repayment) to a permanent shared equity interest in the unit. In these instances the equity position would be based upon the value of the NHIC's contribution toward purchasing the unit. The equity position could last until the unit is sold or refinanced, although the purchaser would have the option of buying out the NHIC at any time.

Because there are so many discouraged home buyers in America today, demand for this program's downpayment assistance should be extensive. An annual appropriation of $1.35 billion could be expected to fund more than 150,000 new and existing home mortgages annually. Ultimately, the combination of loan repayments from prior years' lending and tax revenue generated from the implementation of our total program would make this program self-sustaining.

Mortgage underwriters and insurers will have some reservations regarding the NHIC-assisted mortgages. Mortgage underwriters and insurers consider downpayments contributed by a home buyer, cosigner, or coinvestor, each of whom is liable for the entirety of the mortgage, as equity. However, since the NHIC downpayment equity becomes debt, and since the NHIC is not a cosigner for all the mortgage, mortgage underwriters and insurers will not consider the NHIC assistance as pure equity.

It is likely that mortgage insurers and underwriters will consider NHIC assistance in a manner similar to family gifts and other nonpersonal savings used to make downpayments. The assistance is considered acceptable for all underwriting purposes as long as the first 5 percent of the purchase price is paid for with the borrower's personal savings or assets.

The NHIC would insist on this requirement too, matching the minimum personal investment and creating a 10 percent downpayment on the unit. The NHIC would continue to make matching contributions of up to 10 percent of the unit's purchase price, creating a 20 percent downpayment fund in total. A maximum 20 percent downpayment fund might not eliminate the need for mortgage insurance because the NHIC loan would be discounted at least somewhat; however, affordability would be enhanced by reducing the mortgage principal. Because all mortgages would have at least 5 percent personal equity, all mortgages would be insurable. Thus, the national secondary mortgage markets should have no difficulty trading in NHIC-supported loans.

A second activity that the NHIC should be authorized to explore, and enter into, if feasible, is the making of equity investments in homes costing between 100 percent and 200 percent of a state's median new homes sales price. NHIC participation would be as a lender, similar to those loans made on lower-priced homes, except that, rather than being owed principal and a fixed interest sum at the end of six years, the NHIC would be owed a percentage of the total appreciation of the home.

Because these homes would be more valuable within their respective markets, the 5 percent minimum downpayment requirement would be waived, though a minimum cash downpayment would be required (perhaps $10,000). Because a 5 percent downpayment would not be required, many mortgages participating in this program would not be insurable with existing FHA or private mortgage insurance (PMI) instruments, and new public or private instruments would have to be developed. Furthermore, a national secondary market where this type mortgage could be sold, pooled, and repackaged as FNMA, FHLMC, and the other secondary market purchasers do would have to be developed. Instruments backed by these pools would have yields based upon actuarially expected rates of housing appreciation. Because pools would be organized on a national basis, regional markets where home appreciation lagged behind the national average could participate. Perhaps after the program gains experience, regional pools could be developed with instrument yields based upon actuarial assessments of real estate appreciation within the various regions. Individual home buyers could select a fixed-term agreement with the NHIC that would require a mandatory refinancing of the home in order to recapture the home's appreciation, or the home buyer could seek an open-ended agreement with the NHIC that would give the NHIC a share of the home's appreciation at the time the home changed title. Mortgages could be pooled by term length with yields adjusted accordingly.

Finally, the NHIC should be authorized to make coinvestments for the development of multi-family housing with local or state governmental entities, employers, labor unions, local community development corporations, and religious and other not-for-profit housing sponsors. NHIC investments could be on a deferred loan or shared appreciation basis, with these organizations acquiring complete building ownership over time.

With these powers and functions, the new corporation we envision would be powerful enough to do the job it is intended for, lean enough to do that job efficiently, modern enough to do the job in joint venture with the private sector, and responsive enough to give citizens, local elected officials, and community groups a real role in the process. Like the Federal Housing Administration, the Federal National Mortgage Association, and the Government National Mortgage Association, this new corporation would be a self-supporting entity.

Developing a national mortgage interest-rate buydown program, creating a National Housing Investment Corporation, and assisting states and private-sector entities with the implementation of lease/purchase housing programs would remove many of the barriers to homeownership faced by low- and moderate-income families.

Employer-Assisted Housing

In the 1980s, Americans have been creative in seeking mortgage financing. Prospective homeowners have turned to adjustable rate mortgages, graduated payment mortgages, graduated equity mortgages, and a host of other mortgage instruments designed to lower monthly mortgage costs. States have responded with downpayment assistance programs and lease/purchase homeownership programs. Home builders, home sellers, and the states have, on occasion, offered interest-rate buydown programs. Some housing is being developed as limited equity cooperatives and as community land trusts.

Americans have been creative, but the number of families capable of affording a home purchase continues to decline. While churches, local development corporations, state and local agencies, and foundations have been important in expanding housing affordability, the scope of their efforts is necessarily limited because their financial resources are so limited. Also, their efforts are constricted because few Americans have a direct relationship with local development corporations or national foundations. Indeed, even citizen involvement with churches and public agencies is at a record low according to many surveys.

However, 93 percent of all Americans do have a relationship with an employer. Even in the depth of the 1982–1983 recession more than 8 out of 10 Americans of home-purchasing age were employed. America's employers, particularly those employing more than 100 people, could play a major role in financing housing for millions of working Americans at little public or private cost. Employers have financial resources and lending sophistication that churches, community development corporations (CDCs), and many foundations can never hope to have.

The idea of employer-assisted housing is neither novel nor untried in the United States. Other nations have used this concept successfully, too. Vast numbers of employer-assisted units were built, backed by government grants and other tax incentives, in post-war Germany and Japan. Indeed, today the German and Japanese programs are largely history, because these programs, in the words of a German diplomat, successfully "built to need." [12]

From a public policy perspective, bringing major new financial resources to the housing finance marketplace, at little public cost, must be welcomed. From the employee-borrower perspective, the possibility of creating a housing partnership between employers and employees has, historically, met with ambivalence or hostility. The first mention of employer-assisted housing brings to mind the Pullman company towns of Illinois and the coal towns of late nineteenth- and early twentieth-century Kentucky. Certainly reintroduction of the nineteenth-century company town is not a social innovation that warrants new advocacy. Rather, learning from the American experiences in the late nineteenth and early twentieth centuries, and the post-war experiences of Germany and Japan, we advocate a new kind of employer-assisted housing, one that acknowledges and respects the unique social, political, and economic relationships that exist between employers and employees in this country.

Privacy and due process rights of both the employer and employee must be protected. Borrowers must be afforded the same rights they would have with any other lender. Employers, too, must have the same rights as other lenders to enforce mortgage agreements.

Though building relationships between employers and employees may be good labor relations policy, the mortgage obligations of an employee must be completely separated from the employee's employment obligations. The employee must be able to sell or refinance the unit without employer penalty or involvement unless the employer has a shared equity position. Employers must not make personnel hiring or layoff decisions based upon mortgage loans outstanding.

Another key element in establishing employer-assisted housing programs is a supportive federal policy. Employer-assisted housing programs must be fully deductible for employers, as are other employee benefits, such as health insurance. Without federal tax deductibility, employers will be less willing to become involved in a new benefit program. While it would be preferable also to include housing assistance among those employee benefits that are not taxed as income, undoubtedly many employees would benefit from the program even if it were not tax-advantaged. With these understandings, in an era of lower real wages and higher downpayment and carrying costs, it would seem that employees would welcome a new source of housing finance.

While employer-assisted housing may make good sense from public policy and employee perspectives, there will be little of it unless employers see how they can benefit by providing housing assistance. The bad news is that the conventional business wisdom is that employers aren't and shouldn't be involved with providing housing for their employees. The good news is that America's employers have come to provide a great deal of housing assistance for their employees, albeit in an uncoordinated and sometimes reactive manner.

The President of the Conference Board expressed the conventional wisdom succinctly in 1975: "Housing is typically thought of as something individuals provide for themselves and their families, or as a matter of community concern. Except for companies in the housing business, employers have not been seen as being involved in housing."[13] That is the myth. The reality is that today thousands of corporations are operating or financing housing programs for some or all of their employees. American employers are involved in 17 different types of housing investment programs (see Table 15). These programs include subsidies for homes, apartments, mortgages, and building lots.

It is estimated that U.S. firms are spending at least $20 billion per year on employee housing. Substantial sums are spent for relocation assistance for transferred and newly hired workers, as a company-wide personnel benefit, or as a benefit for senior management. Some employer-financed housing is being built in conjunction with the construction of new company facilities.

These activities do not reach many employees, and they are not generally coordinated with already available state government housing programs. The business community has not yet sought a government policy that will directly complement its own housing activities. Nevertheless the American business community *is* involved in housing for workers. Employer-assisted housing in America, in fact, has become both extensive and expensive. It is a growth industry in itself.

Employers are recognizing that costly housing is hampering their ability to attract, and retain, employees. Perhaps the most publicized recent example of high housing costs' leading to corporate and regional economic problems is found in Long Island, New York. In early 1987 the Grumman Corporation, a defense industry leader and Long Island's largest employer, announced that it was opening or expanding new engineering centers in Florida and Texas, relocating thousands of jobs out of the metropolitan New York City area. Grumman cited high housing costs as one of the key reasons for this decision. A spokesman said, "The engineers we've interviewed . . . simply said 'No, we won't go to Long Island,'" adding that a home near Grumman's new Florida facility that sells for $125,000 costs more than $200,000 on Long Island.[14]

Table 15

Types of Employer-Assisted Housing Programs Operated or Financed by U.S. Corporations, 1986

No.	Program Description	Example or Observed Frequency	Reason for Program	Source of Information
1	Company pays a firm or bank to purchase old home of relocating employee	62% of firms in 1986 Merrill Lynch Survey	Relocation	A
2	Firm purchases old home of relocating employee, directly	14% of firms in 1986 Merrill Lynch Survey	Relocation	A
3	Company provides subsidized loans that can be used by executive personnel	17% of firms in Dartnell Survey	Executive compensation	I
4	Company pays a mortgage interest differential allowance to relocating employees	74% of firms in 1986 Merrill Lynch Survey	Relocation	A
5	Company provides mortgage guarantee for all eligible employees at any time	University of Pennsylvania	Personnel benefit	D
6	Company provides free living quarters for employees	4% of firms in A. S. Hansen Executive Compensating Survey	Executive compensation	E
7	Company sells or leases homes (at discount rates) to all employees at any time (subject to inventory availability)	Hawaii Bell	Personnel benefit	B

Table 15 (cont.)

No.	Program Description	Example or Observed Frequency	Reason for Program	Source of Information
8	Non-realty company sells building lots at discount prices to interested employees	Brown Co. (Berlin, NH), DuPont, Inc. (Seaford, Del.)	Staffing new facility or personnel benefit	B
9	Company builds new housing for sale to employees	9 firms: 2% of in Conference Board Survey	Staffing new plant or special facilities	F, H
10	Company provides down-payment assistance for new home purchase	Less common than mortgage interest difference allowances (no. 2 above); loans in excess of equity are usually interest-bearing and can be recorded as a lien against property Colgate-Palmolive provides match int. points	Relocation	G
11	Company provides direct mortgage assistance and re-coups subsidy cost via a shared equity feature wherein company shares in housing appreciation	"some firms"	Relocation	B
12	"Mortgage buydown": company pays mortgage lender up front or provides limited continuing funds to achieve lower interest rate for relocating employees	15% of firms in Merrill Lynch Survey	Relocation	A

108

				F, H
13	Company stimulates new construction by builders in areas of new facility	2% of firms in Conference Board Survey	Staffing of new plant or special facility	F, H
14	Company contributes to a community "housing partnership" provides affordable housing via a nonprofit housing corporation	National, regional, and local corporations in 20 U.S. cities	Goodwill; community revitalization; expands regional or community supply of affordable housing	J, K
15	Company reimburses relocating employee sale costs of old home	21% of firms in Merrill Lynch Survey	Relocation	A
16	Company reimburses relocating employee for loss on sale of old home	35% of firms in Merrill Lynch Survey	Relocation	A
17	Company reimburses relocating employee for cost of carrying two homes during relocation	Most corporate relocation policies	Relocation	G

Sources of Information:

A. Hagen Marketing Research, Inc., *A Study of Employee Relocation Policies Among Major U.S. Corporations* (White Plains, N.Y.: Merrill Lynch Relocation Management, 1986).

B. Bureau of National Affairs, *Personnel Management*, vol. 2 (Washington, D.C.: The Bureau, 1983).

C. Information made available to the author by a national personnel benefits trade association source.

D. Daniel N. Hoffman, "Employer-Assisted Housing," paper presented to the Rutgers Affordable Housing Conference, New Brunswick, N.J., November 14, 1986.

E. "Results and Findings of Hansen Mini-Survey #4: Executive Compensation and Perquisites," survey by A. S. Hansen Company, 1986.

F. Conference Board, *Corporate Response to Employees' Housing Needs* (New York: The Board, 1975).

G. Commerce Clearing House, *Human Resources Management: Personnel Practices* (Washington, D.C.: The Clearing House, 1984).

H. See Gary Malamud, *Boomtown Communities* (New York: Van Nostrand, 1984), p. 217 ff.

I. Information from a 1985 survey by Dartnell Company made available to the author by a national trade association source.

J. Mary Nenno, *New Money and New Methods* (Washington, D.C.: National Association of Housing and Redevelopment Officials, 1986).

K. Authors' analysis.

Grumman is not alone. Twenty-seven percent of the 606 large firms covered by the 1986 Merrill Lynch Relocation Survey reported having difficulties with recruitment into high-housing-cost areas.[15]

Grumman officials also noted that relocation and other benefits that the company was forced to offer to attract engineers to the Long Island facility often ran as high as 20 percent of salary. "That cost of living differential is an added business expense, . . . a nonproductive use of capital [that] makes it increasingly difficult for [regional] employers to compete in the national market place," one expert concluded.[16]

The head of the Housing Committee of the Long Island Association (a local business organization), said that as many as 30 other area employers were considering similar moves. The Nassau County Planning Director said of the Long Island housing situation, "Long Islanders had better realize that the cost of housing is one of the main reasons why the Island is no longer a good place to do productive work. We are strangling ourselves and not too slowly either." The Grumman decision not to hire 500 additional engineers for its Long Island plant cost the regional economy about $50 million, according to the Planning Director.[17]

The Grumman case is only one example of an increasingly prevalent phenomenon in the New York City region. Mobil Oil, International Paper, and J. C. Penney have all left Manhattan for Richmond, Memphis, and Dallas, respectively, and the Big 8 accounting firm of Deloitte, Haskins & Sells left Manhattan for the New York suburbs; in each case the high cost of housing for employees was cited.[18] Warehouse operators in suburban New Jersey also have had difficulty finding employees who can afford to live within a realistic commute of suburban warehouse sites.[19] Indeed, virtually the whole New York/New Jersey regional economy is seen as endangered by shortage of affordable housing for workers. In 1985 the Regional Plan Association warned that "without adequate housing provision and satisfaction of housing needs, the region may not sustain its projected strong growth in employment and output."[20]

The important and fragile link between affordable housing and economic growth is not limited to conditions in the New York/New Jersey market. Other regional economies such as those in California and Massachusetts are having similar problems. At the start of this decade the *New York Times* reported that "many economists say the high price of housing in California is increasingly turning back would be migrants . . . as well as potential employers in a pattern they say is jeopardizing the state's economic health."[21] In 1981, the California Roundtable said that "the high cost of housing is having a feedback effect on the entire economy and is posing a serious threat to the continued economic growth in California."[22] The impact was judged to be particularly severe in the San Diego, Los Angeles, and San Francisco areas. A January 1983 report of the Bay Area Council, a leading voice of the business/civic community, was devoted to encouraging a wide range of corporate affordable housing activities. This report said, "Problems due to the high price and inadequate supply of housing in the Bay Area are exacting a growing toll on businesses, and threatening the economic vitality of the region at large."[23]

In May 1987, California Assemblyman Dan Hauser, Chairman of the Assembly's Housing and Community Development Committee, said, "While the crisis many were envisioning at the beginning of the decade has not fully materialized, there is a growing problem of job development without a concurrent commitment to low- and moderate-income housing. I fear that if this problem is not thoroughly addressed, California may cease to be the magnet for business expansion that it has traditionally been."[24]

In Boston, housing prices are beginning to cause worries about slowdowns in the growth of the metropolitan economy. High housing costs have already made it more expensive for major employers to recruit needed employees. Although Massachusetts salaries are about 28 percent above the national average, housing price increases are outstripping wage increases. Between 1983 and 1986, housing prices increased an average of 20–38 percent annually, putting the median price of a existing single-family home at $170,000.[25] The result, as in New York, is a personnel recruitment nightmare. The *Boston Globe* published an article called "Boston's a Nice Place to Work In . . . but Who Can Afford to Move Here?" that cited recruitment problems for engineering firms, retailers, computer companies, and colleges.[26] The *New York Times* has reported that Boston hospitals are having to offer housing assistance to attract doctors: "David Trull, Chief Operating Officer of Tufts University's New England Medical Center, said, 'We're aggressively looking for real estate opportunities in our area' to offer subsidized housing to interns, residents and starting faculty." Trull noted that "housing is a very real issue in attracting full-time faculty."[27]

Tufts University's New England Medical Center is not alone in this situation. In 1987, a Harvard-affiliated hospital, Children's Hospital Medical Center, the nation's largest children's hospital, agreed to purchase a nearby apartment building for $22.5 million. An economist with the Federal Home Loan Bank Board of Boston has said, "Ultimately growth could slow. . . . Until we can get salaries up there is obviously a limit on how much the economy can do."[28]

Generally, the very expensive response of business to these problems has been either to bear the cost of recruiting personnel into high-priced areas or to bear the cost of relocating the firm to a less costly area. No business leaders are saying that these responses are ideal, but alternatives so far have been lacking.

Financing Employer-Assisted Housing

Employers are beginning to respond to the housing finance needs of their employees in a variety of ways. Several employer-assisted housing finance programs exist that, if combined with supportive federal and state policies, could serve as model national programs.

One model has been used by the University of Pennsylvania, in Philadelphia, for nearly 15 years. The University of Pennsylvania Mortgage Guarantee Program provides mortgage insurance. Faculty and all other full-time University employees are eligible to participate. The program offers 100 percent mortgage insurance on any conventional mortgage made by a Philadelphia lender. Because the mortgage is 100 percent insured, lenders do not require downpayments, eliminating the barrier that the lack of downpayment poses to many prospective home buyers. Since the University of Pennsylvania is insuring the mortgage, no additional private mortgage insurance is required, saving borrowers monthly mortgage insurance premium charges. From the University's cost perspective, the program is basically costless unless there is a mortgage default. There has only been one default in 15 years of lending. In the case of a default the University is empowered to foreclose on the mortgage and recover its insurance loss. With the exception of publicizing the availability of the program to employees, all other costs of obtaining a mortgage are borne by the private lenders and the borrowers, as is the case in other forms of mortgage lending.

The University of Pennsylvania program is relatively small. As a result, local lenders have been willing to hold the mortgages in their own lending portfolios. Lenders must hold this debt because the mortgages are incapable of being resold on a secondary market, as they carry neither private nor federal mortgage insurance. Such an illiquid program could not gain national banking support. To expand the opportunities for similar employee/employer partnerships, state housing finance agencies should be empowered to purchase employer-insured mortgages from lenders using taxable housing finance agency bonds.

An alternative to having state housing agencies purchase employer-guaranteed mortgages is for the private sector to create a 100 percent employers group mortgage insurance product. Such a product would be analogous to the group health insurance policies that most employers are familiar with. Mortgages whose principals are 100 percent insured by a group policy could be traded on a new national secondary market, solving all liquidity problems.

For the employer, mortgage guarantee programs have little or no cost, unless a borrower defaults. For the employee, the program removes downpayment barriers to homeownership and eliminates the cost of monthly mortgage insurance charges. To further encourage this type of activity, the federal government should also clarify Internal Revenue Service rules so that the expense of defaulted mortgages that firms must redeem can be fully and immediately be deducted from corporate tax liability.

Employer-Assisted Housing as a Personnel Benefit

With a supportive national policy, employer-assisted housing programs could be structured to lower monthly carrying charges as well as provide downpayment assistance. The simplest supportive federal help would be clarification and facilitation of employer assistance for housing as a personnel benefit.

With the increase in two-income families, holding jobs with duplicative personnel benefits, many families want, and firms have begun to offer, flexible and cafeteria-style employee benefit plans. These programs allow employees to choose from among a variety of benefits offered. It is, at best, unclear whether the existing Internal Revenue Service regulations allow firms to offer a housing benefit, even as a taxable benefit within these benefit programs. If a benefit is taxable (for the employee) the federal government ought to allow the greatest possible leeway as to the specific type of benefit. A minimally supportive federal policy would clarify the IRS regulations to permit the offering of a taxable housing benefit within flexible and cafeteria-style benefit plans. If this is done, firms could begin prudently to offer a variety of employer-assisted housing programs, including downpayment assistance accounts, mortgage rate buydown programs of a permanent or temporary nature (which help families qualify for mortgages even if their monthly payments will ultimately rise when the buydown ends), and subsidized mortgage insurance payments.

One benefit form of employer assistance that could be particularly effective is the use of qualified cash or tax deferred arrangement (CODA) plans under Section 401(k) of the Internal Revenue Code, particularly in combination with thrift or profit-sharing plans. A firm offering both benefits could match employee contributions within a deferred compensation program. The employee's contribution would be tax-deferred and the employer's could be taxable or tax-deferred. The employee could then withdraw the funds at some point to use for a downpayment. Current 401(k) regulations prohibit the penalty-free withdrawal of funds from 401(k) accounts prior to age $59\frac{1}{2}$, except for certain emergency situations, principally medical expenses. Tax law should be amended to allow penalty-free withdrawal of funds from 401(k) plans for first-time home buyers. Firms could manage this joint downpayment account in a manner similar to the manner in which pension programs are presently administered.

Having an IRS ruling that housing is a qualified taxable employee benefit would be helpful, but a federal government that truly wanted to encourage employer-assisted housing would grant it tax-exempt status. Current law recognizes the existence of four tax-exempt employee benefits: health insurance, child care (up to $5,000 per year), term life insurance (up to $50,000), and group legal coverage (being phased out as a tax-exempt benefit, though it will still be a taxable benefit).

Offered as a tax-exempt benefit, employees would seek and employers offer housing assistance as a commonplace benefit. As a tax-exempt benefit, firms could offer downpayment contributions, mortgage buydowns or copayments, and mortgage insurance programs. The deferred compensation program referred to above would be even more effective if employer contributions were tax-exempt and employee contributions were tax-deferred.

Firms wishing more extensive involvement could coinvest with employees by loaning the employee a downpayment with the loan and interest due in a specified number of years. Employers' coinvestments could be offered at rates less than those a home buyer could obtain conventionally, because firms lending at below market rates could qualify these loans for limited tax deductibility depending upon the interest rate charged. For short-term loans, firms could pass on their favorable corporate borrowing rates to employee home buyers.

Another mechanism for involving employers as investors is patterned after the Employee Stock Ownership Plan (ESOP). The principle behind the federal government's support of ESOPs through the tax code is that ESOPs give employees a stake in America. Surely if the typical $3,000–$25,000 worth of stock is a stake in America, then owning a home must be considered an important stake as well. The ESOP provisions of the tax code should be expanded to encourage EHOPs, or Employee Homeownership Plans.

In this model, employers could donate (or borrow and donate) funds to a trust, just as they now donate stock in ESOPs, for the purpose of making mortgage loans or downpayment loans or grants to employees. The incentive for making such a donation would be the same as with an ESOP, that the donations received by employees are tax-exempt while the firm's donation is also fully deductible. The Deficit Reduction Act of 1984 allows lenders to exclude from their taxable income 50 percent of the interest they receive on loans to firms financing ESOPs. Employer-borrowers can negotiate with lenders for a share of the lenders' tax savings in the form of reduced borrowing rates, which can be passed on to the ESOP. The extension of this provision in an Employee Homeownership Plan would enhance employer-assisted housing, reducing even further the cost of borrowing and monthly mortgage carrying charges. The ESOP provisions have been retained in the 1986 tax law. Firms that as a result of tax reform have fewer tax deductions and are still subject to corporate and capital gains taxes may want to consider the tax advantages of EHOPs.

An EHOP fashioned after the current ESOP could have an additional business benefit, in that corporations could be allowed to use the trust to take an equity position in a mortgage or pool of mortgages. Home sales and mortgage loans to employees could be structured as conventional loans, or on a shared equity basis. Firms could share in the benefits of appreciation of homes, mortgages, or mortgage pools.

In sum, employer-assisted home financing is happening today in limited ways. In a system that professes to want to maximize private-sector involvement in housing, there is no reason why the federal government cannot actively support the minor legal changes necessary to make employer-assisted housing commonplace. Costs to the federal Treasury for such a program would be minimal in comparison to the expansion of homeownership opportunity that employer-assisted housing could provide for millions of working Americans.

The single-family programs that we advocate, and have described above—mortgage interest-rate buydowns, NHIC downpayment assistance, lease/purchase and employer-assisted housing—have the capacity to assist 330,000 families obtain ownership of either new or existing homes annually. This would admit more than 3.3 million families to the ranks of America's homeowners during the decade of the 1990s.

FEDERAL SPONSORSHIP OF LOW-INCOME MULTI-FAMILY HOUSING

Public Housing

For millions of Americans, however, the dream of homeownership is not practicable. For some, high costs make homeownership unaffordable, while for others, life circumstances make property ownership undesirable. For tens of millions of poor Americans, and for many elderly, single, and handicapped persons, the dream is simply to have decent, safe, affordable rental housing. It is incumbent upon us to offer a program that addresses this dream too.

It was the need to develop decent, safe, affordable housing, and equally importantly to create construction jobs during the Great Depression, that first involved the federal government in public housing programs and policy. Public housing did not start out as housing for the very poor. Senator Robert Wagner of New York, principal author of the Housing Act of 1937 said, "There are some who we cannot expect to serve, . . . those who cannot pay the rent."[29] In the fifty years since the passage of the first housing act, the role of public housing has changed. Public housing is now the housing provider of last resort for those who would otherwise have no shelter.

The public housing tenant of the 1980s is very poor and getting poorer relative to the rest of society. Ten percent of all the nation's renters whose incomes are less than 50 percent of their area's median live in public housing. A 1981 HUD survey indicates that 65 percent of all public housing incomes are between 10 percent and 30 percent of the area median, 89 percent between 10 percent and 50 percent of the area median. Incomes of families living in public housing average about $6,000 per year; elderly tenants (38 percent of all public housing tenants) have even lower annual incomes, averaging about $5,000, with 70 percent having incomes between $3,000 and $6,000 per year. The overall average income of renters in public housing in 1983 was $5,360, or 24 percent of the national median.[30]

As noted earlier, the federal government has supported public housing construction programs since 1937. It has also experimented with a variety of other deep-subsidy housing construction programs during the past 20 years. Some of these programs, such as Section 236, Section 8 New Construction, and the original Public Housing Program, have sought to increase the supply of standard, low-rent housing. Other programs, such as rent vouchers, Section 23, and the Section 8 Existing Certificate Program, have sought to supplement the incomes of poor tenants so that they could afford market-rate rents. In total, more than 4 million households have been assisted by federal housing activities. As we look toward a new housing policy, we need to examine both supplemental income and supply programs.

The theory behind supplemental income rental programs is that even low-income housing consumers should have some choice regarding where they want to live, as long as the unit is not substandard and is rented at a reasonable rate. The theory also holds that, in response to the greater purchasing power of low-income renters, the market will build new standard housing at prices that the rental certificate or voucher holders could afford. However, despite extensive studies there is little evidence to suggest that supplemental income programs have spurred the construction or alleviated shortages of low-cost rental housing. A 1982 HUD report found that more than half of white recipients and nearly three-quarters of minority recipients who received Section 8 Certificates failed to find units.[31] Many local housing authorities report higher failure rates, due to lack of available units. Because these programs have not encouraged additional supply, no residual number of vacated units for other low-income renters has resulted.

There has been no benefit from these programs for low-income renters as a class. Only those who directly receive benefits (as tenants or landlords) are helped by supplemental income housing assistance. Furthermore, even that advantage is short-term. These programs provide assistance for a specified period, during which time substantial public expenditures are made. At the end of the period, assistance may be terminated despite a continuing need. The end result is that a poor family is again without decent, safe, and affordable housing, and a substantial sum of public money is gone. Because these programs do not provide a permanent source of affordable housing either for the program participant or for the taxpayer, whose money has been spent for a fleeting benefit, we believe that supplemental income housing assistance programs are not a worthwhile strategy. We would urge the phasing out of this type of program.

The federal government also has extensive experience with construction programs that do increase the supply of affordable housing. Unlike the certificate or voucher programs, construction programs increase housing availability for those directly housed in a development, as well as for those who are able to occupy units vacated (which may or may not be affordable for low-income tenants). Originally, the principal construction program was public housing, housing owned and operated by public entities. However, in an effort to involve the private sector and reduce the costs of what was perceived to be an expensive program, the federal government established the Section 221(d)(3) Below Market Interest Rate (BMIR), Section 236, Section 8, and Section 515 programs. Under each of these programs, private entities were responsible for owning and operating low-income housing. More than 1.9 million units were produced and made available to low-income renters by these programs.[32]

In return for private participation, the programs were structured to allow private owners to leave the various programs at the end of a 15- or 20-year period, depending on the program. These programs have been providing affordable opportunities during the past 15 and 20 years. But property owners are now choosing to leave these programs in order to take advantage of changed real estate conditions. Thousands of residents have been forced to move and recent analyses by the Congressional Budget Office and the General Accounting Office indicate that hundreds of thousands of units are "at risk" of being lost due to prepayment of mortgages. By 1995, 900,000 tenant households may be threatened with displacement or substantially increased rents. By the year 2025 the at-risk population will include nearly all households living in the 1.9 million Section 221(d)(3) BMIR, 8, 236, and 515 units.[33]

The nation must resolve the conflict between the need for a constant housing stock affordable to low-income renters and investors seeking to maximize income. Current HUD policy toward the disposition of foreclosed properties indicates little interest in protecting low-income housing supplies. Federal law concerning the sale of foreclosed low-income housing requires that HUD consider the impact of a sale on the tenants of the building, as well as the highest price offered for the building at auction. HUD has often disregarded the plight of tenants. In other cases, HUD has purposely underbid private interests, so that properties would go directly to private owners, who are not required to consider the impact of their purchase on current tenants.

Law or regulation must be strengthened to require HUD to dispose of all foreclosed properties in a manner that would keep these properties as part of the nation's low-rent housing supply. In combination with state and local affordable housing efforts HUD should be required to work with public agencies, housing partnerships, nonprofit housing sponsors, mutual housing associations, and community development corporations to restore these projects to financial viability for low-income families.

To secure financially sound projects that are at risk of mortgage prepayment, Congress must take immediate steps to guarantee that contracts for Section 8 Existing Housing Certificates will be renewed when they expire. Tax and mortgage refinancing policies should be established that encourage private owners to continue their participation in the assisted housing programs, and Section 8 Existing Certificates should be made available to tenants in buildings that are being converted to market-rate units. These certificates should be specifically valid in the converted buildings regardless of fair market-rent guidelines.

That the poor will always be with us may prove true. That the poor will be with us after the temporary real estate and income tax advantages of sheltering them have expired has already proved true. Our national housing policy has been shortsighted. Participation by the private sector in the 236, 221(d)(3), and Section 8 New Construction programs was supposed to save the taxpayers money over what would have been spent if the units had been developed as public housing. In fact, the Section 8 New Construction Program's per-unit subsidy is four times greater than the public housing subsidy. Section 236 units may require only about half the subsidy of public housing units, but if they are lost from the nation's low-rent housing stock after 15 or 20 years they will not have been less expensive. Furthermore, Section 236 tenants in 1983 had an average annual income of 43 percent of the national median income, an amount 75 percent greater than that of the typical public housing tenant and high enough to allow them to obtain affordable shelter in a shallow-subsidy state program.[34]

And public housing is an appreciating national asset. Public housing today has a replacement value of more than $70 billion. It is tragic for the families affected that we are faced with the problem of units' reverting to the open market. It is also a scandal that the spending of tax dollars will have resulted in market-rate rental units and condominiums rather than the shelter for the poor that the taxpayers had a right to expect.

The past 20 years of federal housing policy have taught us several lessons. We now know that supplemental income rental assistance programs do not alleviate low-rent housing shortages. We now know that programs that do not permanently add to the low-rent housing stock will create needlessly uncertain futures for poor tenants. We now know that programs that do not permanently add to the low-rent housing stock are more expensive to develop and operate than public housing, particularly considering that these units can disappear from the low-rent housing stock after 15 or 20 years of receiving extensive public subsidies. Finally, we now know that we will need deeply subsidized low-income housing for the foreseeable future.

Based upon 1974–1983 trends, it is projected that by 1993 there will be 7.5 million unsubsidized low-rent units available, but there will be more than 14.3 million families in need of such units.[35] More than 17 million families will need low-rent units by 2003, but only about 7 million units will be in the marketplace.[36] We need a federal housing policy that builds new publicly owned units that will be a permanent part of the nation's low-rent housing stock. Fortunately, we have the makings of such a program; it is public housing. More than 1.3 million families in nearly 3,200 communities call public housing home.[37]

Unfortunately, the Reagan Administration's war against the poor, with Congress' acquiescence, has been most effective when it comes to public housing. In fiscal year 1986 fewer than 4,000 public housing units were built, not including units for Indian Housing Authorities, and the fiscal year 1988 budget calls for no units to be produced.[38]

We call for a reinvigorated public housing program as the basis of a new federal commitment to housing the very poor. The federal government should produce 40,000 public housing units annually. Compared to zero units or 4,000 units, 40,000 units is a lot of housing. However, it is only 90 percent of the number of public housing units produced in 1979.

In restarting housing production at HUD, however, it is important to remember that much of the productive capacity of the agency has been stripped away during the past seven years. Rebuilding the gutted HUD will provide an opportunity to examine how units can be more cost-effectively produced. This opportunity should be taken. The average cost of a newly produced public housing unit is $68,000, an amount that could be considered excessive.[39] Cost containment should be a priority of a reinvigorated public housing program, and the first priority of cost containment must be simplifying HUD reviews and needless bureaucratic delays that drive up the costs of projects.

Site selection controversies have also driven up the cost of public housing. Most public housing has been created through new construction. Developing housing projects through adaptive reuse of vacant and abandoned property should become a HUD priority. Land is scarce and expensive in many urban areas, where abandoned homes, factories, and commercial structures are common. Adaptive reuse projects can be less expensive and are likely to be welcomed by the community because they eliminate a blighted abandoned structure.

Public housing does have a checkered history. Cost containment should be a priority, but it must not come at the expense of proper building design or maintenance. Neither the tenant nor society is advantaged by constructing sparse units that fail to meet the physical, familial, and community needs of tenants. In seeking to build upon public housing's successful experiences, the federal government must develop a system that is sensibly designed and properly maintained. We are all familiar with the high-rise horror stories of Pruitt-Igoe and more recently the demolition of Scudder Homes in Newark. But the fact is that most modern public housing projects, those built during the past 20 years, have averaged well under 100 units in size.[40] HUD should continue to develop modest-sized projects. In addition to modest scale, sensibly designed housing must include modern appliances, landscaping, and recreational and social facilities. Stark housing and the absence of amenities does not encourage communitarian behavior, so vital to the success of public housing.

Maintenance is also a major problem to be addressed in a rein-vigorated public housing program. Much of the extreme building wear and tear is a result of overutilization. Many public housing units are illegally overcrowded. In New York City, public housing has an estimated occupancy rate of 135 percent. More than one-third of all city public housing units are occupied by more than one family.[41] Maintenance under these conditions is difficult. It is made even more difficult by the byzantine system HUD has created for funding building rehabilitation and modernization. Unlike conventional rental housing developments, rehabilitation and modernization financing is not part of the monthly public housing operating budget. Rather, modernization and rehabilitation financing—known as Comprehensive Improvement Assistance Program (CIAP) funding—is subject to a separate legislative appropriation and administrative allocation process. A 1983 Council of Large Public Housing Authorities survey found that it typically took 30 months of planning and preparation to begin CIAP construction, and more than four years elapsed between the time HUD announced the availability of CIAP funding and the completion of the project.[42]

A 1987 Abt Associates study estimates that public housing is in need of more than $9 billion in immediate repairs, and a total modernization effort could cost more than $20 billion.[43] Yet Congress is appropriating only about $1 billion in CIAP funding each year.[44] Consideration should be given to increasing operating budgets, specifically for the purpose of undertaking modernization programs, without reducing CIAP budgets. This additional appropriation would improve housing quality, and might prove a more efficient building rehabilitation process than the cumbersome CIAP process.

In general, the policies we advocate create new housing opportunities for working individuals and families whose incomes place them just out of reach of homeownership or standard, non-cost-burdened rental housing, through the establishment of new partnerships and relationships between federal, state, and local governments, the non-profit sector, and employers. But public housing is a special case. The economic profile of public housing tenants is not that of a tenant on the verge of middle-class status. Rather, most public housing tenants are those mired in the welfare system or employed in low-paying jobs. These individuals cannot be true partners, for they lack the skills and income necessary to become self-sufficient members of society. Programs such as the Section 236, Section 221(d)(3), and Section 8 New Construction programs may be public/private partnerships, but it is one in which the tenants do not, and cannot, participate.

The federal government must be committed to being a partner and a friend of the poor, for the federal government is the only partner capable of providing the resources that the poor need. Helping the poor become self-sufficient and productive members of society should be a national goal. Decent, safe, affordable shelter is a prerequisite for self-sufficiency. It is counterproductive public policy, and indecent moral policy, to reduce direct housing assistance to the poor. We can and must do better.

Federal/State Community-Based Supply Rental Housing

It is not merely preferable that the federal government directly serve the housing needs of the very lowest income families. It is, quite simply, a necessity if these households are to be sheltered. State appropriation and tax-exempt bond programs are less costly, in terms of the tax dollars needed to produce a unit of low-rent housing, than the federal program. But state programs, unaided by private or federal resources, are not able to serve the housing needs of the very poor, those whose income is less than 40 percent of an area's median. Only the federal government has the resources to provide for the housing of those who cannot afford to pay operating expenses, much less the amortizing of a mortgage.

However, during the past 20 years, the states have gained substantial experience in providing housing for tenants whose incomes are between 40 percent and 80 percent of the area median. During this period, states produced more than 635,000 rental units using tax-exempt bond authority. Most of these units, about 385,000, were produced in coordination with federal Section 8, 236, or other programs.[45] However, the remaining units have been built without direct federal assistance. Although the production of non-federally assisted, state-financed rental housing has increased in recent years, in response to local needs and federal program cutbacks, the 20-year average of state production for these units is fewer than 15,000 annually. Clearly this level of production is inadequate to meet the needs of low- and moderate-income families in the absence of Section 8- and 236-type programs.

States can have a more expansive role in implementing a national rental housing production strategy, particularly serving the needs of those whose incomes are between 40 and 80 percent of median income. Active state programs serving these needs will enable federal resources to be better targeted to those whose incomes are even lower.

State Models

As discussed in Chapter 2, several states have established extensive programs for the development of multi-family housing. Two states, Massachusetts and New Jersey, have created programs that by their size and structure command our attention and offer guidance in developing a coordinated state and federal approach to the production of low- and moderate-income housing.

In most states, local housing authorities are municipally controlled entities with direct legal and fiscal relationships to the federal government through HUD. Housing authorities in Massachusetts share this trait; however, state enabling legislation has also created a direct state relationship with the 243 local housing authorities, which manage 63,000 public housing units.[46] This state/local relationship has resulted in the development of more than 10,000 state-financed public housing units since 1983.[47]

The state-assisted public housing program provides grants to local housing authorities for new construction, for adaptive reuse, and for the purchase of units located in privately owned buildings. There are program variants for the development of family, senior citizen, and special needs housing. The linkage of state resources with a locally based–federally related agency is an important new partnership. This new partnership could prove especially useful should a reinvigorated federal housing program enable local housing authorities to combine federal and state resources to develop additional low- and moderate-income housing. A locally administered federal/state partnership could also be structured to encourage the participation of various community and private-sector housing sponsors.

Massachusetts also offers a program to encourage the production of privately owned low-income housing, including those owned by non-profit organizations. The State Housing Assistance for Rental Production, or SHARP, program reduces the interest rate on Massachusetts Housing Finance Agency mortgages to as low as 5 percent.[48] In return for receiving this mortgage, developers must make available at least 25 percent of the units to tenants having incomes less than one-half of the area's median.

In 1984, the New Jersey Housing and Mortgage Finance Agency (HMFA) was created out of the merger of the state's single-family Housing Finance Agency and the multi-family Mortgage Finance Agency. The law that merged the two agencies gave the agency the new authority to create a subsidiary corporation, known as the Housing Assistance Corporation, or HASCO.

The purpose of HASCO is to perform any task necessary to the development of low- and moderate-income housing projects. HASCO began its operations by offering private, non-profit, and public entities various types of technical assistance, but the corporation has become much more powerful than simply a provider of technical assistance. Indeed, HASCO is now becoming the developer and owner of rental property, and can become codeveloper and coowner with public, non-profit, or private development and ownership entities. Since developing and owning low- and moderate-income rental housing is not a guaranteed investment, HASCO is empowered to take investment risks. In return for its risk-taking, the corporation can enter into shared equity agreements with codevelopers that enable the corporation to dispose of its equity over time and receive the appreciation on its investment.

HASCO cannot issue debt—the HMFA does this on the corporation's behalf—but HASCO can go directly to the capital markets and sell stock in projects or groups of projects. The corporation can also receive state and local donations of cash or land. In one recent case a small municipality, with limited development capacity, donated a tract of land on which the corporation will develop and own a 76-unit, mid-rise, low- and moderate-income apartment.

HASCO is not limited to new multi-family construction. The corporation can develop a single-family project and undertake the purchase and rehabilitation of both single- and multi-family housing. The existence of the state's Housing Assistance Corporations means that every community in New Jersey now has the capacity to develop publicly owned housing for low- and moderate-income families. Like the Massachusetts model, HASCO links state resources to community and private-sector resources. If the federal government were to structure its reinvigorated efforts to link with HASCO-type entities in the states, it is likely that a more efficient delivery of state or locally controlled public units would result.

That virtually all states have some multi-family housing finance and development capacity, and that some states are becoming the principal initiators, developers, and owners of low- and moderate-income housing, speaks to the growing sophistication of the states. However, even with the efforts of such states as Massachusetts, New Jersey, and New York (also a major developer of non-federally assisted low- and moderate-income housing) few multi-family units are produced each year without federal financial assistance. States are beginning to have sophistication and technique, but the states also have limited financing capacity.

Because of their limited fiscal capacity, the states need new partners, and both the federal government and the private sector ought to become more active partners. We advocate a federal matching grant program with the states principally for the production of low- and moderate-income rental housing. A federal matching grant program of $2.5 billion per year, matching on a dollar-for-dollar basis state housing trust funds and the contributions of non-profit and employer housing sponsors, could finance construction subsidies for 300,000 multi-family units each year. A program of this magnitude would more than equal all previous state housing finance agency multi-family efforts, including federally and non-federally assisted units, in about three years.

Later in this chapter we will describe how this new federal grant to the states should be established, and how it would operate. But before we do so, it is useful to discuss how the private sector, principally employers, could participate in a low- and moderate-income rental housing production program.

Encouraging Employer-Assisted Rental Housing

The notion of employers' creating rental housing opportunities for employees is a subject that must be approached with great sensitivity, because the history of "company towns" in this country was not a happy one. Yet it is possible to structure development, financing, and ownership arrangements so as to insulate the employer/employee relationship from property maintenance and tenant management relationships. Employers can provide valuable assistance to rental housing projects through agreements with private real estate development companies and specially created employer/employee non-profit housing corporations.

Examples of employer assistance for rental housing could include firms' donating, selling, or leasing surplus corporately owned land, or purchasing land and then donating or leasing at nominal costs or selling the land for employee housing. Land could be sold at a below market cost to a private developer who in return would, through a master lease contract, agree to rent apartments to employees at a reduced cost. Land donated to an employee/employer housing corporation could be used as equity for a mortgage. To encourage firms to purchase or donate land for employee housing the federal tax code should be clarified to ensure that such contributions are fully tax deductible.

Short-term investments by firms could facilitate affordable housing construction as well. For example, a financially strong firm could use its short-term corporate borrowing strength to finance construction financing. Whether a project is being developed by a for-profit or non-profit developer, construction financing is expensive, usually costing several percent more than long-term secured mortgage interest rates. Short-term corporate borrowing is done at or near the prime rate, several percentage points less than long-term mortgage interest rates. If a firm did this borrowing for a developer, thousands of dollars could be saved on a typical project.

Corporations could also invest in employee/employer housing corporations. Unlike individuals, corporations are exempt from the passive loss limitations in the tax code. Investing corporations could obtain tax depreciation rights to the property as well as a direct return on its investment.

In order to support the growth of employer-assisted rental housing, the federal tax code should be amended to make employer assistance a tax-exempt benefit. This is necessary because, without tax-exempt status, the value of rental assistance to the employee would be lost through an IRS-imputed rent-subsidy calculation. (Even without tax-exempt status, a few firms in areas with severe rental shortages may still be willing to provide market-rate housing opportunities as a convenience for employees if the tax laws were clarified or amended to allow employers to provide employee housing as a taxable benefit to employees and a tax-deductible business cost for employers.)

As discussed previously, the federal government should expand the Employer Stock Ownership Program model to allow the development of Employer Home Ownership Programs. A rental EHOP program could be created with employer cash or stock donations being made to an employee housing cooperative. Rents would reimburse the employee trust over the term of the mortgage. The EHOP contribution need not be for the full value of constructing a building, but only an amount necessary to buy down the cost of construction or land to produce affordable rents.

In summary, it is possible to structure employer-sponsored rental housing in a variety of ways so as to insulate employees and employers from property and tenant management conflicts. However, what is needed to encourage the growth of employee rental assistance programs is a supportive set of federal tax laws. Tax law must be amended clearly to permit tax-deductible employer contributions to a housing program, and renting employees must receive the rental assistance as a tax-deductible benefit in order that the value of the benefit not be lost to the employee via additional federal tax liability.

A FEDERAL/STATE PARTNERSHIP FOR SENIOR CITIZEN HOUSING

The fastest-growing segment of the American population is the elderly, particularly the old, or frail, elderly. The frail elderly are mostly homeowners, but they are homeowners with special needs. A 1983 congressional study reported that 12.4 million homes are owned by persons over 65 years of age. Eighty percent of these homes are owned "free and clear." Estimates of the value of elderly-owned housing is placed between $600 billion and $1 trillion.[49]

Elderly homeowners face special problems. Homes purchased 40 years earlier for large families have become difficult to manage for many of the frail elderly. Homes with staircases, high or low cabinet work, or inadequate or inefficient heating or cooling systems become major impediments to safe and comfortable living. For some, selling the home and moving is a necessary or preferable alternative. But many elderly people wish to stay in a familiar home and neighborhood. Many could stay in their own homes if the units were rehabilitated or retrofitted; however, many elderly homeowners, house-rich but cash-poor, are unable to afford the necessary housing rehabilitation or retrofitting that would make remaining in the home a comfortable, viable alternative.

In response to this problem, several states and a number of private firms have begun offering reverse annuity mortgages or reverse mortgages. These instruments enable elderly homeowners to be paid a monthly fee in return for a growing share of the equity in the home. The monthly fee is an important income supplement, enabling the elderly person to pay home maintenance and other necessities.

Among the states that are offering variants of a reverse equity mortgage are Arkansas and Connecticut. The Arkansas program is open to homeowners living in the Little Rock area who are at least 70 years of age and whose annual income is less than 80 percent of the area median income. Participants may receive 25 percent of their home's value as an up-front payment.[50] The remaining value of the home is drawn against according to a formula. The size of the annuity available to the participant is based upon the home's present value minus any repair costs, plus a projection of the value of the home at some future date when the home is likely to be sold. The date is based upon actuarial assumptions; the homeowner is guaranteed a life tenancy and a lifetime income stream. The Arkansas Development Finance Authority is responsible for most repairs for program participants.

The Arkansas program is designed as an annuity program and, as with other annuity instruments, if the recipient dies before an amount equal to the value of the home is received, the remaining equity does not revert to the estate. The ADFA is entitled to all the equity in the home, once a homeowner agrees to participate. This annuity feature has tended to discourage participation, as many elderly people have a desire to leave something to their heirs.

The Connecticut Housing Finance Authority (CHFA) program offers low-income elderly participants 10 years of monthly income supplements. These payments are based on 80 percent of the home's current value plus a calculation to capture the home's appreciation during the 10-year period. Payments from the state to the homeowner carry a modest interest charge, currently 7 percent per year. At the end of the 10-year period, if the home has increased in value by more than the amount anticipated, an additional loan can be structured. If not, the homeowner can continue to live in the home, but no additional payments to the homeowner will be made and the outstanding debt to the state continues to accrue with interest at 7 percent per year.[51]

Seeing the asset value of homes owned by senior citizens, the private sector has also attempted to enter the reverse mortgage market. The national leader is a New Jersey-based mortgage banking firm, American Homestead Mortgage, which offers participants a lifetime income stream and a lifetime tenancy in return for payment upon change of title of the amount loaned, plus an interest amount, plus a share in the appreciation of the home if the particular loan is structured to include the home's appreciated value. Any remaining equity in the home after the debt has been satisfied remains with the estate.[52]

These three examples of reverse mortgages or reverse annuity mortgages are typical of what the public and private sectors are offering to meet the housing and income needs of elderly homeowners. Each of these programs is useful, but each is small, meeting but a fraction of the need. Many elderly people are leery of reverse equity programs. They do represent a new and unfamiliar concept. While the variety of programs allow consumer choice, senior citizens often find the variety of options confusing. Further, many elderly fear displacement, should they exhaust their home equity. Conversely, they also fear that if they should die relatively soon the home's remaining equity will be captured by the lender rather than by the beneficiaries of their estates.

A federal policy on reverse mortgages is needed. The federal government's role should be both regulatory and programmatic. The regulatory role should be to prohibit reverse programs that do not offer lifetime tenancy and a lifetime income stream. Participants should not be in a position of "betting their house" that they will die before their tenancy rights to the property expire or their income is reduced. If elderly people know that such programs are illegal, they will be less hesitant to enter into agreements with reverse annuity mortgage lenders. Annuity programs that seize all housing equity regardless of how much money was paid out to the participant should also be banned. Doing this would assure participants that should they die sooner than later their estate will remain available to their loved ones.

At a programmatic level, the federal government should not immediately offer a comprehensive reverse mortgage program. The states and the private sectors may well be capable, with adequate federal regulation, to provide this needed service. However, the federal government, through the National Housing Investment Corporation (NHIC), should offer a limited reverse mortgage, or deferred loan. The program would not provide a lifetime or even temporary income stream, but rather a one-time cash payment of up to $15,000 for the purpose of rehabilitating or retrofitting the house to make it physically or economically possible for the elderly homeowner to remain in the home. The NHIC would issue these loans through local lending institutions, who would receive a fee for processing

and closing NHIC loans. NHIC loans would accrue interest throughout their term at a rate slightly above Treasury borrowing rates.
Structured as such, NHIC loans would be self-financing, creating a
small public-sector profit.

If the federal government enacted a deferred loan program for
elderly homeowners, we believe that the demand would be substantial, with 140,000 senior citizens each year benefiting from the program. Initial appropriations of $2.1 billion per year would be needed,
but all this money, plus interest, would eventually be returned to
the federal Treasury. When compared to the costs of building new
senior citizen housing or providing nursing home care, an interest-
bearing loan by the federal government is an inexpensive alternative
to help tens of thousands of elderly homeowners live in their own
homes in modest comfort. Enabling and encouraging the frail elderly to remain in their own homes should be the focus of a senior
citizens' housing policy. Tapping the enormous home equity that
the elderly possess will be essential for the success of such a national
policy. The policy described above will benefit many of our senior
citizens, but more than 20 percent of the frail elderly do not have
housing equity to draw upon, either to retrofit a current home or to
provide income for renting or purchasing an alternative dwelling.
These elderly will need standard, non-cost-burdened rental units.

Public housing and Section 8 programs have historically been
important sources of affordable housing for the elderly, though these
programs are not targeted to the special needs of senior citizens. The
Section 202 housing program is specifically targeted to the unique
needs of the elderly. That program, created as part of the Housing
Act of 1959, has produced more than 165,000 units in more than
2,100 projects during its history.[53]

We need to renew and expand our national commitment to the
Section 202 program, making it the lead subsidized rental program
for the nation's low-income elderly. We believe that Section 202
housing is the appropriate vehicle for addressing the rental housing
needs of senior citizens. Developed locally by non-profit sponsors
such as churches, unions, and neighborhood organizations familiar
to seniors, Section 202 housing can play an important role in the
community-based-supply housing strategy discussed in detail in
Chapter 4. This strategy is particularly appropriate for the elderly
since it makes it possible for them to remain in their own neighborhoods. Additionally, since the primary responsibility for senior citizen housing will shift from local housing authorities to non-profit

sponsors, housing authority resources can be better focused on the complex needs of younger, poor families.

As with Section 8, 515, and other similar programs, Section 202 projects are backed by a 20-year Section 8 rental assistance commitment. Because Section 202 projects are owned by non-profit corporations, there will not be a market-driven inclination to convert projects to market-rate units. However, the financial pressure on projects at the conclusion of the 20-year rental assistance agreements will be great and some may be withdrawn from the nation's subsidized housing stock as a result of this financial pressure. The loss of these units due to lack of federal rent subsidies is as unacceptable as the losses of Section 8, 236, and 221(d)(3) BMIR units are to mortgage prepayment. For this reason we advocate a 40-year federal Section 8 commitment that would be renewable for an additional 20 years. A lengthened federal commitment for Section 202 housing will guarantee the existence of subsidized rental housing for the entire economic life, and most of the actual physical life, of the structures built. This is an economically efficient use of the nation's resources, as compared to the extensive sums spent on Section 236 and 221(d)(3) BMIR units, only to have these sums lost from the nation's subsidized housing stock after 20 years.

As we move into the twenty-first century and the "baby boom" generation ages, the nation will need increasing amounts of housing for the frail elderly. By developing housing that will be available for more than 20 years the nation will be preparing for its changing demography. During the second third of the next century the number of elderly people will decline and a loss of subsidized housing stock for the elderly may be demographically appropriate.

NEW MONEY FOR A NEW FEDERAL/STATE HOUSING PARTNERSHIP

Meeting the housing needs of the American people in the 1990s would be staggering to the Treasury if we were to finance and subsidize all the units we seek to build or make affordable as the federal government has in previous decades. We do not propose to stagger the Treasury. The methods we propose are largely self-financing, combining revenue growth generated by new housing, some modest new taxes, some small tax expenditures, and some new appropriations (see Table 16).

Toward a Revolving Tax Recapture Program

Much of this book discusses new ways of dealing with the initial capital expense of housing development. While it is true that housing is capital-intensive, it is also true that housing is labor-intensive. A 1980–1981 study by the Bureau of Labor Statistics found that, for each billion dollars of multi-family construction contract expenditures, 25,400 jobs were created. Similarly, for each billion dollars of single-family construction activity, 22,000 jobs were created.[54]

The program we advocate calls for the annual development in the 1990s of 370,000 rental units at an average cost of $60,000 per unit, 170,000 single-family homes at an average cost of $90,000 per unit, and $2.1 billion of single-family rehabilitation for the frail elderly. Using the BLS job creation rates, we can estimate that approximately 920,000 jobs would be created in each program year. Using an average 1986 construction worker salary of $22,464 and an annual federal income tax rate of 15 percent, the U.S. Treasury could expect more than $3.1 billion dollars annually in additional tax revenue from the jobs created by this housing program.[55]

This job creation estimate is a very conservative figure, for the BLS study does not include planning and design jobs that are part of housing development, nor does it examine the multiplier effects of housing construction on the home appliance, furnishing, service, and related industries. In 1984, the University of Maryland conducted a study of jobs created by the multiplier effect of housing construction.[56] If we update this study for wage increases, the creation of 540,000 additional affordable units would appear to generate an additional 276,000 jobs, producing an additional $123.5 million in tax revenue annually.

Thus, from federal wage taxes alone, the implementation of a national affordable housing program can be expected to generate more than $3.223 billion in new tax revenue annually. Corporate income taxes will add to this total. While there is no need for these revenues to be segregated in the Treasury Department's accounting system, the Treasury should track the jobs and taxes generated by the construction of 540,000 moderate-cost units each year, so that the public will have confidence that much of this program is "pay as you go."

In addition to the jobs generated by new housing construction this program will make the cost of acquiring an existing single-family home accessible to 160,000 families. These sales transactions will generate additional jobs in real estate, mortgage banking, insurance,

Table 16

A Housing Program for America

Program	No. of Units to Be Developed Annually	Average Federal Subsidy Cost/Unit ($)	Total Federal Expenditure/Year (year 1)(billions of $)	Notes
Homeownership programs creating 330,000 affordable units annually				
National Housing Investment Corp.	150,000	9,000	1.35*	All units new construction
Mortgage investment rate buydowns	110,000	13,680	1.50*	All units existing
Employer-assisted housing	50,000	3,300	.165*	All units existing
Lease/purchase	20,000	1,000	.020*	All units new construction
Rental production programs creating 370,000 low- and moderate-income units				
Public housing	40,000	68,000	2.72†	Annual operating subsidy is approximately $50 million

Section 202 housing	30,000	1.34†	Annual operating subsidy is less than $200 million
Community-based supply construction subsidies	300,000	2.265‡	States and frequently non-profits and employers would provide matching funding, so total per-unit subsidy would frequently be in excess of $15,100
Targeting housing rehabilitation			
Housing rehabilitation for the frail elderly	140,000		
Reverse equity loans	15,000	2.1*	Over-time program will become self-financing as loans are repaid with interest

*This activity will require a federal outlay in the first year. In succeeding years new personal income tax revenue generated by the entire proposed program totals $3.3 billion annually. Thus, in subsequent years this activity will be paid for by new tax revenues, making the program self-financing.

†This activity requires a federal outlay from general revenues.

‡This activity is financed by housing trust fund and new program-generated tax revenues.

and a host of affiliated industries such as home repair and remodeling and furniture appliance manufacturing and sales.

The recapture of tax revenue from this stimulated housing construction does, in fact, provide the largest source of revenue needed to finance this additional housing. But recaptured revenue is not, alone, sufficient to fund our entire program. Some additional new revenue is needed.

A Federal Housing Trust Fund

Building on the successes of the states that have adopted housing trust funds, the federal government should follow suit. The purpose of the trust fund would be to expand existing state rental production capacity and to initiate some new programs.

At least 17 states, including California, Florida, and New Jersey, have created housing trust funds in order to provide direct financial support for state housing efforts. The New Jersey housing trust fund, for example, uses dedicated realty transfer taxes. These revenues have subsidized the construction of more than 2,000 housing units in its first year of operation, serving the needs of families whose incomes average between 40 percent and 80 percent of the state median. State housing trust funds are used in various states to expand homeownership, to subsidize the construction and operation of rental housing, and to rehabilitate deteriorated housing.

These state initiatives provide important housing opportunities. However, the small size of the current housing trust funds ($10–$25 million per state) and the small number of states that have adopted them demonstrate the limits of the states' ability to raise tax revenue to meet even moderate-income housing needs adequately.

Creating a Federal Housing Trust Fund

The federal government ought to help raise revenue in a manner that is both responsive and supportive of state efforts. The creation of a federal housing trust fund to be matched by state trust funds on a dollar-for-dollar basis would be both. The concept of a federal trust fund is neither new nor necessarily controversial: Social Security is financed through a trust fund, as are highway construction and environmental cleanup programs. A trust fund accomplishes three goals that a simple annual appropriations bill, even one with continuing budget authority, does not.

First, a trust fund focuses attention on a problem or need in a special way. Prior to Superfund or the Highway Trust Fund, Congress did appropriate some funds for environmental cleanups and highway construction, but when Congress truly became serious about the problem it created a trust fund.

Second, a trust fund provides a sense that there will be a long-term predictable level of funding and housing activity that the states and the private sector can expect. This is particularly useful to the private building and financial sectors. Although Congress need not appropriate all available trust fund dollars in any given year, knowing that trust fund dollars will be available over the long term will enable these sectors to enter into better agreements with suppliers and labor. This will bring added stability and efficiency to the building industry. From a financing perspective, lenders need to know that this program will continue for the foreseeable future in order to create new mortgage products in the primary and secondary marketplaces.

Third, a trust fund emphasizes the pay-as-you-go nature of this housing policy. This is a new housing policy for America, not a new way to "bust" the already broken federal budget.

The federal housing trust fund should be dedicated to the financing and construction of new low- and moderate-income rental units, or the conversion or substantial rehabilitation of buildings that are abandoned or not otherwise used for housing. Only projects that add to the nation's low- and moderate-income housing stock should be eligible for federal housing trust fund financing.

Beyond being a major new source of funding dedicated to the construction of new affordable housing, a trust fund should have the goal of creating a joint federal/state funding and production mechanism that is administratively efficient and programmatically flexible. The recent experiences of the states in providing moderate-income housing suggest that the states are well suited to accomplish these goals, provided that the federal government plays a guiding and supportive role.

We believe that the federal government should play a guiding and supportive role for three reasons. First, the federal government has a fiduciary responsibility to ensure that the federal trust fund dollars reach the intended recipients. A "no-strings attached" housing block grant program does not do this.

Second, the trust fund mechanism employing federal, state, and private resources will require that the states undertake new types of housing development efforts. States will have to be informed of their program options and responsibilities. For example, through their tax-exempt bond programs, downpayment assistance programs, and trust funds, states have figured out how to serve those families whose yearly incomes exceed one-half of the state's median income. However, due in part to inadequate financial resources, states have had a spotty record of serving those whose incomes are between a third and half of the state median. A matching federal share will provide the resources to serve lower-income families and the federal government will want to ensure that they are indeed served. With joint federal/state trust fund financing, rental development options such as construction subsidies, interest rate buydowns, land acquisition, development on community land trusts, joint development with the NHIC, and the conversion of abandoned or non-housing structures to housing will all be possible. As other methods of delivering affordable housing are found to be feasible with trust fund dollars, these programs should be placed on a list of encouraged activities, so that states will be aware of all program options. By taking this "menu approach," states can mold the housing program to meet their unique needs.

Finally, the federal government will want to have a role because states have a mixed record of aiding depressed cities, or depressed rural areas, or other pockets of decline, depending upon the policy of the particular state. The federal government will want to ensure that federal funds address a state's low- and moderate-income housing needs regardless of where that need is located.

One way of assuring that federal funds go to communities of greatest need is to require that a minimum percentage of program activity take place in communities eligible for Urban Development Action Grants (UDAGs). The UDAG-eligible communities are, by HUD definition, the most distressed communities in the nation. These are the communities where most of the poor live and where there is greatest need for low- and moderate-income housing. The federal trust fund should target depressed areas both within the federal allocation formula to the states and within intrastate allocation of funds.

Within the context of creating a flexible program for the states, the federal government should require that minimum percentages of low-income people (below 50 percent of area median income) be served by the federal trust fund, while allowing the program to serve those whose incomes are between 50 percent and 80 percent of the area median income as well.

A federal housing trust fund, matched by state housing trust funds, would be an annually renewable source of money capable of addressing much of the nation's rental housing needs. However, if just the federal and state governments were included in this proposal, we would fail to reach out to all the partners who can play a constructive role. The federal trust fund should encourage states to seek out non-profits and employers. If a state uses its trust fund in combination with the housing efforts of a non-profit housing sponsor or an employer sponsor to develop moderate-income housing, then both the state and the private dollars allocated toward the project should be eligible for federal matching assistance.

Since the inception of the Community Development Block Grant (CDBG) program, many non-profit, community-based groups have demonstrated an ability to build or substantially rehabilitate moderate-income housing, and to do so at low costs per unit. Unfortunately, the construction capacity of the non-profit sector is still limited, creating less than 10,000 units per year. With state and federal trust fund support, the capacity of efficient non-profit housing sponsors could be greatly expanded. Similarly, employer-assisted rental housing programs for low- or moderate-income employees should be eligible to have employer contributions matched by state and federal trust funds, unless the contribution is a tax-advantaged EHOP or shared equity investment.

Trust funds typically establish a link between the thing being taxed and the use of the revenue. In the case of the Highway Trust Fund, gasoline is taxed for road construction; the Social Security Trust Fund taxes income to provide retirement benefits; and the so-called Superfund trust fund taxes polluting industrial firms to pay for environmental cleanup. A federal housing trust fund should be capitalized from a source related to the housing industry.

One new source of revenue that Congress might consider is a 1 percent tax on the issuance of mortgage-backed securities. During 1986 the Federal National Mortgage Association, the Federal Home Loan Mortgage Corporation, and other private mortgage-backed security issuers sold or swapped about $200 billion in mortgage-backed securities. Government National Mortgage Association issues are not included in our consideration, as these issues are already geared to low- and moderate-income housing programs. A 1 percent tax on mortgage-backed securities would generate more than $2 billion annually; with the required state and legislatively encouraged employer and non-profit matches, trust fund resources would be more than $4 billion each year, enough to provide subsidies for 300,000 units.

This tax would be charged only at the initial issuance of the security. It is not a recurring sales tax on mortgage-backed securities. The effect of such a tax in the market ought to be quite limited, but as with first reactions to all taxes, the securities industry is likely to resist the tax. Some persons in the securities industry have suggested that such a tax could result in somewhat higher mortgage interest rates, while others have thought that some of the tax would be absorbed by the issuers and some passed on to mortgage borrowers. However, since the federal housing trust fund would generate several thousand mortgages that would not have been realized had the tax not existed, the taxed industry will be afforded some new opportunities that, if creatively seized, could offset some of this tax burden.

Should Congress want an additional or alternative tax, consideration should be given to elimination of the mortgage interest deduction for vacation and second homes owned by those under 55 years of age. Although Congress has refused to raise additional revenue by restricting the homeowner mortgage deduction, one is hard pressed to defend the deducting of interest on a second home while millions of Americans cannot afford to purchase one home and millions have no home at all, affordable or otherwise.

The exception for those over 55 years of age is urged, since families in this age group frequently purchase a second home for retirement purposes and it is already national public policy to encourage people to prepare for their retirement. The Congressional Research Service estimates that the elimination of mortgage interest-rate deductions on second homes for those under 55 years of age would yield approximately $2.5 billion, an amount similar to that which would be raised by a 1 percent mortgage-backed securities issuance tax.

Clearly it is important for Congress to create a large, dependable source of funding for the nation's assisted housing program. In choosing a source of revenue, however, Congress should be sensitive to the fact that the states will be raising revenues to match this fund. Therefore Congress should not turn to real estate revenue sources that states have used to capitalize housing trust funds. These sources include real estate transfer or recording fees, home sales escrow deposit interest, tenant and utility security deposit fee interest, and escheated and abandoned bank accounts. On the other hand, taxes on the national mortgage-backed securities industry or a change ın the federal tax code are uniquely federal sources of income for the federal housing trust fund.

The Cost-Effectiveness of a Leveraged Federal Housing Trust

Until now, federal sponsorship of housing has meant that the federal government appropriated all funds necessary to build each unit of sponsored housing. Our proposal for the federal housing trust fund is far more cost-effective than previous programs.

First, federal funds will be matched on a dollar-for-dollar basis with state funds. In many cases federal funds will also be matched with private funds from employers and non-profits. However, this sum, only half of which is federal, represents only the project subsidy, not the cost of the project, which is a much greater amount. The balance of development funds needed to complete a project will be obtained through any of the standard financing methods that exist, ranging from tax-exempt bonds to conventional mortgages with private mortgage insurance.

One example is provided by New Jersey, which is developing rental units for moderate-income families with construction subsidies of about $7,500 per unit. The balance of the project financing comes from conventional or state Housing and Mortgage Finance Agency sources, depending upon the project. In this example, with the federal program we advocate, one-half of the subsidy will come from the federal government ($7,500 from a federal trust fund and $7,500 from the state trust fund). However, if the unit cost $60,000, the overall leveraging of the federal funds would be eight to one, a ratio that exceeds even the successful UDAG program.

Modest Federal Expenditures

By enacting a bold national affordable housing program, capable of building or increasing the affordability of 840,000 units each year, the federal government will be creating jobs, the very mechanism that funds most federal action. The policy we advocate will raise about $3.3 billion annually, enough to pay for more than a quarter of the housing activities advocated. The adoption of a Federal Housing Trust Fund will raise more than 2 billion additional dollars. The housing rehabilitation program for the frail elderly, a $2.1-billion-a-year program, will ultimately cost the federal Treasury nothing, be-cause NHIC loans made will bear an interest rate at least equal to federal borrowing costs. These three financing programs, creating 770,000 new or rehabilitated units each year, have no long-term net cost to the federal treasury. It is clear that it is not simply money that is needed to develop new housing opportunities for thousands of American families; a cost-effective federal policy and a real federal commitment to affordable housing are at least as important.

A program that was entirely self-financing would be wonderful, but a program designed to meet the great and diverse housing needs of the American people unfortunately cannot be entirely self-financing. As part of a federal commitment to affordable housing for low- and moderate-income families we advocate a new homelessness pre-vention program. As described in Chapter 6, that program is two to three times more cost-effective than shelters and 10 to 20 times less expensive than welfare motels, but it does require a federal appro-priation. We also call for the restoration of some of the federal hous-ing programs that have been eliminated during the 1980s. We do so because the elimination of these programs has resulted in vastly in-creased homelessness, apartment overcrowding, and families' spending too much of their available income on rent. The very poor, whether young or old, need housing opportunities, and the past seven years have proven that only the federal government has the resources to provide for this need.

Constructing and operating public and Section 202 housing is very expensive. As we have seen, public housing has an average per-unit development cost of about $68,000.[57] To build 40,000 units annually, as was done in 1979, will require annual expenditures of more than $2.7 billion. Furthermore, in addition to the construction costs, the units will require long-term operating subsidies of more than $50 million annually. These units will also receive additional funding throughout their occupancy for major repairs and modern-ization.

Section 202 housing for the elderly is somewhat less expensive to develop, with per-unit costs averaging about $44,800.[58] To con-struct 30,000 units annually will cost in excess of $1.3 billion. Like public housing, tenant rent payments do not cover all mortgage, operational, and building maintenance costs. The federal govern-ment mandates that Section 202 developers set aside a portion of the rents received for a reserve account for maintenance. In return the federal government makes operating subsidy payments of up to $6,912 per unit per year.[59] The development of 30,000 Section 202 units per year could entail an annual operating subsidy of more than $207 million.[60]

A Supportive Federal Tax Policy

Beyond direct expenditures, we will also need a supportive and responsive federal tax code if we are to help the American people meet their shelter requirements in the decade ahead. Recent efforts to make the tax code simpler and fairer are admirable. It should not be the province of tax policy to encourage investments that provide great return for a few at the expense of the many. However, tax policy, when prudently managed, can be an effective tool for encouraging public policies that are good for individuals *and* good for America. Therefore, we do advocate a series of limited tax expenditure policies that, if enacted, will expand homeownership and affordable rental opportunities for thousands of families now deprived of such housing. None of the tax expenditures advocated are particularly extensive or expensive. All the tax expenditures facilitate highly targeted programs and bring major new sources of money to low- and moderate-income housing.

Supportive tax policies are needed to encourage employer-assisted housing. Employer assistance for housing their workers should not increase the tax liabilities of either employers or employees. The principle that some employee benefits are so important that they are encouraged by a federal tax exemption is well established, and Congress, in the recent tax bill, reaffirmed this position.

In a nation so in need of affordable housing, this principle should be expanded to bring the millions of dollars that America's employers would invest to bear on the nation's housing problem. In a tax-exempt environment, we believe that America's employers will assist in the development of 50,000 homes annually. We would expect employer costs to average about $10,000 per unit, with an average unit costing $90,000. This expenditure figure may be overstated, because mortgage guarantees cost a firm nothing unless a default takes place and 100 percent group mortgage insurance products, when developed, may not be as costly either. Nevertheless, for calculation purposes, we assume that employers would spend $500 million to create 50,000 homeownership opportunities. This $.5 billion would not be subject to federal tax. Based upon a corporate tax rate of 3: percent, the revenue loss to the U.S. Treasury would be $165 million. A tax expenditure of $165 million that directly encourages the creation of 50,000 homes would be a very good buy for the public; the Treasury revenue "loss" (i.e., monies foregone) per unit would be only $3,300.

The expansion of lease/purchase housing would also benefit from a supportive federal tax policy. Although lease/purchase housing can be developed in the present legal and financial environment, a supportive tax code could greatly expand lease/purchase housing development, causing, as discussed previously, the creation of more than 20,000 units annually. A tax policy change that specifically supported lease/purchase housing would allow private builders to use tax-exempt financing. Developers would also be allowed to depreciate or syndicate the properties during the two-year lease period, with depreciation being exempt from passive loss limitations. The cost of this policy would be negligible to the Treasury, as long as depreciation is limited to projects receiving tax-exempt construction financing. If 20,000 units were privately developed annually, at $90,000 per unit, the depreciation tax loss would be less than $20 million per year during the two-year lease period. This modest cost, traded off against the economic and social benefits of facilitating home-ownership for families otherwise unable to afford the financial burden, should be acceptable to America's taxpayers and policy-makers.

State Mortgage Revenue Bond Programs

While recent tax reform efforts have been somewhat helpful, one aspect of tax reform may prove to be very hurtful. If we are to have an activist housing policy based, in part, on a supportive tax environment, then Congress must reverse itself and allow a more expansive policy toward the issuance of tax-exempt mortgage revenue and multi-family industrial development bonds that finance low- and moderate-income single- and multi-family housing. By far the largest of the state housing programs, both in terms of dollar expenditures and number of units produced, the state revenue bond programs have been the heart of their housing efforts.

As indicated previously, tax-exempt bond programs are subsidized principally by the federal government in that the interest on these bonds is not subject to federal taxation and, therefore, the federal treasury foregoes revenue that would ordinarily be paid on a taxable investment instrument. Using these tax-exempt vehicles, state and local governments provide below-market mortgages based on the spread between conventional interest rates and the lower interest rates (yields) that tax-exempt bond investors are willing to accept.

Table 17 shows that almost every state in the union uses tax-exempt bonds to facilitate homeownership and rental opportunities for low- and moderate-income families. Figure 9 illustrates the growth of these state and local efforts between 1976 and 1985. During this period more than $122 billion of mortgage revenue and multi-family industrial development bonds were sold. State MRBs enabled the financing of more than 290,000 units during this period.[61] In 1985, the last year before tax reform, more than $38.1 billion in housing revenue bonds were sold, financing more than 100,000 single-family units and 88,400 multi-family units.[62]

During this decade of growth of state and local tax-exempt revenue bond issuances for commercial/industrial as well as housing purposes, a debate took place in Congress over the revenue loss to the federal government. Estimates of direct revenues lost ranged from $15 million to $40 million per $1 billion in bonds issued. In 1985, this resulted in revenue losses of $570 million to $1.44 billion based upon the $38.1 billion in bonding activity.

However, as discussed previously, housing is a labor-intensive industry, and those laborers are paying federal income taxes. Bureau of Labor Statistics data, supplemented by the University of Maryland study concerning the multiplier effect of housing construction on affiliated industries, suggest that the 1985 revenue bond volume of $38.1 billion directly generated about 607,000 jobs, plus another 264,000 jobs in affiliated industries, during 1985. These 871,000 workers paid approximately $3 billion in federal income taxes. Therefore, housing revenue bond programs generated between $1.5 and 2.4 billion for the U.S. Treasury during 1985.

Nevertheless, in 1986, seemingly mesmerized by the budget deficit, Congress decided that there was a revenue loss and that this revenue loss was significant and could not be replaced by other revenue sources. Therefore, Congress took the following actions to limit revenue bond authority of the states:

- It established a total volume cap of private activity revenue bonds (commercial, industrial, and housing) of $75 per capita. This volume limitation forces housing needs to compete against state/private-sector economic development activities.

Table 17
State Housing Finance Agency Involvement in Traditional Programs Funded with Mortgage Revenue Bonds and Multifamily Bonds

State Agency	Homeownership Program	Federally Assisted			State-Assisted	Unassisted	
		Section 8	Section 236	Other		80/20s	80/20s Plus
Alabama	***						
Alaska	***						
Arizona							
Arkansas	***	***		***		***	
California	***	***				***	
Colorado	***	***				***	
Connecticut	***	***	***				***
Delaware	***	***		***	***		
Dist. of Columbia	***	***			***		
Florida	***					***	
Georgia	***					***	
Hawaii	***				***	***	
Idaho	***	***				***	
Illinois	***	***	***	***		***	
Indiana	***	***				***	
Iowa	***	***				***	
Kansas							
Kentucky	***	***	***			***	
Louisiana	***	***	***	***		***	***
Maine	***	***	***	***		***	***
Maryland	***	***	***	***		***	
Massachusetts	***	***	***		***		***
Michigan	***	***	***			***	
Minnesota	***	***	***		***	***	
Mississippi	***		***				
Missouri	***	***				***	***
Montana	***	***					

State / Agency	C1	C2	C3	C4	C5	C6	C7	C8	C9	C10	C11	C12	C13
Nebraska	***												***
Nevada	***												***
New Hampshire	***				***						***		***
New Jersey	***												***
New Mexico					***		***				***	***	***
New York City HDC	***	***			***		***		***		***	***	***
New York State HFA		***			***		***				***		***
New York State MLEAC		***			***		***				***		
State of N.Y. MA	***						***			***			
North Carolina	***	***					***			***			***
North Dakota	***	***											***
Ohio	***	***			***						***		***
Oklahoma	***	***											***
Oregon	***	***			***				***		***		***
Pennsylvania	***	***											
Puerto Rico HFC	***					***							
Puerto Rico HBFA	***	***											
Rhode Island	***	***								***			***
South Carolina	***	***									***		***
South Dakota	***	***									***		***
Tennessee	***										***		***
Texas	***	***			***						***		***
Utah	***	***			***						***		***
Vermont	***	***											
Virgin Islands	***				***					***	***	***	***
Virginia	***				***						***	***	***
Washington	***				***		***						
West Virginia	***	***			***		***			***		***	
Wisconsin	***	***					***						
Wyoming	***	***											

Source: Council of State Housing Agencies, *Production Activities of State Housing Finance Agencies: 1985 and Cumulative* (Washington, D.C.: The Council, 1986).

- As of January 1, 1988, this volume cap is reduced to $50 per capita.
- As of December 31, 1988, states will lose their authority to issue mortgage revenue bonds for single-family homeownership programs. This will effectively end the homeownership dreams of thousands of families each year.

The elimination of state authority to aid low- and moderate-income families in their quest to attain homeownership via the issuance of single-family mortgage revenue bonds is a counterproductive policy, inconsistent with other federal policy choices. For example, citing homeownership as a national goal, Congress chose to retain the mortgage interest rate deduction for both primary and secondary residences, deductions that tend disproportionately to benefit upper-income taxpayers. Eliminating mortgage revenue bonds will discourage homeownership for low- and moderate-income families. Families receiving MRB assistance had modest incomes, averaging $26,713 per year in 1986. And the homes these families bought were modest too, costing an average of $54,353.[63] The tax reform act also discourages the construction of new rental housing. If families are not able to move out of existing rental housing into affordable homes, where will new renters live? Finally, as we have demonstrated above, the construction of revenue bond-assisted housing provides important numbers of jobs for society and revenues for the federal Treasury.

The housing policy we advocate for the most part does not require tax-exempt bonding capacity, though it is needed for lease/purchase housing and would be helpful for a mortgage buydown program. However, the current tax treatment of revenue bonds restricts the growth of affordable housing for no valid fiscal reason. The federal government should act to restore unlimited state authority to sell housing revenue bonds.

Tax Credits

The thrust of federal housing policy throughout the 1980s has been to eliminate direct, appropriated support for low- and moderate-income housing and to reduce the tax expenditure support for moderate-income and market-rate housing. An exception to this pattern, however, was the creation of the "Tax Credit for Low Income Rental Housing" as part of the Tax Reform Act of 1986. This program could bring $10 billion in direct additional support for low-income housing, assisting in the development or rehabilitation of more than 300,000 units.[64]

Unlike other existing or previous tax expenditure programs, this new credit is highly targeted. Previous low-income housing tax incentives have been directed to those with incomes of less than 80 percent of the area median. This new tax credit defines low income as 50 percent or 60 percent of the area median, depending upon how a particular project is structured. The new tax credit program is also highly flexible. The credit can be used to assist new construction, moderate or substantial rehabilitation, acquisition with or without rehabilitation, and property repairs by owners.

There is some debate as to whether targeting the housing needs of very-low-income Americans at the expense of low-income Americans is socially or politically useful public policy. Likewise, there is debate as to whether moderate rehabilitation or acquisition without rehabilitation is the best use of a tax credit program. Whatever the merits of these respective debates, the debate is likely to be brief. The low-income housing tax credit program is but a temporary provision of the tax code; it is scheduled to expire December 31, 1989.

Since the inception of the tax credit program, skepticism has abounded as to its feasibility. There are a number of minor adjustments that Congress could make that would increase investor confidence in the program at little or no additional cost to the Treasury.

First, if a three-year, $10-billion program is good public policy, then surely a four-year, $10-billion program is not bad public policy. Congress should not recapture tax credits not used by the states, particularly 1987 credits. There has been some confusion as to how the credit program would work, and it has taken investors time to learn about the program and how it relates to the rest of the tax changes made in 1986. To penalize the poor who need housing because it takes some time for investors to become familiar with a program is bad policy. Tax credits not used through 1989 should be made available to the states in 1990.

Second, building low-income housing has a number of inherent risks. But this tax credit program creates additional risks for investors that have little to do with building and owning low-income housing and much to do with the way the tax credit program is structured. For example, during the 10-year period when tax credits are received by investors, the income of the investor can change dramatically. If the investor's income declines, interest in the credits or property can be sold. But if the investor's income rises, a combination of passive losses and tax credits may make the tax credits of little value, owing to the tax code's ceiling on passive loss deductions for individuals. While it is true that losses can be carried forward into the next tax year, there is also a value, in some instances, to being able to take credits or losses as those opportunities occur. To encourage greater participation in the tax credit program, restrictions on the amount of passive loss that can be taken by low-income housing tax credit investors should be eased. This will encourage many traditional low-income housing investors to reinvest in such projects.

Another example of risk that the structure of the tax credit places on the investor is the recapture provision. Much has already been written on the feasibility of having a 10-year credit with occupancy and rent-rate restrictions running 15 years. To ease some of the fears regarding recapture of tax credits in the 11–15-year period, investors should be required only to make "good faith efforts" to rent to those of low income. Rent-rate restrictions should remain as presently structured.

A third example of risk to the investor that is a function of how the tax credit program is designed is the method for determining the "present value" of the tax credit during 1988 and 1989. The public interest is not served by developing projects that are not economically viable. Given the constraints on project rental income, it is only fair that investors know the "present value" of the tax credit as the credit has a direct impact on the economic viability of a project for the investor. The current law sets the "present value" of the tax credit at the point when the project is completed. During the 12–18 months that it takes to implement a project, interest rates may change, causing a project to become unfeasible because the value of the credit is reduced. Greater certainty could be given to the investor if the value of the tax credit is set when construction begins on a project, although the 10-year tax credit availability would not begin until the project is completed.

A fourth weakness in the tax credit program that Congress should address is the credit's relationship to mortgage interest rates. The past decade has witnessed unprecedented volatility in mortgage interest rates. A low-income housing project financed at 8–9 percent for a 30-year term may be financially viable with or without a tax credit, but a project financed at 12.5 percent may not be, even with a tax credit. Congress should index the tax credit to mortgage interest rates. This would increase the value of the tax credit and encourage additional low-income rental housing investment in times of higher interest rates. Such indexing could have important countercyclical effects throughout the whole economy, creating both jobs and lower-cost housing at a time when higher interest rates may have induced greater unemployment.

TOWARD A NEW FEDERAL/LOCAL HOUSING PARTNERSHIP

In this chapter, we have emphasized federal/state relationships, describing a plan by which our federal government can build upon, support, and enhance successful housing policy initiatives invented by the states, in a cost-effective manner. In that description, we have made only episodic reference to local governments and local nonprofit, community-based housing development entities. We know full well, however, that America's local governments and local community organizations, all across the nation, have worked very hard and very well in the 1980s to promote affordable housing. These efforts, too, need and deserve families support. In the next chapter, we describe those local housing initiatives that have worked best and detail how these could be incorporated into a new national housing policy. We propose, in that chapter, a new federal/local housing partnership for the 1990s.

4

A New Federal/Local Housing Partnership

All across America, in the 1980s, local governments and local community-based organizations have busied themselves developing new methods to make housing affordable to low- and moderate-income families. Many local governments have put their taxing powers, zoning powers, land, and monies to this purpose. These municipalities have established local housing trust funds, created community land trusts, enacted inclusionary zoning laws, granted zoning density bonuses to developers (in order to bring house prices and rents down), donated municipally owned land to make the housing built on that land less costly, used municipal monies to subsidize construction costs, and adopted zoning laws facilitating the construction of senior citizens' apartments.

Local community-based organizations (e.g., church groups, community development corporations, local labor unions) have acquired substandard buildings and rehabilitated them for low-income housing, created tenant cooperatives, built new homes and apartments for sale or rent to low-income people, established community loan funds for housing rehabilitation, used public and foundation grant funds to help make homeownership affordable to low- and moderate-income families, and administered programs of urban homesteading and sweat equity whereby poor families have converted abandoned slum properties into habitable residential use.

These are mostly small but highly innovative efforts. The great value of these approaches and projects has been recognized by national corporations and national foundations, who have invested hundreds of millions of dollars in them. Several national non-profit corporations and foundations have been formed to assist local governments and neighborhood groups to form community-wide "housing partnerships" and provide investment capital to such partnerships.

Current federal housing policies largely ignore (and sometimes undermine) the new local approaches. National policy should support local efforts, encourage local experimentation, and make working partners of the thousands of local officials and local community groups who have been struggling through the long, dark night of federal neglect.

In addition to those described in Chapter 3, three programs would facilitate a new federal/local housing partnership. First, we advocate a modest federal grant program that would encourage more local governments to form housing partnerships with non-profit groups, to use their surplus land for affordable housing, and to utilize their zoning and taxing powers to help low- and moderate-income families meet their shelter needs. Second, we recommend a series of federally funded regional technical assistance centers to help local community-based organizations acquire the expertise they need to provide a substantially greater number of affordable dwelling units. Finally, we suggest the use of some surplus federal land for affordable housing. These new proposed programs constitute a federal/local housing partnership capable of far greater responsiveness to the American people's housing needs than is possible under our present national housing policies.

New Local Financial Resources for Affordable Housing

Local governments have used a wide variety of tax mechanisms to generate funds with which to subsidize the construction, rehabilitation, and rents of affordable housing for low- and moderate-income families. Two mechanisms, local housing trust funds and linked development taxes or fees for commercial and luxury residential projects, merit consideration at length.

Housing Trust Funds

Trust funds are a predictable and permanent source of revenue for the construction and rehabilitation of low- and moderate-cost housing. Existing trust funds rely on a variety of revenue sources, including real estate transfer fees, sale of public land, interest on real estate mortgage escrow accounts, developer linkage payments, syndication fees, and many other local sources.[1] Some trust funds are at least partially capitalized by an initial or ongoing appropriation. State constitutions and local charters often require appropriation of all resources, even those earmarked in trusts or bond accounts. Trust funds do not revert to the general budget at the end of a fiscal period.

Local trust funds are gaining both popularity and acceptance as a method for financing low- and moderate-income units. They often finance projects designed by local governments, by local non-profits, or by a partnership among these sectors.[2] As federal dollars for cities disappeared, trust funds were developed, using what were previously untapped sources. A number of innovative local trust funds are reviewed here; then three of the largest local trust funds in the nation—those in Boston, Jersey City, and San Francisco—are examined in more detail in the discussion of linked development.

In 1983 the Greater Miami Neighborhoods, Inc., organized a campaign before the state legislature for an increase in the documentary stamp tax, which authorizes certain of Florida's counties to levy a surtax on deeds and other real-estate-related legal documents on commercial properties in the Dade County area. Fifty percent of this surtax, which is a real estate transfer fee, is dedicated to projects for low-income people, the balance for moderate-income projects. This county-level fund supports community development corporations and other programs that assist low- and moderate-income housing construction and rehabilitation. It produces $13 million a year for such uses. In 1986 the legislative authority to create trust funds was extended to all counties in Florida.[3]

In Montgomery County, Maryland, a local trust fund generates revenues from a 4 percent tax on the sale price of rental units converted to condominiums. The county law has raised more than $20 million since it was passed in 1980. Money earned on interest from these receipts is used to subsidize rents in some newly constructed units. Proposed programs include a home purchase assistance program and a finance program for rental rehabilitation.[4]

Denver, Colorado, formed a housing trust fund in 1986 at the urging of local housing advocates. The city has committed $11 million from the sale of land left over from earlier urban renewal efforts.[5] In a unique effort, the fund is administered by the Housing

Trust Council, which includes representatives of the local government, banks, community development corporations, and social service agencies.

Linked Development

In an effort to tap local sources of capital to replace federal money, a growing number of cities with strong real estate markets have linked new commercial and luxury housing development to low-income housing. The rationale for linkage requirements is based on the impact that commercial development has on an already tight housing market. A number of studies have clearly documented the connection between new office space and the increased demand in the market for housing. As more workers compete for a limited housing supply, units become priced beyond the means of many people. Cities, which once had affordable neighborhoods, need an answer to new demands for housing by a larger workforce.

Since 1980, linkage programs have been established in Hartford, Boston, Jersey City, and San Francisco and considered in many others. Linkage programs in these cities take several forms. The four most common forms are formula-based impact fees, the direct construction of low-income units either on or off site, density bonuses, and voluntary agreements between a city and a developer.

Linkage assessments based on square-foot formulas are essentially a new category of development fee. Such fees have long been standard instruments for reducing the costs of public improvements, including such things as sidewalks, streets, and sewers, which are made necessary by new development. Linkage fees carry the concept beyond these traditional requirements to ameliorate the impact of commercial development on the housing market. These fees can be the source of capital for local housing trust funds, or can be targeted in some other fashion to improving the supply of affordable housing in a region.

Three cities—Boston, San Francisco, and Jersey City—have the most experience with linkage. Key features of these programs include a per-square-foot set-aside, an exemption for small developers, and a separate account from general appropriations that administers the use of housing funds.

San Francisco initiated one of the first linkage programs in the nation when it passed a linked development ordinance in 1981. The ordinance requires that commercial developers in the Central Business District either build or renovate a specified number of units or pay a fee of $5.40 per square foot in lieu of units to offset the increased demand on the housing market caused by booming downtown office construction. Initially enacted under authority of the state Environmental Quality Act, the ordinance now derives its authority from the discretionary powers of the San Francisco Planning Commission.[6]

The San Francisco Office of Housing Production program has based its fee requirement formula on a study that indicates that each 250 square feet of new office space resulted in one new employee, 40 percent of whom would desire to live in the city. By the spring of 1986, the San Francisco program had collected funds from 35 office projects and created about 3,800 units of low- and moderate-cost housing. In response to community housing advocates who criticized the program for not producing enough units affordable to low- and moderate-income residents, the San Francisco Planning Department revised the program to require that 62 percent of all the units be affordable to residents whose incomes were less than 120 percent of the area median, and for "in lieu of fees" to go to projects containing 100 percent affordable units.

Boston's linkage program is administered by the city's redevelopment agency. The Boston housing impact fee exacts $6 per square foot for commercial projects larger than 100,000 square feet. The fee is paid over a term of 12 years. In March of 1986 the Massachusetts Superior Court disallowed the impact fee, holding that the fee too closely resembled a Boston city tax preempted by a state law governing the city's taxing power, Boston appealed the decision to the Massachusetts Supreme Court, which found that the original plaintiffs in the case had no standing to bring suit. However, since the ruling did not establish authority to impose an impact fee, new legislation has been drafted to increase Boston's home rule power over taxation, so that the housing impact program can be continued without legal challenge.[7]

Jersey City has a program of voluntary linkage. The Jersey City Office of Economic Development has established mitigation formulas for each type of new construction in the city—residential and luxury condominium buildings and commercial and office buildings. Developers have a choice of building set-aside units on site or off site, or contributing money directly to other developers of affordable housing such as non-profit, community-based groups for financing affordable housing.[8]

Many linked exactions are imposed through the powers given to local governments by local land use ordinances. If local government has excise tax authority, it need only justify developers as a taxable class to impose such ordinances. If there is no tax authority the land use "regulatory" authority will support development fees, but courts usually require a more scientific justification in terms of the causal nature of development burdens on housing and the link to how the money is spent to redress the burden caused by development.

Linkage can only succeed in areas where development pressures are strong enough to overcome the additional economic constraints on the project. Those areas are located primarily in New England, Mid-Atlantic, and West Coast states with booming regional economies, usually driven by service- and financial-sector growth. A linked tax will only work where there is a growth economy that would otherwise externalize certain infrastructure costs. That growth area might be just a few downtown blocks. Whatever its size, developers can bear the tax as long as they can make money. Local politicians can levy it as long as they know it too. Non-growth areas most likely cannot sustain impact taxes, for there would be nothing to tax.

Further study needs to examine the effect that impact fees can have on commercial development. In short, do impact fees have the potential to kill the goose that laid the golden egg? The pro-development answer is "yes," but the answer can change with local economic conditions. Therefore, ongoing analysis and decision making ought to be part of the process. The development-neutral answer is that a development fee is appropriate even if it "kills" marginal projects because development should not be allowed to externalize its true infrastructure costs. The way to ensure equity is to use a cost formula sensitive only to the incremental infrastructure costs and to make the tax or fee responsive to market elasticity and pass-through considerations.

Since it is the impact of increased business activity that puts pressure on the housing market by generating an employee-driven demand for housing, a more equitable approach than exaction exclusively on new construction and new businesses might be housing contributions by the entire business sector. A program of employer-assisted housing mitigating the impact of "hot" regional economies on the cost of housing could resolve the housing affordability problems created in those areas. Linkage to new construction places the burden of affordable housing only on expanding sectors of the business community, when public policy also should be looking at the relationship between existing jobs, new development, employer obligation, and housing.

USING LOCAL GOVERNMENTAL POWERS TO ACHIEVE HOUSING AFFORDABILITY

Some methods have been as important as new money to America's local governments and community groups. The three methods that we feel show the most promise are inclusionary zoning, higher-density zoning, and land trusts.

Inclusionary Zoning

Historically, many American communities have practiced exclusionary zoning—zoning with large lot sizes and other low density requirements that make it economically impossible for low- and moderate-income people to afford housing. But years of civil rights activity, and the tremendous appreciation in real estate values that made it difficult for the sons and daughters of the middle class to afford homes, paved the way for inclusionary zoning.

Inclusionary zoning reverses the practice of exclusion by setting aside land for, and specifically authorizing a portion of, newly developed units for low- and moderate-priced housing. Inclusionary projects have become an important source of affordable housing for low- and moderate-income people. While some inclusionary programs began before the collapse of federal housing policy, they are an even more important instrument for creating affordable units now that few federal subsidies remain.

Most inclusionary housing programs provide for optional or mandatory set-asides of low- and moderate-income housing units. These are often required as a *quid pro quo* for special permits or other actions by zoning or planning boards. Other inclusionary programs provide incentives such as density bonuses or special permit waivers to induce participation in voluntary programs. The development of new low-cost units are directly driven by demand in luxury and commercial markets. They represent one of the most effective methods now available for the production of low- and moderate-cost units.

Although New Jersey's Mount Laurel and Mount Laurel II court cases are the most renowned inclusionary zoning decisions in the nation, most inclusionary zoning programs come through a legislative response to growth patterns, not through judicial intervention. A large number of suburban municipalities throughout the country have instituted inclusionary programs, including Orange County, California, and Montgomery County, Maryland. These programs alone will produce over 10,000 units affordable to lower-income people over the next few years.[9]

The states of Massachusetts and California explicitly outlaw exclusionary practices in their statues governing local land use ordinances. California also requires affirmative action to preserve or replace low-income units affected by development in Coastal Management Zones. A Massachusetts "anti-snob" policy, Executive Order 215, links approval of federal and state discretionary grants to a community's willingness to provide low- and moderate-income housing. Applications for these grants are evaluated on criteria that include the percentage of unmet affordable housing needs, zoning laws, and the presence of lower-income housing opportunities. Those communities with restrictive zoning practices must initiate remedies that create affordable housing opportunities in order to qualify for discretionary state grants.

New Jersey has the most experience with inclusionary zoning, which warrants consideration at length. The Mount Laurel II decision of the New Jersey Supreme Court made inclusionary programs a key part of that state's efforts to create affordable housing for its residents. Mount Laurel II[10] prescribed the use of inclusionary zoning as the chief remedy of past exclusionary practices by New Jersey municipalities.

In Mount Laurel II, the New Jersey Supreme Court held that all municipalities have a constitutional obligation to "affirmatively plan and provide by its land use regulations, the reasonable opportunity for an appropriate variety and choice of housing, including low and moderate cost housing." The court found that the

constitutional power to zone, delegated to the municipalities subject to legislation, is but one portion of the police power and, as such, must be exercised for the general welfare. When the exercise of that power by a municipality affects something as fundamental as housing, the general welfare includes more than the welfare of the municipality and its citizens: it also includes the general welfare—in this case, the housing needs—of those residing outside of the municipality but within the region that contributes to the housing demand within the municipality. Municipal land use regulations that conflict with the general welfare thus defined abuse the police power and are unconstitutional.[11]

Three rather unique legal factors enabled the Mount Laurel suits to be brought before the court. New Jersey utilizes highly flexible criteria for establishing legal standing, allowing parties not directly aggrieved to pursue a remedy from the courts. The New Jersey constitution also clearly gives power to the state to regulate land use for a social benefit. Just as important, the New Jersey State Office of the Public Advocate was able to spend considerable resources preparing the legal work of the case.

The Fair Housing Act of 1985[12] is New Jersey's legislative response to the Mount Laurel court decisions. That law provides the state with the mechanism for assigning affordable housing goals and requirements to each region and municipality. The Act creates a comprehensive planning and implementation process that allows municipalities to determine their fair share housing obligation in a reasonable and orderly fashion.

The Fair Housing Act is New Jersey's attempt at forging an alliance between local governments, non-profit organizations, and private developers in which density, density bonuses, and some state transfer payments are used to leverage private investment in low-cost housing. This bringing together of public/private financing for low- and moderate-income housing calls for creation of local partnerships to implement state policy at the local level. It has laid the groundwork for more formal housing partnerships being organized throughout the state.

The Act establishes the Council on Affordable Housing (COAH), which defines housing regions and establishes each municipality's fair share housing obligation.[13] The Council can work with municipalities to adjust numbers and to negotiate the transfer of a portion of their obligations to other municipalities willing to accept them. The Act is an administrative remedy that allows decisions over low-cost housing to occur in the mediation setting of the Council on Affordable Housing and not in the courts. By participating in the Act, municipalities shield themselves from lawsuits.

Municipalities, with the assistance of the COAH, use a number of tools that directly bring down the cost of building or rehabilitating housing, or that provide subsidy to make homes more affordable. These tools include the use of density bonuses, the rehabilitation of substandard or abandoned structures, participation in Regional Contribution Agreements, and state construction subsidies. Through the use of a Regional Contribution Agreement a municipality may elect to subsidize specific low-income developments in other towns.

New Jersey has recognized that whatever innovative techniques local governments may use to make housing more affordable, some form of state subsidy is usually necessary to bring units within the reach of the lower-income families. To meet this responsibility, the Fair Housing Act appropriated significant funding to the Department of Community Affairs and the Housing and Mortgage Finance Agency. HMFA's affordable housing program began with $15 million available for municipal use and has reserved 25 percent of its bond proceeds for the permanent financing of low- and moderate-cost units. DCA's Neighborhood Preservation Balanced Housing Program is a state trust fund based on a reality transfer fee that provides about $20 million annually.

The long history of Mount Laurel litigation in New Jersey illustrates the difficulty in transferring this approach to other states in the nation. Since the beginning, Mount Laurel requirements have been under increasingly virulent attacks. Even the COAH has used its power to reduce or eliminate the housing requirements of many municipalities. Successful local housing strategies need to rely more directly on building a political consensus around affordable housing strategies rather than depending on imposition by the courts. The Mount Laurel decision, however, did provide the state legislature with the impetus to pass innovative housing legislation and provide low- and moderate-income financing for homes on which it otherwise would not have acted.

Higher-Density Zoning

Higher-density zoning methods such as density bonuses for lower-income projects and accessory apartment permitting procedures could expand greatly the availability of more affordable housing units. Higher densities enable development projects to subsidize low- and moderate-income units internally.

Density bonuses are important tools because land is one of the major components of housing costs. For example, a site valued at $30,000 per acre for single-family dwellings would drop to a per-unit cost of $5,000 if density were raised to six family units per acre. Density also works to reduce infrastructure costs such as sewer, water, and electricity. These factors allow a share of profits to be redirected within the project to help subsidize and make available low-cost units on site.

Zoning that permits or encourages the building of accessory apartments (known as second units, mother-in-law apartments, or granny flats) is considered part of a higher-density zoning strategy, and can substantially contribute to the housing stock in many suburban areas. Accessory units are self-contained living areas created in existing homes. They include separate kitchens and baths and a separate entrance.

Community objections to dividing up large houses include traffic, parking, sewerage loads, and overcrowding. These factors can be controlled through proper planning and regulation. If accessory units are regulated and designed to blend into the neighborhood, property values are maintained and often increase. Legalizing and regulating the conversion of owner-occupied homes to include second living spaces controls the proliferation of illegal conversions, which could threaten community health and building code standards as well as degrade property values.

In suburban communities with large-acre zoning and little space for residential development, creating small apartment units in underutilized homes makes efficient use of the housing stock. Moreover, large homes built to meet the needs of large and growing families often become a burden on older homeowners whose children have moved away. For elderly homeowners accessory apartments are one method of stabilizing a difficult housing situation by bringing in needed income and reducing the size and responsibilities of large living areas. Despite incomes below the national median, many older homeowners are "overhoused." In 1980, people over the age of 65 accounted for 53 percent of all one-person households. Studies by the AARP show that 53 percent of homes with five rooms or more are occupied by older people.[14]

Accessory units also allow a community to remain whole by encouraging a multi-generational population, which is missing from many suburban areas today. Almost everyone fondly recalls the image of the American neighborhood filled with relatives and old friends who took care of each other. Accessory apartments bring us closer to that vision.

California has the nation's most far-reaching accessory apartment policy. California's land use law requires local governments to adopt accessory apartment ordinances that allow occupancy by one or two people 60 years of age or older in units smaller than 640 square feet.[15] In the absence of such a local ordinance, the law establishes state criteria for approval of those units. The law also forbids local governments from prohibiting accessory apartments, except under cases of strict detrimental findings. Rehabilitation loans up to $17,500 are available from the California Housing Finance Agency to owners of single-family homes for the conversion or rehabilitation of an accessory unit for low-income people.

We believe that the federal government should encourage municipalities to adopt zoning practices that facilitate affordable housing via an incentive grant program. Our proposed Federal Housing Trust Fund offers a mechanism for the financing and administration of such a program.

Community Land Trusts

Community land trusts acquire land and hold onto that land to remove it from real estate speculation, for the ultimate benefit of low- and moderate-income families. Land trusts provide opportunities in the future for affordable housing. By retaining control of land, nonprofit community trust corporations remove land from the real estate market in areas with rapidly rising land values. They also provide a buffer against gentrification for low- and moderate-income families wishing to live in established neighborhoods.

Community land trusts assign leases to people that allow housing structures to be bought, sold, rented, or rehabilitated, but that separate out the control of land. Land trusts usually limit the return on equity when houses are sold, in order to keep housing affordable to low- and moderate-income people. In the land trust model, public investment produces low- and moderate-cost dwelling units that remain under public control even after the tenure of the original tenant or owner. This model of limited equity association guarantees to the householder all the protections of homeownership except the ability to receive windfall profits from speculative real estate markets.

In 1979 the Institute for Community Economics created a community investment loan fund to provide a source of finance for community land trusts. The fund has made nearly 100 loans totaling over $2 million for acquisition and development in 15 states.[16] It also provides technical assistance on project financing and production.

In a similar effort Massachusetts has created a land bank. The land bank was formed in 1975 to redevelop land being vacated by the Defense Department, which closed five military bases in the state. After the disposition of the military bases, legislation was passed in 1980 to broaden the powers of the land bank to include the ability to acquire and develop additional state land. Since that time, 714 new units of low- and moderate-income housing have been developed.[17]

Land donations have also been part of the mix of resources that municipalities bring to the affordable housing market. Municipal donations of tax-foreclosed real estate represent a very important resource for community-based organizations that want to provide affordable housing. Bidding against private developers and real estate speculators is usually unsuccessful for non-profits unless municipal authorities intervene in some way.

Municipalities should be using their own land for affordable housing. New Jersey's Fair Housing Act, for example, allows municipal governments to donate land to non-profit organization's to build affordable housing, as opposed to having to sell it at public auction.

The federal government should support community land trusts by donating appropriate surplus land to local trusts and by creating incentives for local governments and private industry to donate property to these institutions. The federal government could encourage private donations of land through the use of various tax incentives, such as support of employer-assisted housing initiatives.

Community-based organizations have long had a problem convincing banks and traditional lending institutions to finance low- and moderate-cost housing projects such as community land trusts. In most cases, the term and interest-rate requirements by banks are much greater than these non-profits can pay. The Institute for Community Economics writes that "it is painfully clear that no amount of local initiative and no amount of technical assistance can have a real impact in communities, unless a new source of capital can be tapped."

Community loan funds initially linked community housing projects in need of financing with concerned institutional and individual investors. There are at least 30 community loan funds now operating across the country, and more are being organized each year. Their combined assets are over $20 million. They make below-market loans to finance low-income housing via community development corporations, community land trusts, and limited equity cooperatives. Lenders include individuals, corporations, religious organizations, foundations, and other socially conscious investors willing to take a lower return on investment in order to fund important public projects.

Community loan funds also provide banks and other private institutions with a relatively simple approach to investing in social responsible projects. High on the list of bank motivatIon for involvement with these funds is the Community Reinvestment Act. Bank investment in a community loan fund helps satisfy CRA obligations.

New Local Partnerships for Affordable Housing

The phrase "public/private partnerships" has described many different relationships between public- and private-sector entities. Local housing partnerships are necessarily decentralized institutions that build on the assets of each particular community. They are sometimes built from the bottom up, sometimes from the top down, usually a little of both—using the resources of banks, non-profit organizations, financial intermediaries, and government. To be successful, local partnerships require strong local neighborhood organizations, community development corporations, municipal and state governments, banks, and private developers, able to work together to meet all their mutual interests.

Perhaps the first form of public/private partnerships appeared in the early 1970s, when many non-profit and community-based development corporations raised funds to buy, develop, and operate low- and moderate-income housing projects. They gained technical expertise by establishing relationships with for-profit developers. By entering into limited partnerships in a process known as syndication, non-profits were able to attract development capital that they had few other ways to obtain.

In syndication, shares of a housing development are sold to investors in the form of limited partnerships. As the rental property depreciates for tax purposes, the lost value offsets or shelters other income of the limited partners. Limited partners—usually wealthy individual investors such as doctors and lawyers—are solicited on the basis of their need to shelter income. It is interesting to note that these "partnerships" often challenge the essential nature of community development organizations. Locally based non-profit groups oriented to serving the poor have their survival linked to tax shelters for the wealthy.

In addition to finding a source of financing, non-profit organizations team up with for-profit developers for many other reasons. Private developers have business experience and good relationships with banks, giving them much easier access to working capital and lines of credit. For commercial lenders, the for-profit track record minimizes their risk. Non-profit, community-based organizations learn development skills and obtain technical assistance from the for-profit partner.

Prior to the Tax Reform Act of 1986, syndications were one of the primary sources of income for low-cost housing development. But changes in depreciation allowances and restrictions on the availability of passive loss deductions for individuals have curtailed the use of this tool. Although syndications are no longer the source of capital that they once were, the use of housing tax credits that were authorized in the Tax Reform Act, discussed in Chapter 3, will fill some of the financing gap caused by revisions in rules regarding syndication. Housing activity generated by the tax credits will equal $10 billion over the next three years if the credit is used to its fullest extent. Ten percent of that amount is allocated by law for use by non-profit groups.

Since 1980, a new type of city-wide housing partnership has been established in more than 20 major metropolitan centers including Baltimore, Boston, Chicago, Cleveland, Denver, Hartford, Madison (Wisconsin), Los Angeles, Newark, New York City, and Minneapolis. These voluntary collaborations between businesses, banks, city governments, and community-based, non-profit development organizations also involve local and national foundations and, increasingly, state governments. Urban housing partnerships represent an estimated $400 million in new funding for low-cost housing.[18] Collectively, the partnership approach to urban revitalization has the capacity to produce many thousands of additional affordable housing units. Housing partnerships constitute a sizeable and growing phenomenon, with the potential to be a significant instrument for the production and delivery of affordable housing.

Partnerships take many different forms and fill varying functions in a community's effort to build affordable housing and renovate older neighborhoods. Here, we briefly review four partnerships and partnership models: those of Boston, Chicago, Baltimore, and Chattanooga. Although these partnerships emphasize different redevelopment strategies, there is a common underlying principle that private resources must be combined with neighborhood initiative and local government involvement to make affordable housing a realistic option.

The Boston Housing Partnership is one of the most well-known and sophisticated partnerships in the nation. In 1986, 1,061 units of affordable housing (rented at an average of $300 per month) were either rehabilitated or newly constructed. The key to the Partnership's success has been the magnitude of public involvement. The Boston Housing Authority, the Massachusetts Housing Finance Agency, and the Boston Redevelopment Agency provide support.[19]

Ten community development corporations thus far have received financing for rehabilitation projects. The Partnership leaves CDCs free to concentrate on direct development concerns, rather than worrying about putting together financial packages. Decisions concerning land acquisition, hiring of contractors, tenant selection, and property management are enough to occupy the staff of these relatively young community non-profit organizations. Although the Partnership's primary responsibility has been to arrange long-term financing for each CDC, it also provides money to cover various predevelopment costs, technical assistance, and coordination with government programs. Local Initiatives Support Corporation (LISC), Community Development Block Grant funds, the Massachusetts Community Development Finance Agency, and annual interest subsidy from the State Housing Assistance for Rental Production (SHARP) program financed the units.

Created in 1985, the Chicago Housing Partnership is a loosely knit collaboration of local foundations, neighborhood advocacy organizations, banks, and city government that plans innovations for low-income housing in Chicago. The Partnership will raise between $50 and $60 million over the next two to three years to rehabilitate 2,000 units of rental housing at an anticipated cost of $30,000 per unit. Rent for these units is targeted at $325 to $350, making housing affordable to families earning $13,000 to $16,000.[20]

The Partnership coordinates project financing and technical assistance with Chicago Equity Assistance Corporation and the Chicago Equity Fund. Coordination among these organizations provides one-stop services for community-based non-profit organizations. Chicago Equity Assistance Corporation, a LISC-sponsored project, provides technical assistance to non-profit developers, reviews construction and rehabilitation proposals, and functions as liaison to the Partnership by structuring acceptable projects and directing them to the Chicago Equity Fund. The Chicago Equity Fund arranges the private capital for these proposed projects. Thirteen Chicago-based corporations including Amoco, Kraft, Sears, and the *Tribune* invested $6.4 million to initially capitalize the fund.[21] The existence of the fund means that community-based nonprofits do not have to directly compete with for-profit developers for financing. Even with the decline of federal support for low-cost housing projects, Chicago has made significant progress through efforts of the fund.

Laurence Fuller, President of Amoco Oil, led the successful fundraising drive. He explains that through the Fund's mechanism, corporations "invest money not just with the expectation of a reasonable rate of return, but with the end product—rehabilitated housing—significantly contributing to the revitalization of Chicago's distressed neighborhoods."[22]

Syndications and other tax advantages, in addition to the revitalization of city neighborhoods, are a large part of corporate motivation to make such significant investments in the Equity Fund. The Equity Fund raises capital through a for-profit general partnership that, in turn, invests as the sole limited partner with each participating community developer. In its first effort, the Equity Fund worked with six non-profit developers to produce 521 low- and moderate-cost multi-family units.

The Baltimore Housing Partnership emphasizes direct rehabilitation of vacant single-family houses and sales to low-income home buyers.[23] The Baltimore program is unique. It owns a development entity—a for-profit subsidiary called the Baltimore Housing Partnership Development Corporation.

The goal of the Partnership is to gather in one place the financial capacity and development ability to renovate the abandoned single-family housing stock in the city. The Partnership plans to acquire, rehabilitate, and resell annually at least 75 homes that are affordable to households earning between $17,000 and $25,000. A city grant to the Partnership capitalizes a revolving loan fund used to cover acquisition and rehabilitation costs. The Partnership also plans a lease/purchase homeownership program for lower-income tenants through pooled syndication of single-family homes.

Chattanooga Neighborhood, Inc., the premier project of the Enterprise Foundation, has a goal to make Chattanooga the first city in the country to make all its housing fit and livable in 10 years. The city has 13,000 substandard housing units, large-scale housing abandonment, and virtually no low- and moderate-income units available for rent. The project will renovate 14,000 units in the city at a cost of $200 million.[24] Chattanooga city government turned over the administration for all its housing programs to the non-profit housing partnership. Private-sector investment and non-profit development corporations will undertake most of the redevelopment, including responsibility for traditional public regulatory functions such as housing code enforcement.

A new federal housing policy should encourage these kinds of housing partnerships in order to fund the activities of a greater number of community-based non-profit developers. Smaller and medium-sized cities, which do not have the administrative and financial resources to establish partnerships on their own, should be targeted for technical assistance as well as federal incentive grants. An effective federal program would provide seed money for establishing individual partnerships, a revolving loan fund for initial property purchases, and an increase in available low-income tax credits.

Community-Based Development Corporations

In the 1980s, hundreds of community-based organizations have formed to provide affordable housing opportunities for low- and moderate-income families. Over the course of the decade, the number, size, financial strength, and sophistication of these entities have grown appreciably. There have been problems and failures, of course, but this non-profit sector could be a major low-cost housing provider as we enter the 1990s.

During the 1970s and early 1980s more than a hundred different non-profit groups across the country have built or renovated some 15,000 dwelling units.[25] These numbers suggest that community-based supply strategies can be one element of an overall plan for expanding the inventory of low-cost housing. For these non-profits to achieve their potential, however, a significant infusion of federal dollars and support is necessary.

In the past, community-based organizations almost exclusively targeted their development activities toward the rental housing market, supported by federal rent subsidies in the 1970 and capital generated from limited partnerships. Present circumstances, however, dictate that community organizations also look toward homeownership as an approach to providing affordable homes.

Many community development organizations have their roots in the problems of mortgage and loan redlining affecting homeowners. They need to go back to some of those initial strategies, now that resources for multi-family rentals are not available.

Homeownership for low- and moderate-income people is an important tool for economic independence. Homeownership is a source of stability in an environment of continuing increasing rents, and is a method of capital accumulation that could help propel lower-income people into the middle class. "Homeownership" can be the foundation of a redevelopment strategy emphasizing neighborhood stability. An aggressive locally initiated homeownership strategy for community organizations could include prepurchase housing and mortgage counseling, delinquency and default counseling for families threatened with foreclosure, tenant ownership programs for landlord-vacated buildings, and limited equity rehabilitation and sales programs.

Recent experience demonstrates that CDCs can effectively provide homes for low- and moderate-income community residents through ownership programs. From the squatting and sweat equity efforts of grassroots organizations like ACORN, to the joint efforts of New York City and the Archdiocese of New York in the Nehemiah Plan, to the growth of neighborhood land trusts around the country, homeownership programs for low-income people have been given high priority by community-based organizations.

Community Development Block Grants

 A new federal/local housing partnership would also be facilitated by some important modifications in the federal Community Development Block Grant (CDBG) program. That program, authorized by Congress in 1975, has been one of the primary methods of federal intervention for promoting a local response to housing and community development. The Act gives local communities and states broad discretion in spending the largest single remaining federal allocation targeted for the community development needs of low- and moderate-income people. Since it was established, the program has distributed over $37 billion to local governments across the country for the benefit of low- and moderate-income people.[26]

Non-profit neighborhood corporations and community development corporations are eligible to receive money for economic development and revitalization activities. CDBG monies are used for land acquisition and assembly, site improvements, and housing renovation. Non-profit groups can use these funds directly for the construction of new housing units.

CDBG has suffered more than a 19 percent cut under the Reagan Administration. The program currently distributes about $3 billion a year, from a high of $3.8 billion in the appropriations of 1980. When inflation and the expanded number of jurisdictions eligible to receive funds are factored in, the real value of the current funding level is less than one-half of the 1980 budget. A reasonable level of CDBG funding only to account for inflation would be upwards of $8 billion.

CDBG's purpose is to improve communities by providing decent housing in a suitable living environment and by expanding economic opportunities, principally for persons of low and moderate income. But because of discretion in the allocation of those funds and increasing competition for public resources under Gramm-Rudman, this money has been channeled away from use by poor people. Congress now requires that, at a minimum, 51 percent of CDBG money be used to benefit persons of low and moderate income. This level should be at least 75 percent.

Local governments have turned to CDBG funds as other federally funded programs have been eliminated and cut back. But CDBG was not designed by Congress to substitute for a substantial housing program. CDBG's role in housing can be described as too little money confronting too great a need.

One benefit of the CDBG process is that local governments charged with allocating funds must submit to HUD a Housing Assistance Plan. Housing Assistance Plans do not now hold local communities to any standard of housing rehabilitation or construction, but they do contain a review of housing conditions, along with a housing needs assessment and housing rehabilitation goals.[27] These housing assistance goals are largely irrelevant, however, because there has been such a severe cutback in federal resources to deal with the almost crisis proportions of housing needs in many areas. These Housing Assistance Plans could be the basis for federal coordination of programs with local governments. Federal incentives and grant programs could be linked to completion of realistic Housing Assistance Plans. Monitoring of those plans across the nation could provide HUD with a nationally coordinated, local approach to housing assistance.

Locally controlled block grants are a resource that needs to be expanded. Although Community Development Block Grants were not designed exclusively for housing programs, they do effectively channel money to local areas for housing. The federal government should increase CDBG funding with the increase targeted directly toward community development organizations for acquisition/purchase of abandoned or tax-foreclosed properties, sweat equity cooperative conversion, below market interest-rate writedowns, and infrastructure improvements in low-income neighborhoods. With improved targeting, CDBG funds can become a substantial resource for community development organizations building for the lowest income sector.

Financial Intermediaries

Several important private-sector intermediary institutions have evolved in the 1980s to help local governments and neighborhood-based community development organizations. These financial intermediaries such as Local Initiatives Support Corporation (LISC), the Enterprise Foundation, and the Neighborhood Reinvestment Corporation do not engage in traditional grant-giving, but actively participate in the design and implementation of the community development projects they support. They have sought to fill some of the gaps left by federal neglect. These intermediary institutions, by their values and actions, strongly influence the goals and activities of a large number of community developers.

LISC is the largest of the national funding intermediaries, making loans to 400 community organizations in 120 cities to build 10,000 new and rehabilitated low-priced housing units. Since it was established with help from the Ford Foundation in 1981, LISC has raised almost $100 million from nearly 300 corporations. Its social investment pool finances housing and economic development projects in distressed cities. By identifying and analyzing worthwhile projects, LISC coordinates the social investment plans of many national corporations. It usually provides below market or higher-risk loans to community development corporations that have established track records but that have difficulty arranging financing with traditional lending institutions. In this way, LISC was instrumental in the creation of the Chicago Equity Fund and the Boston Housing Partnership. According to Paul Grogan, President and founder of LISC, "Our purpose is to create opportunity for conventional lending. It's a pump priming operation, and once it gets going the market may take over. It's got to be an amalgam of public and private efforts that will gradually turn the thing around."[28]

The Enterprise Foundation is a national housing intermediary that works with 68 community groups in 27 cities across the country. It targets families with incomes below $20,000 a year. Established in 1981 by real estate developer James Rouse, the foundation promotes a development program, which directly involves neighborhood people in the decision-making process. The Chattanooga Project is its most ambitious project.

Enterprise is capitalized by the Enterprise Development Corporation, a for-profit subsidiary of the Foundation, which owns seven suburban malls and a number of central city festival marketplaces. Through the Enterprise Social Investment Corporation and the Rehabilitation Work Group, the Foundation provides technical assistance for organizational development and financial assistance in the form of grants and loans. These locally directed initiatives will be discussed further in a later chapter.

The Neighborhood Reinvestment Corporation was created by Congress in 1978 to build and support a nationwide system of local housing partnerships dedicated to neighborhood stability and revitalization. The building blocks of the Neighborhood Reinvestment Corporation, called Neighborhood Housing Services, exist in 205 neighborhoods in 133 cities.[29] Each NHS is composed of neighborhood residents, city officials, and business leaders, who work together to solve neighborhood problems and target public and private investment back into decaying areas. Throughout the history of NHS, local revolving loan funds have invested nearly $87 million in home improvement loans in declining neighborhoods.

Initially, Neighborhood Housing Services grew out of an effort by the Federal Home Loan Bank Board to strengthen its service to urban residential neighborhoods. The first NHS effort in Pittsburgh developed into a successful model that the Neighborhood Reinvestment Act of 1978 permanently institutionalized.

In local NHS partnerships, local residents play a principal role.

They participate on all NHS committees, including the board of directors. They set goals and promote NHS activities throughout their neighborhoods. Local business leaders provide their expertise to the revitalization process, helping with fund-raising, packaging loans, and negotiating development proposals. Local governments supply the financing and political leverage necessary to get the partnership off and running.

The Neighborhood Reinvestment Corporation is aided in the creation of local partnerships by the Neighborhood Housing Services of America (NHSA). NHSA serves as a national technical resource to local NHS organizations and operates a national secondary market for NHS revolving loan funds. It is the national private-sector link to local NHS partnerships, national corporations, banks, and insurance companies seeking to make secure financial investments in our nation's neighborhoods. The Neighborhood Reinvestment Corporation's 1985 annual statement reports that "secondary market gifts helped to bring about more than $17 million in NHS loan fund liquidity because of the catalytic nature of secondary market contributed funds."[30]

NHS success in local neighborhoods comes from willingness to use revolving loan funds for borrowers who do not meet traditional lending criteria. NHS tailors loans to each borrower's special circumstances. This flexible approach for individual loans means that the default rate on NHS loans is somewhat lower than for conventional lenders. It also means that neighborhoods that once were at risk of decay due to the lack of willing investors are being stabilized.

Another model worth noting with respect to both intermediaries and CDCs is the community-oriented development bank. A community-oriented development bank, modeled after the successful South Shore Bank in Chicago, could build in community participation on its board and committees, correspondent relationships with larger banks that are in need of convenient joint ventures to satisfy CRA obligations, and neighborhood savvy and special expertise in small business or housing risk management. It could also establish a bank-held CDC for providing technical assistance to borrowers, and willing participation in SBA and other government loan insurance and secondary market programs.

A NEW FEDERAL/LOCAL HOUSING PARTNERSHIP

Over the past eight years, the federal government has increasingly turned its back on millions of Americans who have had the problem of finding an affordable place to live. Changes in the real estate economy, tax reform, and the defunding of HUD all placed the burden for the maintenance and expansion of the affordable housing stock on a variety of local institutions. State governments, local governments, community-based non-profit organizations, and a new generation of intermediary institutions have tried to respond with new ideas, new programs, and new resources. Local housing partnerships, trust funds, linked development, and inclusionary zoning have enlarged the number of tools available to produce more housing for low- and moderate-income citizens.

But these efforts by local institutions to fill the housing gap should in no way be interpreted as proof that the federal government should have a limited role in producing affordable housing. Ultimately, it is only the federal government that has the political and economic power, and the resources, to substantially influence the nation's housing production.

Certainly the federal government's participation in a partnership with local institutions would enable local programs to overcome adverse economic conditions that otherwise seriously affect their ability to attract capital and financing. Only the federal government can act countercyclically against recessions (as it did not in the recession of the early 1980s) and other economic trends, so that affordable housing development could continue. Only the federal government controls the resources necessary to make a program of housing production and rehabilitation effective at the local level. Locally initiated projects have tested new forms of production assistance and developed track records for local organizations now capable of becoming part of the production program. But these new production vehicles mean very little if they cannot be implemented on a large and comprehensive scale. We need a federal/local partnership that combines the resources of the federal government with the new ideas of local governments and the increased capacity of community-based, non-profit organizations.

The transfer of these programs has been limited to states and local governments with histories of experimentation. Although the initiatives discussed in this chapter exist across the country, they do not constitute a national delivery system for housing. A local/federal system is needed to disseminate ideas, programs, and technical assistance to all areas in the country. The federal government also has the ability to encourage the transfer of programs to areas that might not initially be welcomed by local power interests, but that benefit many lower-income residents.

Federal support for local housing strategies should include strong technical assistance to local governments and organizations as well as the dissemination of ideas. The transfer of program information and affordable housing technology is essential for any housing program to work effectively at the local level. We propose that the federal government fund a network of regional technical assistance centers. Increased technical assistance will make local organizations more effective, and money and resources will be stretched further. CDCs will be able to learn to access their strengths and weaknesses and plan long-term revitalization strategies.

A new federal/local housing policy must channel new resources into local communities. Local governments tend to be most sensitive to community needs and to know the capacity of local groups and to take on new housing responsibilities. We would link federal resources to locally initiated affordable housing programs. The role of the federal government in our recommendations is to establish criteria for local government intervention in the production of affordable housing units and to provide the financial and technical resources to meet those housing goals.

The primary goals of the federal policy as it relates to local organizations and governments should be to reduce housing costs for targeted populations, to ensure that new units remain affordable, and to protect low-income residents in their homes. Specific federal policies should be designed to expand the ability of low- and moderate-income people to become homeowners, to build a new community-based supply of rental units, to guarantee that the current stock of affordable housing units is preserved, and to protect housing-vulnerable residents from avoidable foreclosure and displacement.

The proposed National Housing Investment Corporation would coventure construction and affordability programs for multi-family housing with employers, church groups, community development corporations, and local labor unions. And the proposed Federal Housing Trust Fund would finance an important new affordable rental unit construction program and provide up-front construction subsidies and mortgage buy downs to local non-profit groups for the production of these much-needed apartments.

The proposed Federal Housing Trust Fund would also be the revenue source for a major new matching grant program enabling local governments and non-profit organizations to use their powers and capacities more effectively while maintaining relatively direct accountability and responsiveness to local residents. We advocate this grant program to provide incentives for local governments more fully to apply their taxing, zoning, and partnership-making powers to the task of providing affordable housing. Incentive grants would be provided to local governments on the basis of their activity in the housing field, rewarding those municipal governments that adopt community housing trust funds, effective housing partnerships, cost-reducing regulatory ordinances, local land trusts, community loan funds, and the like. Incentive grants could also attract financial and in-kind contributions for non-profit groups.

Affordable housing is an essential component of human resource and economic development policies that seek the revitalization of low-income urban and suburban neighborhoods. A federal policy that segments housing, that allows a housing policy to be isolated from other factors affecting the life of local communities (such as jobs, schools, recreation, and fair taxes), will succeed neither in stabilizing and bringing back our neighborhoods nor in providing a stock of affordable housing. Without substantial policy shifts by the next administration, the impact of local housing efforts will be minimal at best. Housing policy and financial and technical resources for affordable housing must be part of a comprehensive approach to the redevelopment of our communities.

5

Housing for Senior Citizens

In the 1990s, America will need more housing, better targeted to the life needs of an increasingly diverse population. No group of people more clearly demonstrates this national need than do America's senior citizens. America has experienced, and will continue to experience, a huge boom in the population of the aged and a concomitant increase in the diversity of life needs among that large and fast-growing demographic sector. While the growth rate of the elderly population has increased for decades, the senior population is expected to grow in the next half century at a rate far faster than that of the entire population. By 1990, there will be three times as many elderly households as there were in 1950, and by 1995 there will be 6 million additional senior households as compared to 1980. In the 1990s, the ratio of growth rates for older versus younger households is expected to be three to one.[1]

Demographers predict that almost three-fourths of this population growth will occur amongst the "older old," the population aged 75 and more. From 1980 to 1995, this population group is expected to increase by 52 percent,[2] and much of this increase will be accounted for by older women. Since many of the women in this "older old" category were of childbearing age during the Depression years, when fertility rates were low, there is considerable likelihood that many will find themselves living alone, without offspring to help care for them. The emerging needs of this group are highlighted by a prevailing statistic: the median rent of an elderly woman living alone currently consumes nearly one-half of her income.[3]

EMERGING HOUSING NEEDS OF AMERICA'S ELDERLY

These trends suggest two main policy directions that are imperative for the next decade and beyond. First, we must be sure that there is sufficient housing stock to meet the requirements of the ever-expanding older population. Second, we must help provide both housing and health care services that sustain independent living. These services are obviously needed for the already frail elderly, but they will become increasingly important for a larger number of elderly citizens as the 1990s progress.

We can be reasonably assured that the private housing industry will satisfy many of the needs of those elderly people, frail or healthy, who have substantial means. The best research indicates, however, that about 15 percent of the senior population in the 1990s—3.5 million people—will need help to afford support services, dwelling unit modifications, or new housing units specifically adapted to their level of physical functioning. We should add to this number the approximately 300,000 older Americans residing in nursing homes who could live independently if appropriate facilities were available.[4] Within the next 10 years, we will need about 1.7 million new or substantially rehabilitated units especially designed for the frail elderly. There will also be the need to provide support services, and in some instances minor structural modifications, for approximately 2 million more units.[5]

Once, the overwhelming preponderance of these needs might have been met entirely within the family environment. In the America of the eighteenth and early nineteenth centuries, larger family sizes and limited geographic mobility combined with a universal cultural norm of family responsibility for the care of the elderly to give parents and grandparents reasonable assurance of kinship help in meeting the housing needs of old age. Since the middle of the nineteenth century, however, there has been an increase in solitary living among senior citizens. The development of "old age houses" in the late nineteenth century reflected the trend, and the relentless mobility of twentieth-century life has separated the generations—at least in geographic (and often in value) terms. Today, perhaps one-third of all senior citizens have no direct heir and no close relative who can or will attend to them.[6]

In consequence, government now routinely supplements the family as care-provider, insurer, even guardian for the aged. This responsibility may now often be less personal and more civic, but it is no less real. Wise social policy should still encourage family care for the elderly as much as possible, of course, but a new governmental housing policy to provide needed dwelling units and services for senior citizens is clearly needed: in its absence, too many low- and moderate-income seniors will simply be devoid of adequate housing.

Happily, most elderly Americans already live in good housing, housing that they usually own and have paid off entirely. Seventy-five percent of the 17 million households in this country that are headed by an elderly person are in privately owned homes, and 80 percent of these homes are owned outright. Moreover, contrary to some stereotypes, the trend toward homeownership has actually increased among the older population.[7]

As we noted in Chapter 1, older Americans as a group have probably had fewer housing problems in the 1980s than the population at large. Many older Americans are not cost-burdened, and live in units that are structurally adequate and more than ample in terms of space. Indeed, the financial security that many seniors have been able to enjoy has allowed them to help their sometimes hard-pressed children and grandchildren to purchase homes.[8]

However, this is not a full portrait of the elderly in America. A substantial minority of the aged population do experience housing problems, in terms of both cost and availability. Renters are most vulnerable, but even among those who own, there are real problems. An estimated 20 percent of households headed by aged persons are inadequate or substandard.[9]

For example, among individuals who own homes and live alone, elderly persons comprise more than half of all those living in poverty. Housing is the primary expenditure for most older Americans, with many spending more than one-third of their income on shelter.[10] In addition, many elderly people live in homes of considerable worth, but suffer the irony of having inadequate income.

Dwelling unit modifications for the frail elderly, more housing and housing-related services for other senior citizens, more housing better targeted to the life needs of the elderly—how have our governments dealt with these needs?

HOUSING POLICY FOR THE ELDERLY IN THE 1970S AND 1980S

The Department of Housing and Urban Development (HUD) has been the major governmental impetus behind the construction of rental units for low- and moderate-income elderly persons. Federal involvement in this area dates back to the Housing Act of 1959, which established the Section 202 program to encourage the construction of new units for elderly and handicapped persons. In addition to Section 202, HUD has used Section 236 (Rental Housing Assistance Payments), and Section 8 (Low and Moderate Income Housing) programs to spur new housing for the elderly.

Over the years, HUD has also administered an array of other programs that have influenced housing opportunities for older Americans. Mortgage insurance and home loan programs are aimed primarily at younger, first-time home buyers, but these programs have helped some elderly people buy homes for the first time. HUD also makes available low-interest loans and grants that enable older people to upgrade owner-occupied and rental units. But again, these loan programs have mixed appeal for elderly citizens on fixed incomes.

Elderly housing programs have been slashed by the Reagan Administration, paralleling the sharp reductions in housing assistance administered by HUD. While this policy certainly affects poor older Americans who need housing assistance today, it will have a dramatic effect as the older population in the United States begins to expand rapidly as the baby boom generation ages. This national demographic trend will have a profound influence on the type and character of housing programs beyond the year 2000. The next administration in Washington will face the challenge of an expanding senior population, many of whom cannot afford or cannot find adequate housing to support themselves in an independent manner.

The "elderly boom" of the 1980s and 1990s will place greater demands on Americans as members of families. This is as it should be. Society has obligations borne out of the bond of love and affection that holds families together. Government should supplement these personal bonds only to the extent that families cannot or will not sustain them. But government should act wisely and prudently to help families care for their elders, and help senior citizens care for themselves.

Despite the federal retreat in the 1980s, and to some extent because of it, many state governments have tried to fill the policy gap in the area of housing for the elderly. State governments have created a range of innovative and cost-effective programs that serve as models of what government can and should do. In many cases, these programs are experimental in nature and are restricted because state governments lack the resources to fund them in an adequate fashion. As such, these programs suggest a proper role for an expanded federal commitment in the 1990s—as a partner and as a supporter of creative state and local efforts.

State-level efforts to provide affordable housing for the elderly, before 1980, were dependent on and derived from federal housing policy.[11] While state housing policies have varied widely, until the early 1980s the largest single relevant activity in almost every state was the utilization of federal authority to issue tax-free housing bonds and federal rent subsidies to produce dwelling units for income- or asset-eligible senior citizens.

These programs often produced large benefits for relatively few seniors while ignoring the needs of poorly housed moderate- and middle-income seniors. Similarly, these programs primarily assisted those well elderly capable of independent living to the relative neglect of the arguably more needy frail elderly who did not yet need nursing care. These results did not necessarily reflect the goals of state housing planners and administrators. Their concerns were overridden by the availability of federal funds and the political popularity of the relatively inexpensive new housing these funds helped produce.

The diminution of federal rent subsidies during the Reagan years has forced an extensive rethinking of the states' role in providing adequate, safe, and affordable housing for America's elderly citizens. State policymakers have been encouraged to reconsider their commitment to housing for the elderly, and have often discovered different and better ways to utilize limited resources. In the following sections, we will review a variety of these measures and will provide some detail on programs of particular interest, such as housesharing and reverse annuity mortgages. The programs will be divided into four basic areas: fostering new types of senior citizen housing; helping elderly people stay in their homes; helping elderly people remain near family and friends; expanding the financial sources for senior citizen housing.

FOSTERING NEW TYPES OF SENIOR CITIZENS HOUSING

The growth and increasing diversity of our aging population over the next decade demand that we devote greater attention to providing a wider range of senior citizen housing. Our housing stock must better reflect the evolving physical, financial, and familial needs of elderly citizens. In this section, we will discuss a number of state efforts to provide new housing forms that help maintain independent living for the elderly. In the next section, we will describe some other innovative programs, such as shared housing and accessory apartments, that provide the option of living with family and friends.

Specifically, America's most pressing concern should be to produce more housing opportunities for the increasing population of frail elderly. These opportunities should combine housing with support services that facilitate basic daily activities, such as cooking, housekeeping, and health care. It is hoped that, these services can help the frail elderly live independently as long as possible, and thus avoid costly and often demeaning institutional care.

Congregate Housing

Congregate housing is founded on a shared living environment that combines the shelter and service needs of frail or socially isolated senior citizens who do not require constant supervision or intensive health care. Although congregate housing comes in many forms, one characteristic sets it apart from other housing arrangements: residents are able to partake in meals provided by a central kitchen and often eaten in a central dining facility. A large number of programs also provide space and facilities for social, housekeeping, and personal care needs.

Many congregate housing programs combine independent living in apartments, often in modified public housing, with the availability of support services and congregate dining. A 1984 study found that almost 25 percent of the people living in congregate housing facilities were "vulnerable"; that is, they needed help walking stairs, doing work in the home, or preparing meals.[12] Architectural design modifications such as grab bars and emergency alarms are thus crucial, and are found in apartments as well as in common areas. Although most congregate facilities do provide additional services, escort services, housekeeper help, and personal assistance are often lacking.

A number of states support congregate housing programs that provide some or all of the services mentioned above. In Oregon, for example, the state's Housing Finance Agency has funded 26 congregate care and residential care facilities, which comprise 1,888 units earmarked for low- and moderate-income frail and non-frail elderly.

The congregate facilities provide residents with independent units, along with three meals a day, housekeeping services, and a variety of planned activities.[13]

In Pennsylvania, two retirement communities with congregate services were constructed and permanently financed by the state's Housing Finance Agency. One of these projects, Barnabas Court, is a 58-unit building that was financed through tax-exempt bonds. Along with the federal requirement that 20 percent of the units be occupied by tenants at or below 80 percent of median income, the state mandates that an additional 31 percent of the units must be occupied by tenants with incomes at or below $29,000.[14]

In North Carolina the state is providing financing for three congregate rental developments for senior citizens that are currently under construction. Services will include one to three meals, at the option of the residents, along with transportation and social activities. These services will not be subsidized, and residents will be required to pay a service charge in addition to rent. The charge will vary with the size of the unit, the number of occupants, and the meal plan selected.[15]

Residential Care Centers[16]

This form of senior housing has received increased attention in recent years and is often integrated with congregate care facilities. In some places, it has been described as a "frail elderly retirement center," or as "medically oriented housing." In many respects, this facility resembles a retirement hotel, with a congregate dining room, regular but not continuous physician and nurse services, a supervisory and service staff checking in with residents daily to help with medicines and other life routines, and a homemaker or housekeeper on either a daily or thrice-a-week schedule. This is not a day hospital, both because it is residential and because professional medical attention is not continuously available. Still less is it a nursing home. Since it provides semi-independent living arrangements for the well but frail elderly, a number of state policymakers are coming to believe that we should encourage housing on this model.

As noted above, Oregon's congregate care developments are combined with residential care facilities. People living in these homes, which include completely independent units, share in all the congregate services in addition to limited medical supervision. A nursing staff is also on hand to monitor medications and check blood pressure.

Another, more extended example of residential care housing is the low-income, federally sponsored housing project called Highland Heights in Fall River, Massachusetts. Highland Heights is made up of 110 studio and 98 two-room apartments designed for frail, mostly elderly adults. Replete with architectural modifications, the project also features an outpatient clinic, with physical therapy, occupational therapy, and other treatment rooms. Homemaker, health aid, and visiting nurse services are also available. Lunch is provided daily in a congregate facility.

Studies done over the years suggest that Highland Heights is not only cost-effective but provides a healthier and happier alternative to nursing home care. One study of 51 persons who moved directly to Highland Heights from long-term care facilities found that all but one lived in Highland Heights for more than one year. Indeed, a number of these individuals were able to live at Highland Heights in almost complete independence. Other surveys indicated that the great majority of residents were satisfied with the project's design and services.

Continuing Care Communities[17]

Another variation on this theme is the continuing care community, an arrangement that typically links an apartment complex to an adjacent nursing home. Also called "life care communities," these complexes can be congregate facilities, although for the most part they have not been. Rather they have been independent or semi-independent dwelling units (privately owned or rentals) where residents pay an entrance fee that guarantees them a nursing bed when independent living is no longer feasible.

The up-front entrance fee may range from $6,000 to $100,000 and does not purchase any equity in the community. A refundable entrance fee has gained increased popularity as a marketing approach in recent years. In addition, residents pay significant monthly fees for services that usually include congregate meals and recreational activities, along with personal and medical care. Most continuing care communities no longer require residents to surrender all their assets upon contracting to live in the community.

As of 1986, 16 states had enacted legislation to regulate these communities, and 6 other states had such bills pending in the legislature.[18] Since aged residents must depend on the financial soundness and reliability of these communities, a primary focus of state regulation is economic solvency. In Maryland, for example, the State Office on Aging oversees the mandatory certification of continuing care retirement communities. The state requires maximum disclosure of financial, actuarial, and organizational information, and annually reviews the financial condition of each community. The state also must approve all preliminary plans and feasibility studies for a proposed community.

One such community is currently on the drawing board in Connecticut, and another is already under construction in New Jersey. The proposed Halcyon Towers Congregate Facility in Waterbury, Connecticut, is a 115-unit project aimed at low- and moderate-income residents 55 and over. Tenants will be provided with full apartments, at least one meal per day, transportation, social activities, housekeeping, an around-the-clock emergency intercom service, and an arrangement with a nearby hospital for regular medical care.

In New Jersey, the Housing and Mortgage Finance Agency has provided construction and permanent financing for Leisure Park, a continuing care retirement community in Lakewood. The 219 residential units at Leisure Park will be for independent elderly persons aged 65 and over, with incomes ranging from $22,400 to $32,866. No entrance fee will be required, and residents will pay a monthly fee for rent and services that is expected to comprise 43 percent to 69 percent of their income. Twenty-three percent of the units will be set aside for senior citizens at or below 80 percent of median income. Another 25 percent will be reserved for persons with between 80 percent and 100 percent of median income.

Leisure Park will provide a comprehensive range of services, with two meals a day, social and recreational programs, transportation, housekeeping and linen service, and emergency call systems. Resident nurses and a social worker will be part of the full-time staff. The project will include a convenience store, a beauty salon and barber shop, game rooms, and lounge areas for use by residents only.

Adjoining the residential development will be a nursing home/ assisted living unit facility, which will receive private financing from the same bank securing the construction loan for the residential facility. The nursing center will be a long-term care facility for those residents no longer capable of independent living. The assisted living center will offer a complete range of personal and health services, such as medication monitoring and bathing.

STATE-LEVEL PROGRAMS

With the decline in federal funding for housing activities, state financing for housing has become important. State governments have generally relied on the revenue from tax-free bonds along with direct appropriations from the state treasury to finance new construction, subsidize mortgages, and foster alternative housing arrangements for the elderly.

In most states, housing finance agencies (HFAs) have offered industrial development bonds or municipal bonds, both of which have the attraction of tax-free interest, to induce investments in housing-related programs. Oregon, for example, has financed 26 congregate care facilities with tax-exempt bonds. In Wisconsin, the state Housing and Economic Development Authority has used tax-exempt bonds successfully to finance the Community Housing Alternatives Program (CHAP). CHAP can sponsor a wide range of elderly housing through its ability to provide low-interest loans to non-profit, limited profit, or public agencies committed to establishing community-based housing for elderly and disabled persons.

Direct appropriations from the general revenue, as well as administrative allocation of department funds, support a wide variety of housing programs for older residents on the state level. In Maryland, general revenues support a plethora of senior citizen housing programs, including housesharing, rehabilitation, construction of new rental units, congregate housing, and home repair and maintenance. Massachusetts uses direct appropriations to finance congregate housing along with the construction of new units for the elderly. Similar financing for selected programs can be found in other states, such as California, Ohio, and Minnesota.

Although commonly used, both tax-free bond financing and direct appropriations have some real limitations. The 1986 Tax Reform Act restricts the entities that can own housing facilities through tax-free bonding. These restrictions will limit the states' ability to attract major private firms into cooperative agreements to provide housing.

Helping Senior Citizens Stay in Their Homes

While new housing options for senior citizens are imperative, many elderly Americans do not have to look far for desirable housing. Almost three out of four households in this country that are headed by an elderly person are privately owned, and as countless studies have shown, most older citizens are loathe to move.

For older persons, a house may be a mixed blessing: a place of family memory and psychological comfort, yet financially burdensome and physically inconvenient. Property taxes and energy costs increase economic pressures, and an equity-rich house may still leave its occupants with little available cash. Thus, one of the goals of creative policymakers for the rest of the century should be to find financial mechanisms providing supplemental income to help capable seniors remain in their homes.

Property Tax Relief[18]

All the 50 states provide some form of property tax relief for senior citizens. Generally, this relief falls into two categories, either a "circuit breaker" or a "homestead exemption."

Under the "circuit breaker" approach, property tax relief is adjusted to need by comparing taxpayers' income levels to their property tax liabilities. The State of Vermont grants refunds to homeowners whose property tax payments exceed 3.5–5 percent of household income. The percentage will vary with income, and there is a maximum allowable refund (in 1986, it was $750). The program, which is not limited to seniors, also allows tenants to claim 20 percent of their rent as property tax. Minnesota has a program limited to residents over the age of 65 that provides graduated, capped refunds geared to household income. The refunds may be applied to property taxes or to rent that contributes to such taxes.

Under the second approach, the "homestead exemption," the state excludes a part of the assessed value of a single-family home from the total assessed value before the property tax rate is employed. Louisiana's homestead exemption program, which was made part of the state constitution in 1974, spares most residences from state, parish, and special "ad valorem" taxes up to $3,000 of the assessed valuation. It also authorizes the legislature to extend the homestead exemption to no more than $5,000 of the assessed valuation. The legislature is also permitted to provide tax relief for tenants in the form of credits or rebates.

Over the last decade, some states have also devised other mechanisms of tax relief for the elderly. A few states permit deferral of property taxes until the elderly homeowner dies or sells his or her residence. Wisconsin provides loans to qualified homeowners over the age of 65 to cover the payment of property taxes. The loan principal and 8 percent interest are deferred until homeownership is transferred or the homeowner ceases to occupy it. A few other states freeze the property tax rate when senior citizens reach a certain age, usually 65.

Home Equity Conversions [19]

Estimates of the amount of home equity owned by senior citizens in this country range from $600 billion to over $1 trillion. Four out of five elderly homeowners own their properties outright, and are thus· literally sitting atop a wealth of potential income. And these figures apply to the elderly across the socioeconomic board. A 1984 report of the U.S. Senate Special Committee on Aging found that 25 percent of all low-income elderly homeowners, and 40 percent of low-income homeowners over 75, could raise their incomes over the poverty level by drawing upon the equity in their homes.

Income drawn from home equity could be employed for a variety of purposes, and could be especially useful for the older elderly and widowed population. Studies indicate that Social Security, pension payments, and other sources of income are enough to sustain most senior citizens until their mid-seventies, when a home equity conversion plan becomes most desirable. In New Jersey, for example, the average age of a person seeking a reverse annuity mortgage is 76. Eighty-two percent of this group are single, and 80 percent of the singles are widows. Clearly, home equity conversions are an important resource for a very vulnerable segment of our aged population.

The reverse annuity mortgage (RAM) originated in California, and has since generated considerable interest in other states. The RAM is essentially the opposite of a conventional mortgage. Under a RAM, the homeowner uses the existing equity in the house to draw a loan, which may be received either in monthly payments or as an initial disbursement that can be used to purchase an income-producing annuity. Most lenders who take part in the program restrict the loan to 80 percent of a property's appraised value, or an absolute ceiling of $150,000.

In some cases, a bank will obligate itself to continue payments for as long as a person lives in a home. After death, the title to the home goes into the estate, the mortgage becomes due, and the equity passed on to the heirs is diminished to that extent. RAMs tend to deplete the value of an estate, but do have practical appeal to many elderly people who have to worry about day-to-day expenses. Moreover, one out of three people over the age of 65 does not have a direct heir.

The RAM is a relatively new mechanism, and only a few states are currently working with it. One of these is Connecticut, where the reverse annuity mortgage program is a joint undertaking by the Connecticut Housing Finance Authority (CHFA) and the state Department on Aging. The RAM program provides tax-exempt monthly payments for elderly homeowners for a 10-year period.

To be eligible for the Connecticut program, homeowners must be 65 or older, own and occupy their homes for at least three years, own no other real property, and possess incomes at or below 50 percent of the median income in the area. There is no limit to the value of the property, and the types of property covered may range from a single-family home to a multi-family dwelling in which the borrower occupies a unit.

During the first year of the program, monthly payments usually average about $400. In ensuing years, payments increase at a 3 percent annual rate to keep up with inflation. After 10 years, the owner may continue to reside in the home, with two options. The owner could have the house reappraised, and if the value has increased, a loan extension could be arranged. Alternatively, payments could stop, and the CHFA would continue to hold the loan, with accrued debt paid off when the house is eventually sold.

Since RAM is not only new, but a somewhat complex arrangement, a number of states, including Connecticut, provide counseling for applicants. The Connecticut Department on Aging has a network of retired volunteers who work with the elderly on a variety of housing options. Similar counseling programs exist in Arizona and Arkansas.

A second form of home equity conversion is the sale/leaseback program. One of the oldest methods of home equity conversion, this arrangement has existed for a number of years in France as the "rentes viageres." While it may take a number of different forms, sale/lease-back is basically an arrangement in which a purchaser buys an older person's home but accords the seller life tenancy at a specified rate of payment. The purchaser could be an individual investor, a financial institution, or another family member, and the purchase could be made through an initial lump sum payment, through an annuity-based schedule of payments, or through the senior's holding a mortgage.

A key element of sale/leaseback is that all the terms and rights of the parties need to be indicated in a contract made at the time of sale—most notably, the seller's rights in respect to the future lease. As the elderly person will be placed in a vulnerable position once the property is sold, the lease must protect against all possibilities that could force the senior to leave the home.

The sale/leaseback mechanism has certain tax advantages for investors, but it may have an even greater appeal to elderly home-owners concerned about transferring their equity to the next generation. A number of studies have suggested that many elderly people look upon their homes as a family asset that they are averse to selling to a third party outside their immediate family. Sale/leaseback allows elderly parents to sell a fee simple interest in their home to their children in return for a lease at a fair market rental for life or a specified term.

Another alternative, of course, is that sale/leaseback be contracted with a non-profit or governmental agency. Such an arrangement has recently been implemented in a two-year pilot program started in 1985 in Arkansas. The Arkansas Home Equity Living Plan (AHELP) was developed by the Arkansas Development Finance Authority (ADFA) along with the Arkansas Office of Aging and Adult Services. Under this program, an eligible older person may sell his or her home to ADFA, which in turn will guarantee unlimited tenancy and monthly payments for life to the seller. The program is limited to low- and moderate-income persons who are at least 70 years of age.

AHELP pays the participant in even monthly amounts, based upon a formula that takes into account the present value of estimated future sale proceeds. The seller may also receive a lump sum payment up front of as much as 25 percent of the appraised value of the house, with a subsequent reduction of monthly payments. AHELP assumes responsibility for real estate taxes, hazard insurance, and necessary maintenance. Utility costs, small repairs, law care, and personal property insurance remain the responsibility of the occupant.

Both personal and legal counseling are built into the program. Applicants must meet twice with representatives of the Office of Aging and Adult Services to discuss their range of options regarding their household and personal needs. If applicants want to pursue the sale/leaseback arrangement, they are required to seek legal advice. Low-cost legal counseling with an independent third party has been arranged by two voluntary associations of lawyers.

AHELP has been amply publicized in the Little Rock/North Little Rock area, which is the pilot region for the program. Thus far, one detraction of the program seems to have been its negation of any benefits to heirs. All proceeds from the sale of the house belong to the ADFA, even if the owner dies soon after entering into the sale/leaseback contract and has received but a small amount of income. Since inheritance is an important concern for many elderly citizens, changing this provision might be wise policy in the future.

For senior citizens who want to retain an equity interest in their home, the split equity approach may be a better alternative. This arrangement allows the elderly homeowner to keep a portion of his or her equity along with a guaranteed lifetime tenancy. The other party—which could be a private investor, a corporation, or a public body—becomes the owner of the remaining interest and delivers monthly payments to the owner as part of a long-term installation purchase of the property.

The HELP program, Home Equity Living Plan, Inc., of Buffalo, New York, is a publicly sponsored split equity project, capitalized by $1.3 million in Community Development Block Grant funds. In a typical arrangement, HELP will agree to rehabilitate an elderly participant's home and pay all future maintenance, insurance, and taxes, along with a monthly or yearly cash annuity. The homeowner, in return, agrees to transfer the residual equity in the house to HELP. Upon the death of the homeowner, HELP will gain title to the property and then sell it to recover its investment.

A number of states today also offer some form of deferred payment loan (DPL), which is commonly employed for repair and maintenance costs. These loans permit homeowners to defer payments of principal and interest for a specified term or until the house is sold. In Wisconsin, for example, state revenue funds were used to support a $4.6 million loan program, administered through public and private non-profit agencies, for low-income elderly homeowners.

DPLs are useful because they widen the range of options available to elderly homeowners. In addition to meeting the maintenance costs needed to stay in an existing home, DPLs can also be used to ready a home for sale on the open market, thus allowing the elderly homeowner to remove to another, more convenient domicile. The loans may also allow the homeowner to create an accessory apartment or an income-producing unit within the home.

HELPING OLDER SENIOR CITIZENS STAY NEAR FAMILY AND FRIENDS

The transient nature of modern life takes a toll on all relationships, but it may be a greater hardship on the elderly population. Elderly persons are usually less able and often less willing to move, and may have more to lose from the departure of friends and family. Thus, along with the increased physical discomfort that accompanies old age, many senior citizens dread the loneliness of their advanced years.

The issue is characterized by contradictions that are perhaps typical of American life. Despite the mobility of contemporary society, more than half the population lives relatively close (within 20 miles) to their parents. Despite the fear of loneliness, many studies suggest that the desire for privacy increases with age. Despite the advantages of living with or close to one's peers, many elderly people are reluctant to enter into shared housing or group home situations.

Policymakers in the years to come will have to account for these sometimes contradictory realities. Yet one thing does seem clear: good policy must provide opportunities for those elderly persons who do wish to remain close to familiar supports. Moreover, good policy, without being coercive, should help those senior citizens who have traditionally resisted new housing arrangements realize that there are other options in addition to independent living.

Shared Housing

Shared housing describes a multitude of arrangements, but generally reflects one basic characteristic: unrelated people live together in a shared house or apartment. The dwelling may be owner-occupied, with the other resident or residents living there as tenants, either sharing the same unit with the owner or occupying additional units in the home. Or the residence may be a "group home" in which a group of people live together, paying monthly charges to a non-profit sponsor.

Group homes or residences are somewhat akin to the congregate housing arrangements described in a previous section. While many group residences do provide for individual rooms, the arrangement is more cooperative than congregate housing, and usually involves shared responsibilities and contributions. One study of shared housing found that at least two-thirds of the households required participation based on ability, with frailer occupants being expected to contribute less to daily chores.

There are some obvious personal as well as policy advantages to shared housing. For the senior citizen, shared housing may recreate the best qualities of an extended family—companionship, emotional and physical support, personal security, and affordable living. For the frail elderly, a shared residence may offer a healthy social interdependence, rather than the institutional dependence so characteristic of nursing homes. One study of shared housing supported these presumptions, finding that most elderly occupants emphasized "caring," "dignity," "price," and "independence" as the major attractions of a group residence.

On a policy level, shared housing is a cost-effective way to house older people, requiring no large commitment of capital and using existing housing stock in a highly efficient manner. In addition, homesharing often allows older citizens to remain in their homes and helps maintain the stability and variety of neighborhood life. As federal support for senior housing has ebbed, shared housing has become an increasingly attractive alternative for many state governments.

Before detailing some of the current state programs, we should note two problems that may inhibit their success. One is attitudinal. As already mentioned, many elderly people prefer private living and are suspicious of group arrangements. Their prejudices are reinforced by cultural norms that similarly treat group living as unorthodox and marginal behavior.

These social biases often materialize in the second obstacle to shared housing—legal constraints. In many places municipal zoning codes restrict the number of unrelated persons who may live together under one roof. In New Jersey, for example, as of 1985 only three of the state's 567 municipalities had adopted accessory apartment authorizations in their local zoning ordinances.[20] In addition to these zoning restrictions (which are sometimes disregarded), public welfare programs and federal rent subsidies have tended to deny benefits to individuals living in shared housing arrangements.

Despite these obstacles, shared housing programs have flourished on the state level in recent years.[21] Generally, these programs take two forms. In one type, a group of people share a house or apartment under the sponsorship of a non-profit organization, such as a church, synagogue, or social service agency. The second type of program involves "housemate matching," in which pairs of unrelated individuals are placed together in a shared living arrangements. Operated by public or private agencies, these programs offer information, referral, and counseling to clients who indicate an interest in shared housing.

Shared group homes can be found in a number of states. In Pennsylvania, the National Shared Housing Resource Center (NSHRC) operates a shared housing program that received startup funding from the state Department on Aging, along with continuing support from other state agencies and private foundations. The program embraces 80 buildings with 210 residents, most of whom are over 60 and relatively independent. Most of the houses utilized are still owned by one of the occupants and are often used as equity to provide additional income.

In Ohio, $750,000 in state appropriations has been used to develop shared living homes that can house between 6 and 16 people. Both non-profit organizations and private developers shared in the financing of these homes, which attempt to promote personal independence in a family-like atmosphere. Although the minimum age of tenants is 55, the average age among the 34 residents in the first group of homes was 74. A resident manager and staff are responsible for helping with meals, shopping, cleaning, transportation, laundry, and various household chores. There is no entrance fee for these homes, and monthly charges range from $450 to $650 a person, including all services.

A number of states, among them Georgia, Minnesota, and Vermont, are sponsoring housemate matching programs. In Georgia, for example, the Housemate Match program arranged 113 matches out of 669 applicants in the 1986 budget year. Most of these matches involved a person over the age of 60 and a younger housemate. If other services were needed, they were coordinated through area social service agencies. The program was funded through the Older Americans Act Title III-B, as well as with money from local governments, client contributions, and private donations. Additional volunteer resources are provided by ACTION/VISTA.

Vermont's Project Home is probably the nation's only home-sharing program that emphasizes service to the frail elderly as well as more healthy independent seniors. The program matches people who wish to share housing and expenses, but it also arranges live-in employment, thus providing a range of personal support services. In 1985, the project received 541 inquiries and processed 295 enrollments, of which 107 were home providers and 188 were home seekers. Seventy-nine successful matches were arranged, of which 57 involved live-in companions. Project Home is funded by a mix of public and private sources, including the Vermont Department of Human Services and the Department of Education.

Accessory Apartments and ECHO Housing

Accessory apartments are separate, independent units created within an existing home. For the senior citizen, these apartments may constitute an additional source of income, along with a potential source of companionship and support. From another perspective, an accessory apartment may be created in the home of a child, as a place where an elderly person can live close to familiar supports.

The Census Bureau estimates that there are currently 2.5 million accessory apartments in the United States, bringing in average monthly rents of between $300 and $400.[22] In truth, it is difficult to estimate the number of accessory apartments accurately, since municipal zoning exclusions often discourage their open acknowledgment. Although some places have liberalized their zoning ordinances in favor of these units, fears of increased neighborhood density and declining property values often help maintain old restrictions.

State governments may encourage the creation of accessory apartments through a number of devices.[23] States that offer deferred payment loan programs, or various forms of home equity conversions, are at least indirectly facilitating the development of accessory units. State governments may also have special loan programs to finance the rehabilitation of housing for accessory, shared, and sheltered housing. In Maryland, for example, the Maryland Housing Rehabilitation Program offers loans for these purposes. Similarly, in Maine, the state Housing Authority is currently making permanent a demonstration program that made loans for the creation of accessory apartments. The new program is expected to be financed by the state's housing trust fund, and the loans will carry minimal or no interest.

ECHO housing is an Australian import, and is modeled after the "granny flats" that are common to that nation. The acronym for "elder cottage housing opportunity," ECHO housing is usually a small, compact, removable unit that can be sited in the backyard of an adult child or another relative. ECHO housing is inexpensive, energy-efficient, and versatile. Although it has not yet been attempted, ECHO housing could probably be located in clusters, near a nursing home, for example, or in a village-type setting.

As of this writing, the potential for ECHO housing in this country remains untapped. There have been a few small efforts by private entrepreneurs, and only a scant number of reported state programs that barely exceed demonstration projects. In Iowa, the state used federal funds to finance the construction and display of a prototype echo unit. In New Jersey, a small-scale ECHO program for low-income elderly people who need to live near their families is being planned by the Warren County Office on Aging.

At this point, the development of accessory apartments and ECHO housing might best be served by state policies that induce or pressure local governments to alter their restrictive zoning ordinances. One way to do this would be to link state housing grants to favorable changes in municipal zoning laws. Another approach, which has been utilized in California and Massachusetts, would be to enact state land use laws that can be used to influence or override local ordinances.

Expanded Financing for Senior Citizen Housing[24]

Although commonly used, both tax-free bond financing and direct appropriations have some real limitations. The 1986 Tax Reform Act restricts the entities that can own housing facilities through tax-free bonding. These restrictions will limit the states' ability to attract major private firms into cooperative agreements to provide housing.

A New Federal Housing Policy for Older Americans

There was no separate, national senior citizens housing policy until the Housing Act of 1959, which created the Section 202 subsidized rental housing construction program. The program has developed more than 165,000 units since its establishment. However, a policy that has produced, on average, fewer than 6,000 apartments for the nation's elderly each year is not a policy that is serious about meeting the elderly's growing need for affordable housing.

Though federal efforts have been meager, the states have shown considerable interest and creativity in meeting the special needs of the elderly. But, like many other state housing programs, programs for the elderly are small in scale, and meet just a fraction of the need. The federal policy for meeting the housing needs of elderly Americans should support and expand upon the efforts of state and community-based non-profit sponsors.

We propose a three-point program that links federal efforts to those of state and non-profit providers, and to the will of the elderly to live independently for as long as it is physically possible.

First, a national effort must be made to enable the elderly to gain access to their housing equity. The elderly have housing equity valued at between $600 billion and $1 trillion. This equity remains almost entirely untapped as few financial instruments exist that enable the elderly to borrow cash based upon the value of their homes. The federal government need not offer a reverse equity program tailored to the income maintenance needs of the elderly, as expanding state and private sector programs can meet this need. However, federal regulation of reverse equity mortgage providers should be increased. The goal of this regulation would be to assure the elderly that all reverse equity programs offer life tenancy and return of remaining equity to the estate should the participant leave the home before all of the home's equity has been drawn against. If federal regulation prohibited reverse equity programs that didn't guarantee life tenancy, and return of unborrowed equity to the estate, the elderly might become more willing to use these types of programs. Furthermore, private lenders could advertise that their program meets these federal standards, in a manner similar to how banks or savings and loans advertise that their deposits are federally insured for customers' protection. This too would help build visibility and confidence in reverse annuity programs.

Second, a national program of increasing housing affordability and quality for the elderly should include incentives for the elderly to live in their own homes for as long as possible, for this is where most senior citizens want to live. Though a publicly financed federal reverse equity program for supplemental income purposes is unnecessary, a program that would lend the elderly up to $15,000 for home rehabilitation and retrofitting so that the home can be adapted to the changing physical capacity of the frail elderly should be a federal priority. We believe that a National Housing Investment Corporation should be created by Congress and capitalized with an appropriation of $2.1 billion in each of seen successive years for the purpose of capitalizing this program. Thereafter, the program would be self-financing as loans would be repaid, with interest, as the elderly vacate their homes. Approximately 140,000 elderly homeowners could be served by such a program annually.

Third, we call for a major commitment to the federal 202 subsidized rental housing program. Although most elderly own their own homes, and have housing equity that could be drawn upon to provide for changing shelter needs and supplemental income, more than 20 percent of all elderly do not own a home and do not have housing equity. Many of these elderly need standard, non-cost burdened housing. The Section 202 program is one that if adequately funded can meet the rental housing needs of the low-income elderly. A program of building 30,000 Section 202 units annually would meet this need.

Section 202 housing is only developed by community-based nonprofit sponsors, sponsors who have no financial stake in prepaying federal loans and converting the rents to market rates. Thus, the housing remains available for low-income elderly for the 20-year life of the federal rent subsidy commitment. However, recognizing that the elderly population is the fastest growing segment of the population, we believe that this federal commitment should be extended to 40 years, with an additional, optional, 20-year rent subsidy commitment possible after that.

The expansion of the Section 202 program, which relies on nonprofit sponsors will also help to expand the capacity of community-based organizations, who will also be sponsoring shallow-subsidy rental housing projects for low- and moderate-income families, because the Section 202 program carries with it long-term fiscal support. With long-term rent subsidy commitments, Section 202 housing, like public housing and other community-based supply, shallow-subsidy rental housing will become a permanent part of the nation's low-cost housing stock.

Finally, although a housing policy designed specifically to meet the needs of the elderly is a national necessity, we must also remember that housing for elderly persons will often depend on their ability to obtain good and affordable shelter during the earlier stages of life. Thus a farsighted national housing policy for senior citizens is ultimately inseparable from a farsighted housing policy for all Americans.

6

Housing for the Homeless

The 1980s witnessed the appearance of a multitude of homeless Americans, numbering in the millions, growing rapidly, staying homeless longer. The country has not seen anything like this, or like the shelters and soup kitchens that reappeared to serve them, since the Depression of the 1930s.

Why has this happened? What can we do, what should we do about it? This chapter advances an explanation for the explosive growth of homelessness in our time and predicts that much greater homelessness will occur unless effective action is taken. Thereafter we suggest a three-part plan for the prevention, treatment, and cure of homelessness in America.

HOMELESSNESS IN THE 1980s

From its peak in the 1930s, when federal agencies were assisting hundreds of thousands of people per month, American homelessness declined in the 1940s, 1950s, 1960s, and 1970s to the point of virtual disappearance as a widespread societal problem. Skid row areas shrank in number, size, and population, coming to be places in which a rather small number of older single men, mostly alcoholics, were housed in missions and single-room-occupancy residential hotels.[1] For most of the rest of the housing-vulnerable population, expansions in the economy and in social welfare programs served well enough to provide at least a roof over their heads.

201

In the 1980s, however, worsening economic, familial, and health conditions for lower-income Americans combined with major public policy changes to bring about an explosion in homelessness. As indicated in Chapter 1, we estimate the current number of homeless persons at about 1 million, and the present annual growth rate in homelessness at 20–30 percent.[2]

The recession of the early 1980s produced unemployment levels not seen since the Depression. Unsurprisingly, homelessness grew as a direct result. Proof of this unemployment-to-homelessness linkage abounds. A 1983 National Governors Association report, for example, found America's homeless population to be increasingly comprised of the (then) newly unemployed. Similarly, a national survey of shelter populations in 1984 revealed that 35 percent of the homeless had become unemployed during the previous nine-month period.[7] In that same time frame, unemployment was listed as a major cause of homelessness in 100 percent of cities surveyed by the U.S. Conference of Mayors and as *the* major cause in six out of seven Southwestern cities reported on by the General Accounting Office (1985). HUD data suggests that 35–40 percent of American homelessness in the early and mid-1980s was attributable to evictions and foreclosures relating to job loss.[3]

Since 1984, however, unemployment fell but homelessness rose. Why? Part of the reason is the increase in permanent layoffs. Between 1981 and 1985 more than 11 million Americans were terminated from their jobs: 12 percent of our workforce experienced dislocation. Over one-third of the dislocated workers experienced a pay cut of 25 percent or more in their subsequent jobs. For every layoff, 1.4 additional jobs are lost.[4] More permanently unemployed workers, more workers with a lot less money—those are the natural preconditions of an increase in homelessness (see Figure 10).

A good part of the increase in homelessness, however, was attributable not to economic forces alone, but also to changed governmental policies. In 1981, as the American economy was going into deep recession, with homelessness rising, the President and Congress were making deep cuts in social welfare and housing assistance programs. Huge reductions were legislated in the amounts and eligibility for federal income assistance to the poor, Medicaid, day care, and food stamps. These legislated cuts reduced needed disposable income for millions of poor families. By administrative action, several hundred thousand more persons—some of them too ill to respond to termination notices—were stricken from the rolls of those receiving disability income under Social Security.[5]

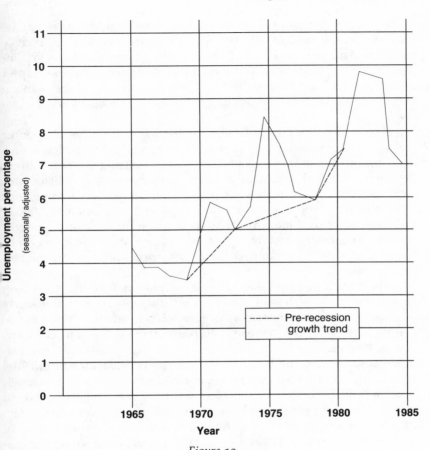

Figure 10
Losing Ground to Structural Unemployment: Growth in Pre-recession
Unemployment, 1965–1985
Source: *Ways and Means*, newsletter of National Center for Policy Alternatives, Spring 1987, p. 3.

In the early 1980s, proponents of these cuts said they hoped the states would expand funding so as to cope with any suffering that the poor might undergo as a result. The states did no such thing. Most of the state governments acted so as to effect little or no restoration of funds.[6] Indeed, from 1979 to 1983, the state governments *reduced* case welfare benefits by almost 20 percent.[7]

The millions of Americans who were newly falling below the poverty line in the last recession, like the scores of millions already there, faced not only social welfare cuts but huge diminutions in federal housing assistance. In the 1980s, federal funds for rental assistance to new units were slashed, as was the eligibility to receive benefits. And federal support for the construction of new low-income dwelling units was all but eliminated. As indicated in Chapter 1, the federal government has cut back on housing more than on any other activity, now providing infinitesimal amounts of new assistance.

If federal policies in the 1980s were making poor people poorer and more housing-vulnerable, federal and local public policies have been prompting a shortage of low-income housing for some time. Between 1970 and 1982, for example, urban renewal policies and local zoning and tax abatement policies contributed to a 50 percent reduction in the number of single-room-occupancy (SRO) units available in America.[8] New York, Boston, Chicago, Denver, Seattle, Rochester, and many other cities lost 50–85 percent of their SRO stock to planned land clearance and tax-advantaged gentrification.[9]

The dearth of affordable housing for poor people has been seen as a major cause of homelessness in our time by every major study and responsible commentator on the subject, among them several committees of the U.S. House of Representatives, the National Governors Association, HUD, the U.S. Conference of Mayors, the National Coalition for the Homeless, the New York Partnership for the Homeless,[10] and a host of scholars and housing analysts. And most, if not all, of these studies and commentators see the cuts in federal welfare, housing construction, and rental assistance as a major factor contributing to the rise in homelessness.[11] Our own analysis of the limited available shelter-based data confirms this view: the majority of those forced to seek emergency shelter would have qualified for one or more of the cut federal programs; many homeless people could have avoided displacement if more expansive federal safety net policies had remained in effect. Much homelessness in America, then, can properly be labeled, "Government Issue."

Certainly this is true for that portion of the deinstitutionalized mental patient population that has become homeless. The state governments began to adopt deinstitutionalization as a policy in the 1950s, when new forms of drug treatments gave promise that even seriously ill psychotic patients could be treated in the community: it seemed like a way to give mentally ill people their freedom while humanely reducing state expenditures. And when Congress, in 1963, promised to fund community mental health centers, the movement to release mentally ill patients from state hospitals really took off.

More than 400,000 patients were discharged in the 30-year period from 1955 to 1985.[12]

Tens of thousands of these people have become homeless. Why? Fewer than 800 of the 2,000 planned community mental health centers were ever built. And while a great many patients have been very well treated in community centers, fewer than 25 percent have remained in any mental health program: too many seem never to have been referred to community programs.[13] Moreover, the various levels of government did not provide the group homes or halfway houses the patients needed. In some states, the number of halfway houses decreased in the 1970s and 1980s even while those state governments continued to dump thousands more patients out of the hospitals.

Funding has not followed patients out of the hospitals and into the communities. The patient-to-staff ratio in state mental hospitals has dropped from 50:1 in the 1960s to something approaching 1:1 now; yet state mental health budgets are still disproportionately hospital, not community care, budgets. In 1979, after two decades of deinstitutionalization had reduced hospital patients from 550,000 to about 150,000, more than 40 percent of mental health expenditures were spent by state hospitals and less than 20 percent by federal outpatient clinics.[14]

Some of the deinstitutionalized also became homeless because, once out of the hospital, they shunned aftercare in fear of forcible reinstitutionalization or in the often mistaken belief that they required no further help. When a crisis occurred, they lacked the supportive social services needed to avoid homelessness.[15]

The mentally ill probably constitute 20–30 percent or more of the homeless population.[16] Not all of these homeless people are deinstitutionalized mental patients. Many have never been treated for their mental and/or emotional problems. Life on the streets undoubtedly created some, and exacerbated most, of those problems.

In the early 1980s, families constituted about 20 percent of the homeless population.[17] Today, families—many, if not most, one-parent, female-headed families—are a higher percentage than that, waxing as a proportion of the homeless all through the 1980s, growing by 20 percent to 30 percent per year and more in the middle 1980s.[18] Cuts in Aid to Families with Dependent Children (AFDC) programs, inadequate and poorly implemented child support laws, indifferently enforced domestic violence statutes—all these contribute to this trend.

Women and their children also constitute a disproportionately

high share of the hidden homeless and the housing-vulnerable. B
hidden homeless we mean the 4–14 million or more American fam
ilies doubled and tripled up, mostly in the overcrowded apartment
of family and friends. In New York City, more than 10 percent o
the Housing Authority's 150,000 public housing units are double
up; Governor Mario Cuomo estimated 500,000 such families in Nev
York State alone.[19] The National Coalition, in 1985, estimated th
figures at 10–20 million American families doubled up.[20]

The homeless of the 1980s, then, are disproportionately draw
from the ranks of structurally unemployed workers, poor and dis
abled elderly persons, poor working mothers and their children
lower-income families needing housing assistance, and mentally i
people. This is close to, if not exactly, a cross-section of our povert
population:

> What makes the 1980s feel like the 1930s is the make-up of the homeles
> population. Now, as in the Depression, the homeless represent a broad cros
> section of American society—the young and old, single people and families
> the mentally and physically disabled, and the able-bodied. The most dra
> matic change in the last 10 years has been a sharp increase in the numbe
> of women, children, young men and families.[21]

In the early 1980s, perhaps two-thirds of the homeless were on th
streets due to some short-term and obviously temporary calamity–
a fire perhaps, or a burst boiler—and only one-third had been evicte
from a previous residence. Today, that ratio has been reversed: abou
two-thirds of the homeless are without shelter for reasons that ar
chronic in character.[22]

America's homeless population, in the 1980s, then, is alread
huge and growing at 20 percent a year or more; it is staying hom
less longer and diversifying, but is increasingly composed of fam
lies, chronically poor families. Waiting but not wanting to join the
on the streets, if effective action is not taken, is a reserve army
hidden homeless families, almost equally poor.

It is a tragedy. The death certificates rarely list homelessness a
the cause (mostly they call it by a medical term like hypothermia
pneumonia or by a forensic term like homicide), but homelessnes
kills and is killing Americans in our time. Similarly, the unemploy
ment forms and divorce decrees and foster adoption papers don
typically name homelessness as a reason for job loss or the breaku
of families, but they could—because homelessness does those thing
too.

It is a tragedy, and it is also a moral outrage. Homelessness is a preventable condition. The public policies of our states and nation in the 1980s could have recognized and ameliorated rather than ignored and exacerbated the economic, familial, and health problems of poor Americans. Certainly our public policies in the 1990s should do so. Unless and until they do, increased homelessness will be America's future.

PREVENTING HOMELESSNESS

A strategy of homelessness prevention, a series of measures designed to avert the eviction of families on the verge of destitution, should be developed and implemented as the first order of business in preparing a new housing policy for America. Such a strategy is needed not merely to stop the suffering but also to avoid the social costs of emergency treatments after the tragedy of homelessness has already occurred. Prevention is simply cheaper, as well as more humane, than treatment and cure. Some of the prevention programs we describe in this section are many times cheaper than shelters, welfare motels, and other forms of assistance. Some of the money now used (wasted?) on emergency welfare motel placement might be better used to avoid the need for such placements. How, then, might we proceed, as a nation, to prevent homelessness?

A simple reversal of the public policies that have contributed to the problem would be a good start, but only a start, in preventing further homelessness. Federal cuts in income assistance to poor people, disability payments to handicapped people, Medicaid funds for sick people, food stamps for hungry people, and rental assistance to housing-vulnerable people have contributed relatively little to budget deficit reductions and less to our national security but much to the emiseration, hunger, and homelessness of poor Americans. A continuation of these policies is likely to mean continued suffering and homelessness for the poor; on the other hand, restoration of some or all of these funds would help prevent homelessness. In addition, better laws and better law enforcement on behalf of dislocated workers, female-headed households, and the mentally ill would help prevent and reduce homelessness in America. Most of all, a restored expansive construction subsidy program to get much-needed low-income housing built would help prevent future homelessness.

But there are a number of new state and local programs that are

more tightly targeted to preventing homelessness than are any o
the general assistance programs cut in the early 1980s. New Jersey
Pennsylvania, and Maryland have adopted programs that make timel
intervention by way of short-term loans and grants to stave off evic
tions or mortgage foreclosures. Massachusetts has a limited home
lessness prevention program for welfare mothers. At the local level,
Allegheny County (Pennsylvania), St. Louis, and New York City have
developed innovative prevention programs. These efforts warran
brief description.

New Jersey's Homelessness Prevention Program[23]

The purpose of New Jersey's Homelessness Prevention Program is
to provide temporary assistance of last resort to households facing
imminent eviction or foreclosure because they lack adequate funds
for reasons beyond their control. Reasons include loss of employ
ment, medical emergency, governmentally imposed and fault-free
loss or delay in benefit payments, natural disaster, crime victimiza
tion, forced displacement by illegal landlord actions, non-payment
of child support, threatened eviction of a doubled-up family by the
primary tenant, and permanent divorce or separation resulting in
income loss. The program requires strict documentation of imminent
homelessness (eviction subpoena, mortgage foreclosure notice) and
strict documentation that all reasonable efforts to receive alternative
funding have been made (unemployment benefits filed for, child
support sued for, etc.).

The program makes loans and grants for tenant security depos
its, rent arrearages, forward rent payments, and second mortgage
loans. Program assistance is structured in the form of loans when
ever feasible (all mortgage assistance is so structured) but poor fam
ilies whose rent exceeds 50 percent of income receive grants.

The program was legislatively authorized and begun in 1984
Between December 1984 and June 1987, 6,000 households (abou
15,000 persons) were helped to avoid homelessness, at an average
cost per household approximating $1,000 (on a total expenditure o
about $6.5 million). Preliminary evaluations have shown that the
program has about a two-third success rate (in that the family is stil
in the apartment or home or moved by choice one year after assis
tance was terminated), that it is two to three times more cost-effec
tive than shelters and 10 to 20 times more cost-effective than the use

of emergency or welfare motels, and that it is in need of improvement in collecting on its loans. Anecdotal data suggest that a rather high and increasing percentage of assisted households wind up back on their feet economically (rather than on some form of public welfare) after program assistance terminates.

One of the things learned from running this program, however, is that some homelessness is caused by government delays in benefit payments. Families living on the knife-edge of poverty often cannot continue to make rent payments while waiting six weeks to six months for unemployment checks, disability payments, welfare payments, and Supplemental Social Security benefit checks to arrive. Streamlining eligibility analyses and check disbursement schedule may not seem like major policy initiatives, but they would reduce homelessness in America and ought to be accomplished.

Seventy percent of the households helped to avoid homelessness by the New Jersey program are not on any form of public assistance. Hard-working people can—and do—become homeless in America today. Tens of thousands of families struggle from paycheck to paycheck and sometimes can't make ends meet. For those families, a layoff, or an unexpected illness, or an accident, poses the threat of being thrown into the streets because the rent or mortgage cannot be paid. It makes more sense, both morally and economically, to help these families stay in their own homes than to house them in shelters or in expensive "welfare motels." That is the prime lesson learned from New Jersey's Homelessness Prevention Program.

Other State Prevention Programs

The same important lesson has been abundantly demonstrated in a package of Pennsylvania programs.[24] In 1983, the Commonwealth initiated its Homeowner's Emergency Mortgage Assistance Program when the legislature appropriated $75 million to help delinquent homeowners. Between December 1983 and July 1987, the program helped 6,200 families to maintain homeownership, providing loans averaging $9,430 at 9 percent interest but with flexible repayment schedules.

The program is open only to persons who can show notice of imminent foreclosure, at least 60 days of delinquency, financial hardship beyond their personal control, reasonable likelihood of ability to resume full mortgage payments within 36 months, and a favorable previous mortgage credit history. These requirements enhance the fiscal viability of the program (i.e., provide reasonable assurance of timely repayment) but they do mean that only about one out of every three housing-vulnerable applicants has his or her emergency loan approved. The program's obvious successes, and the financial responsibility shown by its personnel, has won the legislature's support; the program has been extended through 1989 and additional appropriations are expected.

In 1986 and 1987, Pennsylvania began two other homelessness prevention efforts. First, 17 new or rehabilitated single-room-occupancy apartment buildings have been started, using $5.5 million in appropriations to the Pennsylvania Department of Community Affairs. Second, a housing assistance program in the state's Department of Welfare pays up to $750 in rent, security deposits, or utility bills to keep tenants from becoming homeless (pretty much on the model of the New Jersey effort described above). This program has had $3 million dedicated to it in the 1987–1988 period and is a demonstration effort, not yet a state-wide program.

Maryland operates two small prevention programs[25]—one for homeowners and one for tenants. The eviction prevention effort for renters is a small, welfare-oriented effort. The Homeowner's Emergency Assistance Program, begun in 1985, assists householders who have been unable to keep their mortgage payments current because of involuntary unemployment. It does so by providing financial counseling and last-resort loans. Unemployment is the only condition that triggers eligibility; householders suffering income loss due to disability, family breakup, failure of child support payments, and so on cannot obtain financial assistance.

The program has had a modest level of funding (about $2.5 million) and has closed fewer than 100 loans in the first two-and-a-half years of operation. The authorizing legislation required payment of loans within two years but permitted flexibility in determining interest rates. In practice, loans (which have averaged $7,000 to $8,000) have been made at 6 percent interest for an average duration of about one year.

Other states are trying to prevent homelessness, too. Massachusetts, for example, is now providing child welfare payments, for a time, to poor women whose children have been temporarily placed in foster care in order to avert homelessness for the mothers and permanent breakup of families. A majority of the states are trying to use federal welfare payments ("emergency assistance" under the Social Security Act) in ways that are consistent with homelessness prevention efforts. Some states are using federal rent assistance vouchers and certificates for persons threatened by eviction. Only very few states provide state-funded rental assistance that can be used to avoid homelessness.

All these efforts are laudable in motive but woefully underfunded in comparison to the need. The New Jersey and Pennsylvania efforts are coping with perhaps 10 percent of the documented need or less. A federal homelessness prevention program, or block grant, is, we think, required.

Local Prevention Programs

Federal homelessness prevention efforts, however, should be flexible enough to encourage policy and program innovation at the local level, because it is there that successful innovations are to be found. Recent initiatives in Allegheny County (Pennsylvania), St. Louis, and New York City commend themselves to our attention.

The most successful local efforts involve state and city governments and non-profit community groups working together as partners in preventing homelessness. A 1985 report of Allegheny County's ACTION-Housing deserves quotation at some length on this point.

During the past two years, several new housing assistance programs have been created by local nonprofit housing and social service agencies to help lower income families, unemployed people and other populations at risk to resolve specific problems which threatened their dislocation from existing houses and apartments. For example, the Urban League of Pittsburgh established a rental assistance program with State, County and FEMA funding which has helped more than 900 lower income and unemployed families avoid evictions. This was accomplished through direct financial assistance to these families enabling them to partially cover their delinquent rental payments. The Dollar Energy Fund, created in 1983 by 31 local religious groups and social service agencies, has helped families to pay their delinquent utility bills and retain essential gas and electric service. ACTION-Housing's mortgage assistance program has helped more than 2,000 unemployed families in Allegheny County to save their homes from mortgage foreclosure through a combination of free financial and legal counseling, negotiated partial payment plans with lenders, and direct financial assistance from the agency's $250,000 Mortgage Foreclosure Prevention Fund. This locally designed program has recently been augmented by the state funded PA Homeowners Emergency Mortgage Assistance Program, which has assisted an additional 1,000 + unemployed homeowners in Pittsburgh and Allegheny County since March, 1984.

The successful implementation of these preventive programs enabled Pittsburgh and Allegheny County to avoid a far larger and more complex homeless problem such as that which is now plaguing Boston, Philadelphia, Cleveland, Seattle and many major urban areas around the country. Due to the strategic importance of these programs and services in preventing homelessness and keeping the overall problem at a manageable size, efforts should be made to strengthen, expand and/or modify them in an effort to maximize their effectiveness and impact. In addition, other appropriate programs and services need to be established to assist families and individuals who are faced with the prospect of losing their existing homes or apartments.[26]

Successful city-level homelessness prevention programs tend to emphasize timely identification of families likely to be plunged suddenly into homelessness, and city/private partnerships. New York City, for example, has developed a program called Housing Alert in an effort to prevent an increase in homelessness in two target sites— the South Bronx and Washington Heights (in northern Manhattan).[27] Using a combination of two main indicators, a pattern of multiple moves, and a pattern of multiple administrative closings to public assistance, the program identifies public assistance recipients who are at a high risk of losing their housing. Persons and families so identified are then interviewed in order to make a final determination of whether or not a housing stability problem exists.

Families determined to be at high risk work with a case worker, who facilitates the receipt of any and all types of aid for which they are eligible. If the present housing situation is potentially explosive or is congested, respite care such as weekend camps, babysitting services, or food allowances may be made available.

The program also includes "housing specialists" who find alternative housing in the community for participating families. Appeals to area churches have provided a good network for locating available housing. As case workers become more familiar with landlords in the area, it is hoped that a network will be established between them. Housing Alert is looking into the idea of shared housing as another alternative.

St. Louis' city government established a "homeless reception center," accepting calls and visits from housing-vulnerable as well as already homeless persons. Center personnel categorize visitors and callers into at least three major groups: those already on the streets, those at immediate risk of homelessness (0–48 hours), and those likely to be at risk witin 2–30 days. Of the first 6,500 cases, two-thirds fell into the second and third categories. Crisis intervention counseling is provided by city personnel; cash and in-kind assistance is sought from church groups and other non-profit organizations. More is needed, but the program is working. Some homelessness is being prevented in St. Louis.[28]

The federal government and many state and city governments are now being pressured to provide funds to shelter homeless people. These governments would do well, we think, to prevent homelessness in the first place and to begin by preventing the homelessness they are themselves causing to occur.

Useful and modest-cost federal actions might include amending federal statutes to prohibit termination of federal disability benefits unless it is shown that the beneficiary is able to work and work is available, amending the federal policy on AFDC to remove the time limit on the disregard of earnings as a work incentive when calculating eligibility and benefits, acting to exempt all children's earnings from the determination of eligibility and benefits, and raising the limit on resources a family may own and still qualify to $2,250 (the current limit is $1,000). Providing prerelease procedures for SSI and food stamp benefits and extending SSI presumptive disability to persons suffering from severe mental illness would also prevent homelessness.

Useful and modest-cost actions by state and city governments would include better state/community coordination to help persons released from mental and penal institutions avoid homelessness and preservation of needed low-income housing.

But the principal homelessness prevention programs that must come if America is to avoid an increase in homelessness are two: a major new effort to provide temporary assistance to avert evictions and foreclosures, and a major new construction program to provide needed new low-income housing. And these programs can only be financed at the level of need, by the federal government.

But prevention, the least costly and most humane approach, is almost totally absent from the legislation on homelessness that Congress passed and the President signed in 1987. That legislation, the Urgent Relief for the Homeless Act, provided $355 million for emer-

gency shelters, food, medical treatment, and demonstration programs to aid homeless persons and families. It did not, however,
include a major new temporary rental assistance program to avert
evictions or a temporary mortgage assistance program to avert foreclosures or a new construction program targeted to need. It did not
borrow or build on or support state and city homelessness prevention programs.

America's current housing policy, then, does not yet treat
homelessness prevention seriously. In the absence of such treatment, it is very important that we understand our national policy
toward emergency shelter for the homeless—because, without prevention, there are likely to be many more homeless people to fill up
our emergency shelters.

PROVIDING EMERGENCY SHELTER

America's housing policy for most of the 1980s has done much to
cause, little to prevent, and almost nothing to cure the homelessness
that afflicts millions of American citizens. Likewise, national policy
on providing emergency shelter to homeless people has been largely
uncoordinated and ungenerous. In consequence, there is now an
immense shortage of shelter beds in this country. Major federal legislation signed in 1987, the Urgent Relief for the Homeless Act, provides some, but too little, of the needed resources and coordination
of effort. Thousands of Americans will still be turned away from
overcrowded shelters into bitterly cold streets this winter and we
still have a very long way to go before the merest beginnings of a
decent public policy on homelessness—sufficient temporary shelters—is achieved.

The shelter bed shortage is acute and growing. In 1984, HUD
found some 91,000 beds nationwide,[29] only one for every three or
four persons whom HUD's very conservative studies found likely to
be homeless on any given night. Other federal agencies, analysts,
and advocates put the likely number of homeless persons at 1–3
million in 1984, so HUD's shelter bed count might have meant one
bed for every 10 or more homeless Americans.

In some localities, the shortage of shelter beds is simply stupe-
fying. In 1986, Los Angeles County had a bed to need ratio of 1:15.
For Chicago's relatively constant number of 10,000 homeless youths,
there were reportedly 30 available emergency beds.[30] Little wonder

then that Los Angeles, in 1987, witnessed the rise of tent cities where hundreds of homeless persons and families recreated scenes most of us associate with third world poverty or Depression-era movies. Chicago's streets, jails, hospital emergency rooms, and morgues are filled with homeless people.

Most analysts make a distinction between "emergency shelters" and "transitional housing." "Emergency shelters" are facilities suitable for very short-term stays—providing a warm, safe environment and, hopefully, identification of longer-term needs such as job training, housing counseling, health care services, and so on. "Transitional housing" denotes facilities designed for longer occupancy where needed services are provided to get the homeless person or family ready for independent living again. Most of the money and media attention have been directed toward the emergency shelter need, which is both logically and humanely prior to the need for transitional housing. But far more must be done to provide both transitional and permanent housing if we are to avoid the long-term institutionalization, in "temporary" shelters, of millions of Americans.

Ironically, it is often cheaper to provide transitional or permanent housing than to use welfare motels or even to build and run barracks-type emergency shelters. The 1986 American Society of Architects report gives examples of longer-term housing developed in New York City at half the capital costs and two-thirds the operating costs of city shelters and at a small fraction of traditional federal subsidies.[31]

For most of the 1980s, federal policy toward sheltering the homeless consisted of minimizing the problem, and denying responsibility for dealing with it. The federal government spent less money each year on direct aid to the entire country's homeless populations than New York City spent. The federal government did offer Department of Defense facilities as shelters to 380 local governments, which, however, overwhelmingly declined the offer because they did not have adequate funds to operate the shelters. National policy makers declared that homeless people are on the streets by choice; their studies limited themselves to showing that some local governments were using some of the cut-back federal block grants to shelter the homeless.[32]

However, in 1987, the Urgent Relief for the Homeless Act was passed, which creates an Interagency Council on the Homeless to review federal homelessness programs, recommend improvements in federal, state, local, and private homelessness relief programs, provide technical assistance, to states, local governments, and non-profit organizations, develop innovative homelessness programs, and to reduce duplication of federal agency programs. The Council would also assess the level of federal assistance necessary to meet the needs of the homeless and recommend actions to help resolve the homelessness problem.

The Act provides $180 million for HUD housing efforts—$50 million for emergency shelters, $80 million in transitional housing demonstrations, $35 million for Section 8 moderate rehabilitation rent subsidies, $15 million in supplemental assistance grants. Beyond these much-needed dollars, the bill requires governors to design coherent strategies for meeting the needs of homeless people in their jurisdictions. The Act requires them to submit comprehensive homelessness assistance housing plans to the Interagency Council for review and approval. It ensures that funds under the housing title are provided only in ways that are consistent with each jurisdiction's strategy.

The state plans have five characteristics. They assess the size and characteristics of the homeless population. They describe available services. They set forth the jurisdiction's strategy for matching the needs of homeless people with available services and for meeting the needs of special groups of homeless people, such as families with children, the elderly, mentally ill persons, and veterans. They explain how federal assistance provided under this Act will complement and enhance other available services. And they include other information the Interagency Council determines is necessary for the plans to serve as a useful basis for program monitoring and evaluation.

The Urgent Relief Act begins to provide the services needed in transitional and permanent housing for the homeless. It appropriates $50.6 million to the Alcohol, Drug Abuse, and Mental Health Services Block Grant for community support demonstration efforts; $46 million is to be spent by the Department of Health and Human Services for outpatient and mental health services; $20 million is included in the Veterans Administration medical care program for the homeless; and $11.5 is targeted to educational services for the homeless. In addition, the bill appropriates $10 million for emergency food programs and $36.8 million for community services block grant activities to house and service homeless people. In all, some $355 million is provided to a more diverse, better targeted, increasingly coordinated set of programs to aid the homeless.

This bill is not a solution to America's homelessness crisis. It is neither preventative (having no reference to the not yet homeless

but housing-vulnerable) and it is not curative (making no commitment to the new construction needed to supply sufficient low-income housing even to the already homeless, still less to the housing-
vulnerable). It is not even an effective national treatment for homelessness, for it is still seriously underfunded. But the essential features
of the Urgent Relief Bill—planning, housing, and services—could lead
us beyond the treatment of homelessness to prevention and to cure,
because they are precisely what is needed to eliminate the problem.

ELIMINATING HOMELESSNESS

Earlier in this chapter, we outlined the elements of a national plan
to prevent homelessness via a targeted emergency rent and mortgage assistance program and the reversal of harmful public policies.
In Chapter 3, a program to stimulate the annual construction of
350,000 units of low-income housing was described. Together, these
efforts would go far to eliminate homelessness in America, because
affordable housing is the essential factor in both prevention and cure.

But for many homeless and housing-vulnerable people, it will
be necessary to provide and to integrate social services and specialized facilities into our affordable housing program. Group homes,
halfway houses, congregate care centers, multi-generational shared
living arrangements, specialized medical or mental health services
integrated into housing complexes—all the things that were discussed above for elderly and handicapped persons and at-risk families—will be needed to eliminate homelessness from our midst.
Housing plus services, the theme of all the chapters in this section,
will be increasingly required in the 1990s.

Through a new national housing policy, we *can* prevent, treat
and cure the disease, the epidemic, of homelessness in American.
Because we can, we must!

7

Housing for At-Risk Women and Children

Housing programs to suit the particular needs of women will be an important part of a comprehensive national housing program for the nation in the 1990s. The feminization of poverty, greater female participation in the workforce, increases in divorce, increases in the numbers of single women raising children and older women outliving their husbands—in short, the breaking apart of the traditional nuclear family—have created an array of housing needs that are not addressed by the policies of the past. These shelter problems exist for women in four different substantive areas: unaffordability of decent housing; rental and credit discrimination; the lack of housing during various life crises; and the inappropriateness of current housing design for many contemporary families.

The majority of women living alone or as single parents with children have much lower than median incomes. Furthermore, women and children do not have access to many existing rental units because of discrimination against children, which prevents even those who could afford today's rents from finding a home. Practices that deny women credit make it difficult for them to qualify for home mortgages, and divorce laws that dissolve family homes in order to get out appreciated housing equity decrease the shelter standard of women and children.

Additionally, the nature and character of a dwelling unit itself determines many quality-of-life issues for women and their families. Our concept of housing should go beyond simple shelter concerns to include services linked to shelter such as child care and transportation to employment. Size, room configuration, and the possibility of sharing arrangements with flexible public and private spaces are important methods that can meet the needs of women and their children.

THE UNAFFORDABILITY OF HOUSING

The income and social characteristics of the 91 million adult women who live in the United States indicate the special need that women have for affordable and appropriately designed, homes. Women in this country live in 80 million housing units; 9.6 million of the total are substandard according to HUD definitions.[1] Half of the female population belongs to a high-risk social group: the single-parent head of household, the single or widowed elderly person, the wife in a dual career family.

Single-parent females and elderly females living alone reside in 16 percent of the 80 million units. One-third of these single women with children work. Of the single female parents and elderly female householders in these 13 million units, 6 million are burdened by shelter payments judged by HUD housing affordability standards. In these units renters spend more than 30 percent of their incomes on housing, and homeowners spend more than 40 percent—placing economic hardship on those women and putting them at housing risk.[2]

The growth in number and problems of female-headed households has been dramatic. As we noted in Chapter 1, these households have increased from about 3.5 million in 1950 (9 percent) to over 9 million in 1980 (15.3 percent) of which about two-thirds are single-parent households. The number of female-headed households has risen by 65 percent in the 1970–1980 period and is expected to grow by almost one-half in the 1990s.[3] These households, according to HUD's 1981 *Annual Housing Survey*, are substantially more likely to live in inadequate, crowded, or cost-burdened dwelling units than are most Americans, and they have extremely low median incomes ($9,210) to cope with their housing problems. Only 40 percent of these families owned their own homes in the 1980s,[4] compared to 60-plus percent for the general population; they tend to be renters and to be concentrated in urban areas, especially central cities.

The affordable housing burden on women who are heads of household must be addressed by a national housing policy. The most significant change in family composition over the past 15 years has been the quantum increase in the number of one-parent families. Today, over 25 percent of all families with children are headed by single parents, and over 55 percent of all black families are maintained by single women heads of household.[5]

Twenty-five percent of all wives work, adding the burden of finding an appropriate child care system to other responsibilities. But even married women are not protected from housing risk. Only 48 percent of all women own their homes compared with 65 percent of all U.S. households.[6] Women are at risk from changes in their family structure due to the death of their husbands or divorce.

One of the principle conditions that affects the ability of many women to find a home is their lack of economic power. Single women who care for their children and single women who are elderly have a fundamental problem obtaining and maintaining an appropriate housing unit. These single women are disproportionately poor. Seventy-five percent of all female-headed households earn under $15,000 a year, and half earn under $10,000 a year. Seventy-five percent of all married couples earn more than $15,000 a year; only 11 percent earn less than $10,000 a year. The median income for a single parent is $9,000 a year; the median income for elderly women is less than $5,000; U.S. median income is over $20,000 a year.[7] These tremendous income disparities account for the feminization of poverty in this country, and bear directly on the acute housing affordability crisis that women face as a class.

The issue of affordable housing for women is at such a point of crisis that our nation's public housing program primarily houses single women and their children. The National Low Income Housing Coalition in their 1980 report, *Triple Jeopardy*, describes the connection between single parents, poverty, and public housing:

Although not generally thought of as such, both the Section 8 program and public housing are predominantly women's programs. Female-headed households make up over three-fourths of the participants in the Section 8 program for existing housing. Fifty-three percent of the participants are female-headed households. Likewise, about 75% of those households who have been approved for the program but have been unable to find a suitable unit are female-headed households. Public housing also has a majority of female-headed households in residence. Three out of four households in public housing are headed by single adults and experience tells us a vast majority of these women are either elderly women living alone or young mothers raising families alone.[8]

Many more women and their children are in poverty today due to cuts in human service, job training, and welfare support programs.

A new, expansive housing policy must give public housing authorities, as a primary houser of poor women and their children, the opportunity to package shelter plus social service programs targeted to women's needs. Women in public housing suffer more frequently than most from child and wife abuse, teenage pregnancy, high rates of divorce, and drug and alcohol addiction. Women in public units also tend to need day care, job counseling, transportation, and financial planning help that will enable many of them to move off welfare.

At the present time social welfare programs, which include Aid to Families with Dependent Children (AFDC), Social Security (SSI), and General Assistance, spend an estimated $10 billion a year on direct and indirect housing subsidies.[9] This money is not coordinated by any federal policy or program to relate to the housing programs originating in HUD. This lack of federal program coordination means that no money is available for either better housing programs in HUD or enhanced social services in Health and Human Services. Because of low benefit levels women on public assistance are forced to use HUD resources for income support. This money could be better spent by HUD on new construction, rehabilitation, modernization, and maintenance for expansion of the nation's low-income housing system. A reformed social welfare system should peg payments to an appropriate standard of need, increase job training and employment opportunities, establish child care centers, and fund a variety of other programs designed to lift people out of poverty.

A new housing policy will need to address the relationship between the role of welfare and that of public housing. Public housing programs are poor substitutes for an inadequate welfare system that does not provide realistic shelter expenses or the social supports necessary to help give women the ability to become independent of public assistance. A public housing policy cannot be a replacement for a proper welfare and income support system. An incomes policy, however, that simply addresses the financial pressures that put women at housing risk ignores the non-economic problems that confront women as primary care-givers in society.

HOUSING DISCRIMINATION

Discrimination in the rental housing market against families with children is a serious problem in all parts of our country. Single women with children are those least likely to be able to buy a house. They are forced to seek rental housing and become the most frequent object of this form of discrimination. And to the extent that these single-parent families are black and poor, discrimination translates across lines of race and class.

While this type of discrimination is widely practiced and affects thousands of families, it goes against the grain of the family tradition and American values. It goes against the grain, but it is not against the law—that is, not against federal law. Even though the Civil Rights Act of 1968 was amended in 1974 to make it unlawful to discriminate in renting or selling a housing unit because of gender, the act does not prohibit discrimination against families with children.

A report commissioned by HUD and released in 1980 on rental practices affecting families found that landlords actually acknowledged exclusionary practices against families with children in one out of four rental situations.[10] In California, children were barred from 70 percent of the housing units surveyed. Local studies reveal similar levels of restriction on children in Texas and New Jersey.[11] HUD also reported that newer and better-maintained apartment complexes were more likely to exclude children.

Many families are forced to place their children "voluntarily" in the temporary custody of state agencies because they are unable to locate available housing that accepts children. In New Jersey, the Division of Youth and Family Services, which is charged with the care of at-risk children, found that up to 40 percent of the children placed in foster care were there because housing for the family was unaffordable or unavailable.

Discrimination against children is certainly an essential women's issue because women, for the most part, are the primary givers of child care in this society. It is unconscionable that children and their mothers are not properly housed because they are not allowed to live in some places. Anti-discrimination language to protect families with children must be part of a national housing policy and passed as a key element of a new Federal Fair Housing Act.

LIFE CRISES AND THE HOUSING OF WOMEN

Divorce

Divorce is one of the principal factors in the unprecedented growth in single-parent families in recent years. The divorce rate is currently at 50 percent; 24 percent of all women who have been married have been divorced at least once.[12]

Until recent changes in divorce statutes concerning the joint custody of dependent children, women with young children were traditionally given custody and, as primary caretakers of the children, they also were given the family home. New divorce laws in many states, however, dictate dissolution of family assets and division of property. These laws work in ways that threaten the homes, and even the ability to pay for any shelter, for displaced and divorced women.

For the average working American family, it is homeownership and housing equity that help maintain middle-class status. But in separation and dissolution of a marriage, women lose access to much of that equity and the housing unit itself, and many times fall from their once comfortable middle-class status. Even given their share of half the equity in a house, many divorced women still do not have enough money to put down a downpayment on a comparable dwelling, and none of the income to replace their home with another. The MIT-Harvard Joint Center for Housing Studies found that women on the average moved three times after a divorce, and each time they stepped down the housing quality ladder.[13]

By denying divorced women a place in their established homes, we do more than force them to move down the housing ladder. Since an important source of their identity is broken, a vital part of the community is broken at the same time. Instead of creating a social holding place for displaced homemakers and their children, current policies dissolve their social contacts and communities and add them to the group of improperly housed people. Federal policy should preserve the family home for women and their children after divorce, or create suitable living environments that would allow them to maintain an appropriate standard of shelter. Such federal initiatives should emphasize expansion of transitional housing programs and the increased availability of reverse annuity mortgages that would enable women and their families to remain in their homes.

Widowhood

Elderly women, most of them widows, are an important segment of the female population that are at extreme housing risk. Women over the age of 65 are almost three times more likely than men to live alone.[14]

Older women also suffer from some of the lowest incomes in society, averaging less than $500 a month of available income to cover food, clothing, utilities, housing, and medical expenses. Few older women have pensions or substantial savings on which to rely. The historic economic discrimination against women in employment and in the credit markets comes to a head after the husband dies and accumulated assets become an essential aspect of maintaining a decent quality of life. The financial ability of elderly women to seek appropriate housing is therefore even more constrained than that of elderly men or single-parent households.

Twenty-one percent of elderly female householders own the homes in which they live, and many face problems trying to maintain those homes properly.[15] These women may have more house than they need or can afford. Even if the mortgage is paid, the cost of paying property taxes and utilities in addition to standard maintenance is beyond the means of many older women. For others, the physical burden of essential, everyday tasks such as cooking, cleaning, and basic household chores makes continued long-term living in their established home problematic.

For elderly women, living in a one-person household can be emotionally, as well as financially, difficult. Isolation and loneliness due to the lack of companionship and mobility compound the problem of poverty.

In developing a national housing policy we need to help shelter elderly women in ways that preserve their dignity and place in the communities in which they live. This means establishing programs for accessory apartments, retrofitting of homes, and shared housing. A national program supporting conversion of seniors' homes to contain accessory apartments would enable many women to pay the costs of maintaining their homes. A grant program or loan payable when the property is sold, for conversion of homes to contain second units, would be a cost-effective, compassionate, and efficient use of housing resources. The use of a National Housing Investment Corporation to fund retrofitting of homes with life care systems would permit frail elderly women to remain in their homes rather than being forced into nursing homes. Regulation of reverse annuity mortgages would produce confidence in a financial mechanism capable of producing an income for low-income but house-rich elderly women. Finally, support for local shared housing programs, in some circumstances, can produce the right mix of companionship, decreased household chore burdens, and additional income for elderly women homeowners that can keep them in their homes.

Homelessness

As we saw in Chapter 6, significant numbers of the new homeless are women and children. A HUD report on homeless and emergency shelters issued in 1984 reported that "single men still make up the largest category of the homeless, but that a significant portion are now in family groups."[16] Local homeless advocacy groups report increasing numbers of women and children seeking emergency shelter. The number of homeless women could be anywhere from 45,000 to 340,000, making up 13 percent of the homeless singles and 21 percent of people in families.[17] The Women's Institute for Housing and Economic Development estimates that across the nation over 500 emergency shelters serve 250,000 women and children.[18] The substitution of vouchers for Section 8 subsidies where low vacancy rates make units impossible to find, rental discrimination against families with children, and the very low income of many women, particularly black and hispanic women, all add to the pressures that are pushing more women into homelessness.

Battered Women

Many times women remain in their abusive situations because they have nowhere else to go. The absence of affordable housing and the low income of many women, combined with the lack of available space in shelters for battered women, often leave these women no option other than to remain home with the abuser. A study of homeless women in New York City by *City Limits* found that 10 percent of the women sheltered by New York's Red Cross Emergency Center were abused. Although battered women's shelters do exist, average stays are often limited to less than 90 days. The New York State Coalition Against Domestic Violence reports that during 1984–1985 women and children were refused shelter by 77 percent of the domestic violence programs in New York City.[19] Women are then forced into emergency shelters or other facilities designed to shelter homeless people. Nationwide there are fewer than 8,000 beds available for abused women, certainly far fewer than the number of women who need shelter from abuse.

TRANSITIONAL HOUSING

Transitional housing bridges the move from short-term emergency shelter to a long-term, permanent, and affordable home. Transitional housing provides for shelter beyond immediate emergency needs by helping to stabilize women who have been displaced from their homes because of changes in their family structure. Divorced, abandoned, separated, and abused women, as well as women who are drug- and alcohol-dependent, newly released women prisoners, and disabled women are in need of the type of support that transitional housing can effectively furnish.

Typical services included in transitional housing are child care, job search, personal financial management, and the teaching of life-planning skills. The goal is to enable women to become self-sufficient in a period of time ranging from three months to two years. Various transitional housing programs range in size and structure from converted single-family homes suitable for a few women to large projects serving 200 or more people as part of an integrated living and rehabilitation environment.

Transitional residences usually combine private and community space in ways that maximize self-sufficiency and reduce economic costs. Sponsoring groups usually are churches, YWCAs, or women's groups; funding comes from private sources, usually United Way and similar local charitable givers. Federal and state rent subsidy programs are sought. In all programs, residents pay rent and otherwise contribute to the cost of running their non-traditional housing arrangement.

Services such as day care, transportation, and food preparation are all critically important to women who must juggle child-rearing and a full-time job. In Europe many mutual housing associations provide child care as part of their responsibilities; some also include other congregate services such as prepared food and laundry. In the United States, however, virtually no permanent service and shelter arrangements exist other than those for elderly and handicapped persons.

The YWCA of Jersey City sponsors the Fairmount Housing[20] Corporation for single women who are heads of household. The unique financing package combines land donations from the city, Community Development Block Grant funds, a grant from the New Jersey Department of Community Affairs. Included in the project's mortgageable costs were funds for a full range of social support services. In addition a VISTA contract will train 10 low-income residents of the project in building maintenance and management and child care services. The VISTA stipend does not count against Social Security or welfare support.

The Family Housing Demonstration Fund before the California State Legislature[21] links state-financed housing with shelter-plus-service initiatives. The demonstration program will fund the design of new living environments and social and economic programs so that working parents, job-seeking parents, and homeless parents have the opportunity to build productive lives. Provisions of the legislation include financing for job and economic development, support services, and affordable housing.

The Family Housing Demonstration Program funded by the legislation provides for the construction or rehabilitation of "community housing" and "congregate housing" by non-profit organizations and public agencies. Community housing is defined as 20 or more rental or cooperative units on one or more sites that include social and economic services. Congregate housing projects are new or rehabilitated large multi-bedroom structures in which three to six families share common areas and household duties including child care.

This proposal essentially calls for the creation of a new housing type not generally found in this country—community and congregate housing—that connects child care services, job training, and other social support services to shared facilities such as kitchens and laundries.

One of the nation's most established transitional housing projects is Warren Village, founded by a Methodist Church group in Denver, Colorado. Warren Village opened its doors in 1974 and since that time has become a model facility for the nation. Its original 95 apartment units were financed by HUD. An additional 106 units were financed in a joint effort by the Colorado Housing Finance Agency, UDAG funds, and grants from local foundations. The project was designed as a mixed-use development, combining the apartment units with a large child care center and 10,000 square feet of commercial space available for rent. The commercial space helps subsidize the rents on the women's apartments, and may enable the Village residents to start their own businesses. An evaluation of Warren Village residents reports that the percentage of employed residents increased from 47 percent of those moving into the Village to 94 percent of those leaving, and the number of public assistance dropped from 65 percent to 6 percent.[22]

If we are to overcome the deterioriating housing conditions that face single women and their families in this country, emergency support is not enough. Transitional housing projects are an essential component of any national policy that attempts to meet the needs of battered and homeless women and their households. National legislation based on the California Demonstration Project should make grant money available for similar demonstrations in each region of the country. Support should also be given to the development of privately operated transitional projects like Fairmount Housing Corporation and Warren Village.

INAPPROPRIATENESS OF CURRENT HOUSING DESIGN

Housing design, like the availability of services, schools, and employment, influences the quality of women's lives and the suitability of their living situation. Housing for single parents, battered women, and transitional units for the homeless needs to take new forms—structures different from the traditional three-bedroom, one-and-a-half bath, and family-room dwelling.

The physical structure and design of a house should also relate to the special needs of single-parent households. Jacqueline Leavitt, Professor of Planning at UCLA, promotes the concept of "Shelter Plus"[23] to respond to the needs of female-headed households beyond that of simple affordable places to live. Collaborating with Troy West, an architect at the New Jersey Institute of Technology, Leavitt designed a prototype flexible house that integrates services and shared living arrangements for single parents.[24] The prototype, based on feedback and critique from the League of Women Voters and Parents Without Partners, consisted of a two-and-one-half-story infill unit that could be fitted into a traditional suburban neighborhood. Internally, the house is designed around the concepts of private and congregate spaces that have flexible uses. The house could be shared by four adults and six children, each with his or her private space.

That women are developing a new notion of housing with a different character was documented in the April 1986 issue of *Ms* magazine in a feature story on "Women's Dream Houses." *Ms* surveyed 6,000 women on their housing dreams and desires. The response showed a willingness and interest to share some living space with others in a community or congregate arrangement. This response cut across all age and income categories and recognized that housing must now reflect the new roles and responsibilities of women in society.

National policy should also promote a new type of housing for single parents who cannot afford to live in a traditional single-family structure but who have no desire to live in a public housing project. New structure designs for the renovation of larger abandoned buildings, retrofitting of existing homes, and new construction of infill housing in established neighborhoods would be promoted through national design competitions and grant awards to architects and community planners. HUD should fund demonstration projects around the country and disseminate prototype plans to community non-profits, churches, and housing cooperatives for replication. New funds through a federal housing trust fund and a national housing investment corporation would be available to support these housing programs.

A national program promoting accessory apartments, described in Chapter 5, could also serve many of the needs of single-parent households. For single-parent families, separate living units within an already existing home would be affordable.

HOUSING AMERICA'S WOMEN AND CHILDREN

Our national housing policy will create new rental and home-ownership opportunities for women. It will produce shelter-linked services connected to expanded public housing programs, community development corporations, limited equity cooperatives, and mutual housing associations.

The center of community life in this country is based on women and children. Neighborhood organizations, schools, religious associations, all get their everyday sustenance from the activities of women. When a woman has no home, we destroy not only the woman, but the family and community as well. A progressive national housing policy would challenge the conditions that make women the least well-housed members of society, and strengthen our families and communities.

The future character of America's housing policy for the next decade will, of necessity, respond to the changes in the make-up of the family and the special needs of the growing population of women who must work to support themselves and their children and of elderly women living alone. Just as women organized the Garden Club movement in the 1920s to build parks across the United States, which helped foster more livable communities, the demands of women for housing more appropriate to their present lifestyle will change the way the nation conceives its housing programs.

8
Housing in Low-Income Urban Neighborhoods

In many of America's urban neighborhoods, the absence of affordable housing has reached crisis proportions. These are the districts of the housing-vulnerable, where most of the homeless come from and many camp out, the mean streets in which poor people struggle with too little money to keep up their properties in the shadows of abandoned, dilapidated buildings. They are the grey areas that are often redlined by the banks and blackballed by the realtors, places caught between the contrasting dangers of deterioration and gentrification. These are the communities where more and more poor families, with less and less money, seek fewer available apartments of declining quality at ever higher rents. To these communities, the federal policy of near abandonment of new housing activity has been more than a failure; it has been a disaster.

But as the federal government pulled back, neighborhood people organized and pushed forward. Local community organizations, tenant groups, religious institutions, labor unions, and ad hoc coalitions have tried to fill the gap created by federal withdrawal, pressing demands for fair access to housing credit, for use and control of vacant buildings, and for tenant management or ownership of private properties and declining public housing projects. In this chapter we review six neighborhood-level housing movements of the 1980s and then identify federal housing policies to advance the goals of those movements. The six movements are efforts to obtain needed mortgage and home repair loans, improve vacant buildings by urban homesteading, permit tenants to manage or own apartment buildings cooperatively, involve religious organizations in the construction or rehabilitation of housing, work with labor unions to expand affordable housing in the community, and form and operate mutual housing associations. These community-based movements have sought directly and pragmatically to improve the quality of life for neighborhood residents, finding or forging local solutions that have produced a little of the affordable housing needed in the area, and a lot more than what would have been produced in their absence. But, in addition to meeting immediate shelter needs, these movements try to change the economic and political circumstances that have led to the affordable housing crisis. They center on notions of equity, self-help, and community empowerment.

THE MOVEMENT FOR NEIGHBORHOOD HOUSING CREDIT

In the mid-1970s one of the first of these movements confronted very limited availability of home mortgages and rehabilitation loans in city neighborhoods. Originating in Chicago with a coalition led by Gale Cincotta, demands for greater neighborhood investment by banks soon spread to cities across the country. Community-oriented researchers documented redlining—the practice of denying loans based solely on geographic information—in most older urban regions.[1]

Access to credit is a critical aspect of community health and local ability to revitalize urban housing stock. Capital for housing is a cornerstone of neighborhood stability and vitality. Lending institutions have often denied credit to certain neighborhoods based on arbitrary criteria such as racial composition, geography, or age of the housing stock without regard for the credit applicants' ability to pay. Redlining continues to occur in all our cities despite the best efforts of community groups and concerned lenders to target financing to areas in need. Disinvestment leads to deterioration and the eventual loss of affordable housing in low- and moderate-income neighborhoods.

In response to demands by neighborhood organizations for equitable treatment by commercial lenders, Congress enacted two laws to deal with the problems of neighborhood divestment—the Community Reinvestment Act (CRA) and the Home Mortgage Disclosure Act (HMDA). Both of these laws have been effectively used by community groups and local residents, despite statutory weaknesses, to encourage investment in their neighborhoods.

The Home Mortgage Disclosure Law,[2] enacted by Congress in 1975, requires banks, savings and loans, and credit unions to disclose the distribution of home mortgage and home improvement lending on a geographic basis every year. The goal of the act was to produce the information necessary for community groups, government regulators, and lending institutions to evaluate the access of certain areas to private capital for housing rehabilitation and purchase. Community groups hoped that by having access to investment data they would be able to identify and create new opportunities for lending in their areas.

The Community Reinvestment Act,[3] passed by Congress in 1977, states that all banks "have a continuing and affirmative obligation to help meet the credit needs of the local community in which they are chartered, including low- and moderate-income communities." Federal regulators, under CRA powers, evaluate lenders' records of community investment when banks seek approvals for mergers, acquisitions, and new branch openings. The Federal Reserve Board and other federal regulators can deny the application of banks to develop new markets based on a poor neighborhood investment record.

The HMDA and the CRA give the public access to the data necessary for a true public/private dialogue about the nature and need for capital investment in our communities. Community organizations have used these laws to create an opening at the negotiating table that fulfills the spirit as well as the form of partnerships. These public/private partnerships can be the vehicles for the future production and rehabilitation of affordable housing.

CRA is a cost-effective and principled alternative to large government financing programs. With the information provided by CRA and HMDA, community groups have the ability to challenge effectively the applications of lending institutions with poor track records in low-income neighborhoods and, thereafter, to make something happen to enhance affordable housing opportunities in poor neighborhoods.

Since CRA's enactment, over 100 protests have been filed by community organizations seeking greater bank investment in their areas. Professor Calvin Bradford, a leading expert on CRA at the Humphrey Institute at the University of Minnesota, estimates that $3.7 billion has been invested in low- and moderate-income neighborhoods as the result of CRA protests.[4] Nearly $1.6 billion has been committed by banks involved in special loan programs agreed upon by lending institutions and community groups. Billions more in investment dollars have been generated from bankers' increased awareness of investment responsibilities to areas in which their depositors live.

ACORN, a national organization of low- and moderate-income people organized in over 25 states, makes aggressive use of CRA. In 1986, ACORN negotiated over $400 million in new investment in city neighborhoods. Agreements have been signed by 12 banks, and others continue to be negotiated.[5]

Perhaps the largest CRA settlement on record came out of a challenge by the Chicago Reinvestment Alliance, a grassroots coalition of neighborhood-based developers, citizen groups, and technical assistance organizations, and three Chicago banks.[6] In March of 1984, First Chicago agreed to make $120 million in loans to various low- and moderate-income neighborhoods in return for an agreement not to protest their plan to acquire the American National Bank of Chicago. Within a short period of time, a community coalition led by the National Information Training Center negotiated another $50 million in community reinvestment from two other Chicago banks that were planning mergers. In the First Chicago agreement, the bank created a new department to oversee its community investment program and neighborhood organizations became involved in soliciting and screening loan applications.

Many of the lending agreements reached as a result of the CRA negotiations became the funding source for public/private partnerships in the city. For example, the Chicago Equity Fund combined Community Development Block Grant money and a low-interest mortgage from a community reinvestment agreement to finance the conversion of an old hotel to 115 units of low-income housing.

The only enforcement mechanism under CRA is that it requires the Federal Reserve Board and other bank regulators to consider compliance with the goals of the act when reviewing bank applications for expansion and merger. With the new wave of bank mergers brought about by deregulation, CRA challenges have become an effective method for community groups to target more investment into their neighborhoods.

Tha banking system in this country historically has been substantially decentralized. As a result of recent deregulation, however, banking has become increasingly consolidated and competitive.[7] Banks and other lending institutions are expanding across state lines and are moving toward a regional, and perhaps eventually a national, system of lending and credit allocation. The issue of credit allocation will become an important concern of local communities, who no longer will have direct contact with top bank management. As the banking institutions become more regional or national in character, their concerns for the financial health of any particular community are likely to decrease.

A new federal policy should require lending institutions to provide detailed community development plans indicating how they intend to address the credit needs of each low-income community in the areas they serve. CRA also needs to be expanded to include disclosure of commercial lending practices. Commercial activity in a neighborhood—local mom and pop stores, tailors, shoe stores, and laundromats—are essential to neighborhood life and a key aspect of stabilizing and preserving low- and moderate-income housing units. These neighborhood entrepreneurs are the life blood of vibrant urban economies.

One of the side effects of centralization in the financial services industry is that banks are predominantly making mortgage loans that can be sold on the secondary market, which means they must be standardized. As a result, banks spend less time with people who could qualify for credit, but who need loans customized to their circumstances.

Banks ought to be encouraged to write more flexible loan packages, corresponding to the budgets of low- and moderate-income households. Many more people could afford to buy houses or fix up the homes they live in if banks would structure something other than their recently standardized mortgages. This flexibility could include items such as rehabilitation below present loan-size requirements and considering income sources such as permanent part-time jobs, food stamps, and various types of government support. A CRA review should require examination of a lender's flexibility.

Deregulation, however, can present greater opportunities for socially responsible community investment. The expansion of banking territory and new bank products should correlate with a greater obligation for community reinvestment. This principle was ratified in the House Banking Subcommittee version of the Interstate Banking Bill, but the bill never came before the House of Representatives for a vote.

A national housing program to promote increased neighbor-

hood investment should authorize lending institution regulators t(
determine which banks will be allowed expanded powers such a:
underwriting securities, opening additional branches, or offering in
surance, based on a strong CRA record. Bank regulators could als(
require non-banks, such as insurance companies, and mortgage bank:
to invest a certain percentage of their funds in a Federal Housin§
Trust Fund.

A trust fund investment would alleviate the problem of deter
mining which low-income communities these institutions serve, thei
proper level of investment, and how loans could be serviced. And i
trust fund would be a direct and obvious place for community-base(
organizations to go to get project financing. Rather than spendin§
time and energy seeking financing, a trust fund capitalized by CR/
requirements would provide one-stop financing for community de
velopers. In this investment model, regional or national institution
would invest in a national trust fund. They would be guaranteed i
rate of return, based on prime plus an agreed-upon number. Sucl
an investment would presumptively fulfill CRA requirements.

As mortgage banks control an increasing portion of the housin;
mortgage market, and are not covered by CRA or HMDA, thes
federal acts are decreasingly useful in channeling investment int(
poor neighborhoods. Thirteen of the 25 largest mortgage banks i
America are subsidiaries of bank holding companies; their share c
the mortgage market has risen to over 30 percent and it continue
to increase.

In some cases, lenders have been able to avoid their communit
lending obligations by transferring their lending activities to mor
gage bank subsidiaries. Deregulation has also enabled the bankin
industry to transfer lending activity to mortgage banking companie:
Between 1980 and 1983 the FHA collected data on loans made b
mortgage banks, since most loans by mortgage banks were insure
by the FHA. The FHA, however, under the Reagan Administration'
direction has stopped collecting lending information.

Federal policy should establish lending requirements for mor
gage bankers and other investors such as insurance companie:
Mortgage banks, which are subsidiaries of commercial bank holdin
companies, could have their community lending practices linked t
the community deposits of all the holding company subsidiaries. Bι
many mortgage banks and insurance companies do not have a dej
ository community to which housing investment could be linked. I
these cases, again, a contribution to a federal housing trust func

ould be the standard against which community investment is mea-
ured. As the nation's financial system moves away from any geo-
raphic anchor, new reinvestment tools such as trust funds and re-
ional development corporations become necessary tools for
hanneling capital into housing in low- and moderate-income neigh-
orhoods.

Congress also ought to extend the Home Mortgage Disclosure
ct to require disclosure of deposits within SMSAs by census tracts
nd of loans made outside the SMSAs by zip code. To improve the
vestment record of the emerging interstate banking system, lead-
g institutions also should be required to disclose the origin of their
eposits. Such depository reporting requirements would encourage
e extension of fair lending practices, insuring that local money is
sed to improve the local housing stock rather than downtown de-
elopment or overseas investment.

HE URBAN HOMESTEADING MOVEMENT

cities across the country, poor people, desperate for decent hous-
g and willing to work to make abandoned units fit for their fami-
es, have become squatters. They have used their labor and the do-
ated labor of their friends to rehabilitate abandoned buildings. These
omesteading and sweat equity efforts have increased in number,
support for housing from the federal government has dwindled.
hese efforts have been both individual attempts to find a home by
eople who have no better place to live and organized campaigns
y poor people's organizations demanding a government response
the housing crisis. For low-income families in many areas, sweat
quity is the only route to homeownership.

The federal government responded to initial grassroots home-
eading activities by authorizing the Federal Homesteading Dem-
stration Program—Section 810 of the Community and Redevel-
oment Act of 1974. As amended in 1983, the program targets
rticipation to large low-income families who live in substandard
wellings and pay more than 30 percent of their income for shelter.
1986, the homesteading program spent $12.3 million to acquire
o abandoned units and turn them over to low-income people at a
st of approximately $18,000 a piece.[8]

The goal of the Section 810 homesteading program is to turn

abandoned properties into homes for poor people at minimal cost to the federal government. Local urban homesteading agencies, usually Public Housing Authorities, identify abandoned units within their jurisdiction, acquire properties, and turn them over to eligible low income families. The homesteaders agree to bring the property up to code standards and occupy the building for at least five years When used in conjunction with sweat equity, subsidized rehabilitation loans, or private forms of assistance, homesteading can produce livable family-sized units fulfilling all building code requirements for as little as $15,000. With a low-interest mortgage such units could be sold for $200 a month—affordable to even very-low-income families

Although the Section 810 program has been dramatically under funded, urban homesteading has the potential to house the homeless and tap the nation's stock of abandoned houses. Homesteading has important advantages as a very-low-income housing program. It is cost-effective (providing units for under $20,000 per unit), is able to meet immediate housing needs, and has enjoyed a track record of success for more than 10 years.

In cities across the country, local community and tenant groups continue to press HUD and local administrations to turn over tax delinquent and other abandoned properties in their inventory. New York City has thousands of individual squatters. In addition to these individual actions, well-organized homesteader campaigns transferred thousands of units for low-income families.

Organized homesteading campaigns have launched affordable housing actions in Atlanta, Chicago, Washington, D.C., Phoenix Detroit, and New York City. In 1980, ACORN, the Kensington Joint Action Council, and a number of other community organizations in Philadelphia began aggressive squatting in an effort to get the city government to turn over a number of the 26,000 abandoned housing units in the city's inventory.[9] The campaign led to a series of agreements with the city to provide homesteading units to qualified low income people. Local community development corporations train tenants in sweat equity techniques, work with the city to transfer abandoned units to low-income people, and work out financing with banks. Typical of their affordable project design, Philadelphia home steaders received 50 houses and $200,000 of CDBG money from the city, which they combined with sweat equity and bank loans based on CRA agreements to provide houses at an average cost of $15,000 dollars. In these unique agreements, banks have accepted sweat equity as a portion of downpayment requirements and have agreed t include food stamps and part-time jobs in income calculation for mortgages.

After a long campaign in Detroit, community leaders successfully negotiated with the city to implement a homesteading program. In Chicago, homesteaders drafted an agreement with the Department of Housing that would allow them legally to reside in abandoned units as "nuisance abatement contractors." Homesteaders would be paid to fix up their homes by giving them title to the property.

In New York City, the Urban Homesteading Assistance Board[10] helps tenants and community organizations use homesteading and sweat equity techniques by running interference with the city bureaucracy and by providing technical support. UHAB has successfully lobbied the New York City administration to reduce the foreclosure period on vacant, tax-delinquent land from up to six years to one year. Since the project began in 1973, UHAB has assisted in the redevelopment of approximately 15,000 tenant-sponsored cooperatives and sweat equity homesteads.

The federal government controlled more than 37,000 properties at the end of 1986. There are an estimated 50,000 abandoned units in New York City—10,000 of which are owned by the local government. In addition, FHA, VA, and FmHA foreclosures transferred nearly 50,000 thousand units to government ownership in 1986.[11] This is an inventory of housing ripe for additional homesteading.

Federal policy should encourage cities to turn over privately owned tax-delinquent buildings to low- and moderate-income people in an orderly and timely fashion. In order for projects to be affordable for very-low-income people, HUD should reconsider its rehabilitation standards. Present HUD building standards require almost complete gut rehabilitation, making these rehabilitated units too expensive for many poor residents.

The success of sweat equity projects takes more than the energy of a homesteader. Homesteaders need skills, training, money for materials, and construction assistance to complete projects. The federal government must design and create a program for very-low-income tenants that would transfer to them abandoned and tax-delinquent properties. This policy calls for expansion of the Section 810 program and establishment of an Affordable Housing and Homeownership Program that would help low-income individuals and community organizations acquire ownership interests in abandoned units, as either individual homeowners or as cooperative owners. The program would coordinate training in construction skill with ownership skills such as budget counseling. At the local level the program would designate contractors for technical rehabilitation such as plumbing and electrical work. Finally, this program would provide low-interest loans for construction materials.

THE TENANT MANAGEMENT/OWNERSHIP MOVEMENT

Across the country, in both private and public housing projects, tenants have organized to manage (and in some cases, to own) the buildings in which they live. Although there is no necessary link between proposals for tenant management and tenant ownership, they are both potential strategies for providing tenants more control of the affordable housing stock. The roots of tenant-controlled buildings stem from the late 1960s and early 1970s, when urban slumlords and some housing authorities reneged on their managment responsibilities.

In New York City, private landlords had abandoned low-income buildings by the thousands because tax liens and code violations cost them more than the buildings were worth. Tenants, sometimes in a desperate effort to preserve their homes, to keep the water running and the boiler fixed, were left with no option but to run the buildings themselves. In the short term many apartment buildings were stabilized and tenants learned the fundamentals of property management. For the most part, this tenant activity was limited to local initiatives designed to rescue single buildings and never developed into a city-wide or publicly supported program of tenant ownership.

Tenant management in public housing had a similar evolution, originating with the 1969 rent strike against the St. Louis Housing Authority.[12] The St. Louis Housing Authority had a record of deplorable housing conditions and an unresponsive administration. When the Housing Authority attempted to raise rents in 1969, the tenants responded by organizing a rent strike. After a number of months, the rent strike succeeded in bankrupting the Authority. During the months of the rent strike the tenants became managers by default; they had to learn how to make the buildings operate. HUD put the bankrupt Authority into receivership and, as part of the settlement, required that tenants have a significant role to play in the management of the project. The tenant management corpora-ion now operates 3,000 apartments and constitutes the most well-known experiment in tenant management.

Based on the St. Louis experience and at the urging of the Ford Foundation, HUD initiated a tenant management demonstration project in 1976 that examined the feasibility of turning the management of public housing projects over to tenants. In an effort to improve the management of public housing, and to address many of the problems associated with a sometimes overwhelming bureaucracy, tenants have taken over the management in a number of demonstration projects. The study concluded that low-income tenants could master the skills necessary to manage housing. The study also clearly demonstrated, however, that tenant groups would fail if not provided with sufficient continuing subsidies and other support from the federal government.[13]

After backing into various management arrangements, the tenants began to examine ways of doing major building repairs and improvements. It was one thing to put locks on the doors and have the floor swept, but quite another to replace a roof or repair a boiler. Tenants found that, in order to get loans, they needed collateral, and for that they needed to own their buildings. With the help of Legal Services lawyers and an array of technical assistance organizations, tenants organized their buildings into cooperatives.

In St. Louis the need for capital became the engine for social invention, as tenants looked toward ownership as a tool for economic development. Day care centers and catering businesses were established, and 700 units of newly constructed apartments are being planned. Most important, these institutions took on a life of their own as they became a new and important force in their neighborhoods for community development.

Tenant-run housing, whether public or tenement, has much to recommend it. In many cases, tenants are the only people around who care enough to run buildings after owners walk away from them. The St. Louis experience documents that, in some situations, residents also can do a better job than management. Residents live on site; they know what's going on. They have a self-interest in seeing that the buildings are managed effectively, and when financial resources are limited, they understand what priorities should be established. Moreover, in cases of tenant management, peer pressure works as a tool to diminish drug use, graffiti, and crime.

The history of tenant ownership is more mixed. Sometimes tenant ownership has proved desirable, or has been demanded by necessity, and at other times it has been a bad policy for the tenants and for the long-term survival of a public affordable housing stock. Questions of ownership should respond in a practical manner to each of those needs. Certainly, many housing authorities are failing in many of those areas, but a broad range of response can provide the solutions to the problems of employment, safe and healthy shelter, and social pathology. The issue of tenant ownership should be clearly decoupled from questions of management.

HUD's current move to embrace tenant management and ownership programs could endanger the United States' long-term affordable housing goals. Tenant ownership programs could be used as a device to reduce the national public housing system, and ultimately remove units from the low- and moderate-income housing inventory. If not given necessary support for operating and maintenance subsidies, tenant-managed units will continue to deteriorate just as they did under housing authority management.

Low-income housing policy cannot responsibly trade off increased tenant control over their housing conditions for fewer and less reliable resources. Conversely, public resources should not be transferred to private owners without resale and profit controls. Tenant-owned units, especially in gentrifying areas, could be sold off after a number of years, producing a windfall for the owners at the expense of public investment and a reduction in the available affordable housing stock.

Public policy toward tenant involvement in the management of public housing units should consider the particular conditions surrounding each housing project, the character of the public investment in the stock, and the need to preserve and expand the number of low-income units in the nation. Each decision made about the final disposition of public housing units should stress tenant participation in project management and the need to construct a true partnership between tenant organizations and public housing authority administration.

Tenant advisory councils are a minimum level for tenant participation; they presently exist in housing authority administrative structures, but are not often used effectively. In order to use their advisory councils, tenants need to organize to have an impact on the system. In addition, housing authority administrations have to be willing to turn some decision-making power over to tenant representatives.

Resident management corporations create a much greater role

for tenants in the operation of their housing units. Problems exist with the professional ability of some resident corporations to make important financial and staff decisions. Massive amounts of technical assistance are necessary to train tenant leaders. And after leaders develop the necessary management skills, they often use those skills to leave the low-income project. The sometimes adversarial relationship between the resident managers and housing authority staff makes a well-run resident management corporation difficult to achieve.

Transforming public housing projects into limited equity cooperatives preserves the low- and moderate-income units for the long term. Present administration policy toward these limited equity private cooperatives, however, may cut tham adrift without the financial resources or technical support necessary to guarantee their survival. HUD requires conversion projects to continue to serve at least 50 percent of low-income residents and to limit rents to 30 percent of income. However, this allows a considerable reduction in low-income units and the conditions are often waived.

A number of major issues need to be addressed by public housing cooperative conversion strategies. In the initial HUD demonstration projects, buildings were transferred to tenant owners without the continuing operating subsidies for which HUD projects are eligible, making it difficult to serve a very-low-income population. Restricting rents to 30 percent of income preserves tenant budgets, but does not create a large enough financial foundation for a project to succeed. Property in private hands of tenants is also liable to local property taxes rather than HUD payments in lieu of taxes, further increasing tenant costs.

To keep units affordable to low-income residents, conversion schemes that preserve annual contribution contracts with HUD need to be designed. Furthermore, cooperative conversion should only be established under conditions that provide sufficient reserves to repair and maintain buildings, as well as the rent subsidies necessary for low-income tenants.

Should tenant coop conversions fail because of the lack of continued support from the federal government, an important and valuable housing resource would be lost. Alternatives such as opening up cooperatives to higher-income tenants may stabilize a cooperative financial base, but ultimately erode our stock of low-income units if there is not a corresponding production program. A responsible national housing policy would increase the absolute supply of low-income units by incorporating them into a larger number of mixed-income projects. In this way, more low-income units would be spread over a greater number of housing projects. Rather than being ghettoized, the poor would become part of a larger community. This program would insure that housing was decent, appropriate, and affordable.

The Role of Religious Institutions

Local church organizations have become involved in neighborhoods throughout the country advocating, organizing, and building housing for low- and moderate-income people. For the churches, affordable housing is a not theoretical problem debated in Washington, but a problem confronting members of parishes and congregations daily. Jarred into action by the growing numbers of homeless people, many churches have joined with other local community leaders to establish non-profit housing organizations.

Church involvement and commitment to issues of shelter, affordable housing, and community stability rest on religious traditions that uphold the dignity of human beings and the imperative of social justice. The Bishops' Letter on Housing and the policy statement of the United States Catholic Conference articulate a clear role for the public, private, and religious community in the provision of housing and the creation of a new comprehensive housing policy:

The United States is in the midst of a severe housing crisis. This is a broader, more pervasive and more complicated phenomenon than the customary photographs of urban slums and rural shacks indicate. It involves more people, more neighborhoods and communities than was thought to be the case even a few years ago. It touches millions of poor families who live in inhuman conditions, but it also involves many middle income families whose ability to provide themselves with decent housing is being painfully tested. Rising costs of shelter, maintenance and utilities—as well as high interest rates and regressive property taxes—are forcing many families to live in inadequate housing or to do without other basic essentials. Other low and middle income families have been confined to neighborhoods without adequate services, minimal safety or necessary community life.[14]

Churches have traditionally interpreted their role as one of combatting alienation and isolation in the communities they serve. They are often the institutions of most significance to stabilizing neighborhoods, crucial to the mending of a social fabric torn by poverty and economic abandonment. Neighborhoods and church congregations and parishes have often grown up together. These special ties between religious organizations and city neighborhoods give churches special obligations and opportunities to become leaders in affordable housing efforts.

But churches are very limited in the financial support that they can give to housing. Most city churches that deal with the problems of homelessness, decay, and displacement every day are as poor as the communities they serve. They struggle in their ministry to low-income groups, running soup kitchens, distributing clothing, and coordinating youth programs, while maintaining church buildings and traditional religious functions. State and local governments, commercial lenders, banks, and employers must follow the leadership of church revitalization efforts and provide the resources to make large-scale housing revitalization possible.

Church-Sponsored Housing Efforts

The Nehemiah Plan—named after the Biblical builder of Jerusalem—is the most well-known and most expansive church-based housing project in the nation, located in Brooklyn, New York. The ecumenical coalition of 52 churches called East Brooklyn Churches Local Organizing Project will build 5,000 single-family houses that will be owner-occupied and affordable for families that have combined incomes of $20,000 a year. Nehemiah units have an average unit selling price of $50,000 on land that once was a blighted neighborhood filled with empty lots and abandoned buildings. In order to make the units affordable for prospective moderate-income homeowners, national church bodies contributed $12 million for zero-interest construction loans; the city contributed 30 blocks of land, a ten-year tax abatement, and a $10,000 downpayment loan; and the state provided low-interest mortgage loans. It took several years for churches to raise the initial money it cost to hire the Industrial Areas Foundation to initiate a community-organizing program enabling the East Brooklyn Churches to pressure the city and state to provide the resources that made the project possible.[15]

Although the scope of Nehemiah may only be possible in large cities, many ecumenical housing efforts have sprung up around the country. The Interfaith Task Force in Wilmington, Delaware, and

Hope Communities in Denver are two examples of other churches working together to meet housing needs in their communities. Altogether there are hundreds of local church-centered housing efforts in the country.

Jubilee Housing, Inc., is an ecumenical church-based housing project formed in 1973 that has become a prototype low-income housing system for the Enterprise Foundation. Rents charged in Jubilee units are affordable to even very-low-income tenants. Though Jubilee receives no Section 8 subsidies, the average income of its tenants is about $8,500. Housing rehabilitation costs are kept to a minimum through the use of donated tenant labor, the pro bono efforts of housing professionals, and corporate donations of staff. To date Jubilee has renovated over 1,000 units of low-income housing.[16]

Jubilee raises most of its building funds from grants and zero- or low-interest loans from socially concerned individuals. The money raised by the project is stretched to cover as many buildings as possible through a renovation strategy that calls for bringing units up to code, but not for extensive gut or cosmetic rehabilitation. In this way building systems such as plumbing and heating are replaced over time, rather than as part of up-front costs.

Jubilee's unique approach to housing also attempts to give low-income tenants a variety of the social supports they require to sustain a market-level rent after a number of years. These supports include job placement and financial counseling in addition to child and health care services. The Enterprise Foundation has expanded the number of Jubilee-style projects to Annapolis, Maryland, Lousiville, Kentucky, and Minneapolis.

The New York Archdiocese Office of Neighborhood Preservation manages a $1 million housing fund that is used for the rehabilitation of abandoned city-owned buildings, and has initiated a far-reaching homeownership project that would construct 2,000 new homes for households with maximum gross incomes of $25,000.[17] The goal of the program is to make the homes available to families living in public housing and federally assisted projects. Vacated units would then become available to low-income families on waiting lists. Each housing unit will be owned as a cooperative or condominium. To assure continuing affordability, certain resale restrictions will be applied to each of the units.

The role of the Archdiocese is to establish partnerships with local church-based housing organizations to sponsor the construction of homes, identify sites, and assist in finding buyers for each of the units. Together, the Archdiocese and local sponsors plan to develop prepurchase and postpurchase counseling programs.

Habitat for Humanity is an ecumenical Christian international housing program aimed at enabling home ownership for low-income families who are living in inadequate shelter. Habitat directly applies Christian religious teaching to building housing for the poor, as described by the Habitat motto: "A decent house in a decent community for God's people in need."[18] Habitat projects are sponsored by local groups in over 170 cities in the United States, as well as in many third world countries. Every major Protestant denomination and many local Roman Catholic churches support Habitat projects by sponsoring volunteers or helping to finance local projects.

Habitat houses are built with the significant involvement of volunteer time. The two philosophical bases of housing activity are that, in order to quality for a Habitat house, a family must not be able to purchase a house by conventional means and that units are financed with no interest, profit, or finance charge. Families are chosen early in the construction process and are required to work on their homes for a specified number of sweat equity hours.

Habitat accepts no government funds, but does solicit properties from local governments. It provides another type of partnership that links affluent and low-income people, and provides the opportunities for skilled people to donate their labor and talent. But Habitat's weakness is that its projects are very small and extremely time- and volunteer-intensive. While Habitat's vision and moral wisdom raise awareness about the necessity of shelter, it does not provide a model capable of housing the hundreds of thousands of ill-housed in our society.

Church Pension Fund Investments

National church organizations also provide an alternative source of capital for community loan funds, land trusts, and grants and loans to other types of community-based housing initiatives. Church pension funds, for example, total over $9 billion.[19] Churches could be an important pool of alternative investment capital that takes into account the "social" as well as fiduciary responsibilities of investment decisions.

The McAuley Institute, established in 1982 by the Sisters of Mercy,[20] administers one of the largest and fastest-growing housing investment pools. The Institute is a national non-profit organization that assists local church-based housing efforts through technical support and its revolving loan fund. The loan fund totals over $2 million and is capitalized by contributions from a number of Catholic orders in addition to the Sisters of Mercy, including the Paulist Fathers, the Sulpician Fathers, and the Trinitarians. The demand for loans by local church projects is twice the available lending pool.

Today nearly $1 million has been invested by the revolving fund, leveraging $12 in financing for every $1 lent by the program. New church networks are being sought to increase the size of the fund substantially. The revolving fund targets its resources to low-income homeownership programs, limited equity cooperatives, and mutual housing associations. McAuley identifies its mission as a Catholic housing institute to "advocate with the poor and homeless, to mobilize and leverage church resources to promote the dignity of each person and alleviate the shelter needs of the ill-housed and homeless."

The largest national denominational response to the need for alternate investment funds occurred with the merger of the American Lutheran Church, the Lutheran Church of America, and the Association of Evangelical Lutheran Churches.[21] The merger agreement between these branches of the Lutheran faith calls for investment of some significant portion of their pension funds in socially responsible endeavors. It will mark the first national commitment of church pension fund investments for all regions of the country.

The Lutheran commitment to housing grew out of an innovative program for downpayment assistance to first-time home buyers. It was sponsored by the Rocky Mountain Synod of the Lutheran Church in America, the Central District American Lutheran Church, and the Association of Evangelical Lutheran Churches. Each of the churches solicited their members as part of a social ministry program to loan $100 for at least a year to the church. Interest from the account is used to provide low-income families with a grant up to $1,800, or one-half of the required downpayment to buy homes.

In addition to the housing efforts of national churches, many hundreds of local churches and synagogues, unconnected to any national program, have used their own skills and resources to create affordable housing opportunities in their areas. Even with the limitations of small urban houses of worship, they have found ways of producing at least some needed dwelling units. With the almost epidemic size of homelessness, an immediate response to housing issues has been a priority in both low-income and gentrifying neighborhoods.

Religious institutions are located in every community in the country. People congregate to fulfill their spiritual needs, but also to express their best dreams of a just and good society. They certainly can and should be part of the building blocks that put our nation's housing policies back in order. Our national housing policy must continue to encourage the leadership of churches and synagogues, as they work to stabilize decaying neighborhoods and transform them into vibrant communities.

Just as the successes of Nehemiah, the McAuley Institute, and Habitat for Humanity lie not merely in the creation of some number of new affordable housing units, but in building new structures of influence for low-income communities, national policy should be oriented to community participation in the neighborhood revitalization decision-making process. National housing programs can give churches the tools to be leaders, making their involvement in housing issues important and essential to program development. When local communities have an authentic voice in federal/neighborhood programs, they will effectively use the financial and technical resources advocated in our proposals for a new housing policy.

LABOR AND AFFORDABLE HOUSING

Organized labor in America has a historic commitment to government policies that built and provided housing for poor and working people. The passage of the landmark housing bills of 1937 and 1948 would not have been possible if it were not for a labor-led housing coalition. But in more recent years, labor's role in housing programs has been generally limited to a small number of unions that have put together financing packages and experimented with methods that create jobs as well as affordable housing. Today unions are realizing that labor, again, can and must do more to build housing for its members, that labor can provide new sources of housing finance, can support traditional union housing concepts such as cooperatives and mutual housing associations, and can negotiate with employers for housing benefits.

Labor's concern with housing for its members and all working people originated with the housing cooperatives built by the Amalgamated Clothing and Textile Workers Union in the 1930s, and struggles for broader social programs during the Depression. During that time the textile workers and other unions sponsored thousands of cooperative units.

During the Depression, when thousands of people lost their jobs, they also lost their ability to pay the rent. With millions facing eviction, labor led the call to action. Affordable, decent shelter became a centerpiece of labor's political program.

The CIO established a labor housing committee that, along with the AFL, successfully lobbied for the passage of the first public housing act in 1937. Not only did organized labor support the legislation that created these policies, but it actively participated in the local, state, and federal programs that produced affordable housing. Much of the housing built by unions participating in these programs was unique, not only because it was organized as cooperatives, but because of a design that was sensitive to open space and public areas. Union housing included day care facilities for working women and other support services important to families with two breadwinners.

The CIO lobbied for a public housing construction program that would produce a million units a year for 10 years. Their political goal was for housing affordable for working people, not the housing of last resort that public housing has become today. They made the argument that it was government's obligation to provide housing for the nation, that housing was a right.

Following World War II, with housing availability getting tighter as the soldiers returned from Europe and Asia, unions invested large sums of money from pension and welfare funds and dues money in housing. Unions built substantial numbers of cooperatives and affordable apartment units. Labor played the role of catalyst, innovator, and initiator of many of our nation's low- and moderate-income housing programs.

Since the mid-1950s, however, most organized workers achieved the ability to live in a single-family suburban home and came to expect that their children would have housing better than their own. Organized labor's power to influence government decision-making on issues of concern to poor and working people, and its ability to bargain for substantial wage and benefit packages, propelled many working people into homeownership. It is also a testament to government policy that working Americans became middle-class, due in part to our nation's housing programs. FHA insurance and VA mortgages enabled millions of average working people to buy homes. And it has been the equity built up in the appreciation of working people's homes that has allowed them to borrow to send their children to college and pay for retirement and medical expenses as they age.

Clearly, the economic status of the young American worker is changing. In 1949, a 30-year-old earning an average salary could afford to buy the average-priced house with 14 percent of the paycheck. Today, monthly carrying costs on the average house costs nearly 50 percent of earnings. The fastest-growing sectors of our economy are minimum-wage and low-paying service jobs. For these workers, house prices and rents are increasingly unaffordable. Today it is not uncommon to find single working mothers living in shelters because they can afford no other places to live. With those changes in working people's economic circumstances, labor should once again put affordable housing at the top of its political and social agendas.

Unions in the 1960s and 1970s supported the establishment of non-profit housing programs such as the Section 202 Housing for the Elderly and Handicapped Program, FHA, and the Section 8 Existing and New Construction programs. Unions building and managing properties under these programs simply administered them in conformity with federal law. As with all other HUD-related programs, the past growth and present shrinkage in union housing activity directly correspond to HUD's budget.

Organized labor has begun to carve out a new housing agenda for itself. At the grassroots level individual unions and the AFL-CIO have developed responses on their own that build low-cost units and channel finance capital into working and poor people's housing. If these efforts could be expanded throughout the labor movement, they would have the potential for altering the housing production system in the country.

Construction trade unions have led the way for renewed labor involvement in the actual development of housing projects for working people. In Boston, the Bricklayers and Laborers Union has undertaken a demonstration project to show that union labor can build projects at an affordable price and at union-scale wages. In their first effort, the Bricklayers Union constructed 17 brick townhouses. The 1,200-square-foot, 2-bedroom units sold for $70,000 in a market where similar units sell for over $140,000.[22] By using the leverage of their pension fund investment with a local bank, the Bricklayers negotiated a below-market construction loan for the project. The union's pension fund placed $1.2 million in certificates of deposit earning between 6.5 and 7 percent. In return, the local bank made below market construction loans available for the project. The city contributed land, which was combined with state mortgage subsidies, rent subsidies, and linkage fees to cover basic infrastructure costs. The units will remain affordable in the long term because clauses in the deed limit appreciation on the units. Based on the success of the original 17 units, the union has begun construction of two additional projects providing more than 200 units. Union plans include a mixed-income project and sale of units to the Boston Housing Authority for use by low-income tenants.

Pension Funds

Labor union pension funds can provide new sources of capital for low- and moderate-income housing. In the United States today, total pension fund assets exceed $1 trillion, and are expected to double by the year 1990.[23] Pension funds invested in affordable housing programs could provide retirement plans with an acceptable return and long-term stability. Most pension funds have gone untapped due to struct requirements for high-yield returns and long-term financial stability. New investment models designed both by AFL-CIO unions and by state administrators of public employee pension funds offer realistic opportunities for this major new source of money to be brought into a national housing program.

The AFL-CIO Housing Investment Trust is a joint labor/management trust that makes FHA-insured loans, rental housing loans, and nursing home loans. The stipulation is that construction must be done with union labor. The trust is presently capitalized at about $154 million, and is open as an investment vehicle to any labor union pension fund. Although the growth of the investment trust had been slow, it has been growing steadily in recent years. The existence of over 450,000 private employee pension funds makes the potential investment pool by labor in housing quite significant.[24]

The construction trade unions have a pension fund investment program that invests in real estate projects that create jobs for their members. Many multi-employer pension funds have established investment financing foundations through which they finance housing

Table 18
Construction Foundations Across the Nation

No.	Year Formed	Name	Amount Invested* (millions of $)
1	1980	Development Foundation of Southern California	125
2	1980	Northern California Pension Investment Foundation	15
3	1980	Massachusetts Construction Industry Development Finance Foundation	12
4	1980	Syracuse Building Trades Investment Group	6
5	1981	Buffalo and Western New York Building Trades Investment Foundation	20
6	1982	Florida Affirmative Investment Roundtable (includes Palm Coast Affirmative Investment Roundtable)	20
7	1982	Pacific Northwest Construction Financing Forum	12
8	1983	Minnesota Construction Industry Foundation	30
9	1984	Tri-State Investment Foundation	0
10	Pending	Northwest Ohio Building and Construction Industry Foundation	—
11	Pending	Baton Rouge Building and Construction Industry Foundation	—

*Approximations provided by the foundations.
Source: AFL-CIO Industrial Union Department, *Labor and Investments* 5, no. 4 (1985).

developments in the local regions. Since 1980, over $230 million has been invested through nine regional foundations throughout the country.[25] (See Table 18.)

In another example of the creative use of union pension funds for housing, the Detroit Metropolitian AFL-CIO has initiated the first publicly traded real estate investment trust for unions. The Metropolitian Realty Corporation, established in conjunction with the city and local businesses, will be traded on the American Stock Exchange and securities will be marketed to private- and public-sector pension funds. The Metropolitian Realty Corporation will provide mortgage and equity financing in single- and multi-family homes; at least 50 percent will be in first mortgages. Seven of 18 Board members are union representatives, and all projects will be built by construction unions at prevailing wages. All housing projects will be located in the greater Detroit area, and fill the need for equity financing left by bank redlining of city neighborhoods.

The key to unlocking the large amount of capital contained in labor pension funds is meeting fiduciary responsibility established in the Employee Retirement Income Security Act of 1974 (ERISA). ERISA stipulates that pension funds must be invested prudently and for the sole benefit of plan participants and beneficiaries. Tradition-ally, investment in affordable housing has not qualified as an eligible ERISA investment. However, recent innovative approaches to pension fund use have enabled labor investment foundations established by the construction trades to move capital toward the housing sector. Also, public employee pensions funds in New York, Connecticut, and Hawaii have created such investment vehicles.[26] These new investment structures lower the risk to the pension funds, provide acceptable rates of return, and, at the same time, make housing loans available for moderate-income people.

The New York State AFL-CIO targeted $20 million in public and private pension fund assets into the rehabilitation of 350 vacant and abandoned city-owned properties in the Crown Heights neighborhood of Brooklyn.[27] The project, sponsored by Brooklyn Ecumenical Cooperatives, a partnership of labor, church, and government agencies, established a local church-based housing corporation that would receive and rehabilitate the vacant property. The purchase and rehabilitation loans were leveraged by a $20 million pension fund investment in certificates of deposit, issued by a local financial institution. The CDs give a market rate of return and are 100 percent guaranteed by the Federal Deposit Insurance Corporation (FDIC) up to $100,000 per plan participant, thus meeting all ERISA investment criteria. This linked pension agreement, similar to the Boston Bricklayers' program, meets the "prudent" pension investment rule. The banks, in turn, committed themselves to make construction and rehabilitation loans that financed the rehabilitation of structures. Similar leveraged models are being put in place by each of the regional trade union investment foundations.

States have begun to use the resources of their public employee retirement systems to supply mortgage money for affordable housing. While union pension funds make substantial investments in securities from the Government National Mortgage Association, only a few states have provided similar vehicles for public employee pension fund investment. While a majority of states still use private mortgage investment firms to invest their public employee retire-nent funds, five states—Connecticut, Hawaii, North Carolina, Colorado, and Michigan—have created their own state vehicles for pension investment in state housing opportunities.

Connecticut offers a Pooled Mortgage Investment Program (Yankee MAC) backed by home-mortgage pools.[28] The State of Connecticut, as sole purchaser of the pools, sets the terms and conditions of each mortgage and targets benefits. The State Treasurer, who is responsible for the administration of all state pension funds, invests the funds in state securities backed by these mortgage pools. To date, pension funds have earned an above-average return. Mortgages are targeted to pension fund participants, who also have priority for 5 percent and 10 percent downpayment mortgages. The teachers union, for example, which participates in the program, has been targeted to receive over 1,000 low-interest loans for its members in a recent offering.

The International Brotherhood of Teamsters has made retiree housing one of the union's major nationwide priorities, with affordable housing available for their retired members in projects located in Wisconsin and Michigan. The Teamsters Union is one of the few labor organizations that has directly used pension funds to build such housing for its membership and families.

New national housing programs need to be able to access the very large pools of pension fund capital for housing construction and mortgage loans. Changes in ERISA requirements that do not sacrifice essential protections for retirement income must be established along with important fiduciary guarantees. Public policy must make pension system investment in low- and moderate-income housing stock a prudent and productive investment for pension participants and the communities in which they live.

Housing and Jobs

Construction trades have also participated in creating employment opportunities and opening membership into well-paying trade unions for residents of low-income neighborhoods. The link between housing and jobs has always been an important community development tool. Workers can build housing, which they then can afford to buy or rent. In addition, wages circulate in the neighborhood, spurring increasing small business activity and in turn producing more jobs.

The Humboldt Construction Company in Chicago is an example

of a successful partnership between a community-based developer, a non-profit construction program, and a construction trade union It can be a model for national programs that relate the production of affordable housing to local jobs. The Humboldt Construction Company was established in 1981 to be the for-profit subsidiary of the Bickerdike Redevelopment Corporation (BRC), a non-profit, community-based, low-income housing developer.[29] Bickerdike was organized in 1967 by a local church/community coalition to address the low-cost housing shortage in a predominately hispanic neighborhood. BRC has built over 250 new and rehabilitated low-income units.

Humboldt helps BRC meet its housing goals by providing quality rehab construction workers for BRC and other area sponsors of low-income housing. A key aspect of the subsidiary is that it employs unemployed and underemployed local residents who have no other means of access to good jobs in the construction industry. In 1986, BRC and Humboldt signed an agreement with the Chicago-Northeast Illinois District Council of Carpenters, AFL-CIO, that enabled BRC/Humboldt employees to become union members. The agreement guarantees union wages, participation in the carpenters apprenticeship program, and neighborhood hiring of Humboldt employees.

The contract between a community-based low-income sponsor and a trade union can be a model for future agreements that produce both housing and jobs. Labor participation with community development corporations opens the door for direct improvement in the quality of life of low-income people.

Employee Benefits

Of the $20 billion that employers spend on housing benefits every year, relatively little goes to low- and middle-income workers, who encounter the greatest difficulty in buying a home or paying the rent. Yet one of the most pressing problems faced by these wage earners is finding a decent, affordable place to live near their jobs Recent studies in expanding economies such as San Francisco, Jersey City, and Boston demonstrate the pressure that the business demand for workers puts on the housing market.

Unions could play a major role in opening up corporate dollars for housing investment in low- and moderate-income units by including housing assistance demands as part of collective bargaining packages. Many urban governments have residency requirements for teachers, firefighters, police, and other public employees. As finding affordable housing in those cities becomes more difficult, public employee unions may be forced to look at what types of housing benefits could be appropriately negotiated.

The recent economic transition in the United States away from a manufacturing and toward a service economy also has had a dramatic effect on housing affordability for average wage workers. Especially in expanding regional economies, lower-wage service workers find escalating rents and home prices increasingly unaffordable. Higher housing costs have caused a decline in the real spendable wage of both organized and unorganized workers.

Service-sector jobs such as hospital and clerical jobs often cannot support rents or house payments in the regions in which they are located. A strategy for organizing these people by including housing demands can lead to a revitalized labor movement that directly improves the daily quality of life for low-income workers. It may be that employers and employees can reach common agreement that affordable housing near places of work is worth the investment of America's business community. The truly vast potential of defining housing assistance as an employee benefit could be tapped by workers during contract negotiations, or by community development corporations in search of new capital.

COMMUNITY DEVELOPMENT AND MUTUAL HOUSING ASSOCIATIONS

Mutual housing associations offer solutions to the housing affordability problem for moderate-income people who are not at the lowest end of the economic scale and so cannot qualify for public housing but, on the other hand, do not have enough money to buy their own homes.[30] Key aspects of all mutual housing programs include resident participation in the development and management of units, a large-scale ability to build and renovate large areas of deteriorated neighborhoods, and an emphasis on affordability for low- and moderate-income members.

A Mutual Housing Association is similar to a cooperative, except that membership is open to both individuals and organizations. Each mutual housing association member has one vote for electing a board of directors, which sets policy, controls finances, and oversees operations. This structure enables banks, housing authorities, and CDC to become part of a Mutual Association. They can lend resource and advice without taking control away from resident "owners."

Mutual Housing Associations can be an alternative to publi housing cooperative conversion because they combine the benefit of tenant management and ownership with continued housing au thority involvement and increased financial protection for the low cost housing stock. The structure of Mutual Housing Authorities al lows a flexible approach to control and ownership issues. Using thi model, housing authorities with a minority role on a Mutual Hous ing board of directors could lease public housing units to the Mutua Association, thereby retaining HUD subsidies but turning decision making over to tenants and a larger community of interest. Simila relationships could be included in MHA contracts, which could pre serve public money but guarantee local accountability for project op erations.

In Europe, West Germany, Sweden, and Denmark have bui housing that meets the needs of their populations using a simila cooperative association model. For over 100 years, a system of nor profit organizations linked into regional and national federations ha built and managed housing projects. This system is distinct fror public housing: it is run by the working and moderate-income mem bers. In those countries, national legislation regulates the functio and operations of the non-profit housing sector and addresses issue such as rent levels, maintenance, and occupancy rights. In Scand navian countries, 25 percent of all housing built after World War was developed by cooperative associations.[31] In West Germany housing enterprises between private industry and workers form partnerships with the government and community non-profit orga nizations such as Mutual Housing Associations. This non-profit se tor has the strong support of organizations representing the feder railway and the postal communication systems as well as industri and commercial enterprises and trade unions.

One of the first American demonstrations of the mutual housin concept is in Baltimore, Maryland.[32] The Mutual Housing Associa tion of Baltimore develops, owns, and manages low- and moderat income housing projects. Alameda Place, the Association's first de velopment, is a demonstration project, funded by HUD, based o the Western European model. As of 1987, the complex had 49 town houses, containing one-, two-, and three-bedroom units. The Balt more Neighborhood Housing Services and the Neighborhood Rei

estment Corporation provided financing. The Association controls
ffordable housing units and rents them to Association members.
he one-time membership fee is equal to about 5 percent of the unit
ost. Residents also pay a monthly fee that covers the cost of debt,
naintenance, and a fund for expansion of mutual housing. A resi-
ent owns an unrestricted right to live in the coop permanently.

The mutual housing approach to meeting our national housing
eeds requires the input of national financial resources and technical
upport as well as an integrated system of planning that truly does
orm new partnerships between employers and employees, tenants
nd housing authorities, non-profits and governments, and federal,
tate, and local government intervention in the housing market. The
nost appropriate role for the federal government is to help build but
ot to manage new housing projects. The central theme of such a
ommunity-based supply program is control of the affordable hous-
ng inventory by residents or responsible groups in the community.
n most cases, community control will take the form of tenant man-
gement or ownership of subsidized units, conversion to tenant co-
peratives of privately owned units, or individual homeownership.

defining characteristic of community supply is that the housing
mains affordable through restrictions that remove newly con-
ructed or renovated units from the often speculative urban real
tate market through deed restriction and other limitations on eq-
ty accumulation. Whether the affordable housing model is a land
nk, mutual housing association, or deed-restricted ownership unit,
rivate equity based on public capital investment ought to be limited
nd shielded from the market as the demand for land continues to
crease. Without such controls public investment for affordable
ousing will eventually be lost to either speculators or everyday
arket turnover.

FEDERAL NEIGHBORHOOD HOUSING PARTNERSHIP

hatever else a new national housing policy must do, it must build
n and enhance the energies of neighborhood groups, religious or-
nizations, and labor unions who have energized much housing
dvocacy and spearheaded new movements for housing equity and
stice. A new National Housing Investment Corporation could be a
orking, an equity-sharing, and a risk-sharing partner with these
cal non-profit development entities.

A national Old Buildings, New Communities Act, to coventur the production of affordable apartments via the conversion and re habilitation of empty buildings, should also be enacted and properl funded. The act could provide local community organizations witl the funds and technical assistance they require to preserve neede new housing and neighborhood stores and businesses. This bill woul differ substantially from existing rental rehabilitation programs in thre ways: by emphasizing a partnership with non-profit communit groups, labor unions, and church-based development groups; b concentrating on empty and abandoned buildings so as to eliminat displacement effects; and by encouraging mixed-use projects to in clude viable neighborhood stores and service businesses. This par nership between the federal government and local development en tities could be a catalyst for the rebirth of many urban neighborhoods

A national network of well-funded and technically competen community development corporations could provide the essentia institutional framework for bringing low-income housing and sma business revitalization back into local communities. Evolving out c the original self-help labor movements of the Depression, the Grea Society initiatives of the 1960s, and the historic church regard fc healthy and decent neighborhoods, community-based housing in tiatives can effectively provide an appropriate flow of affordabl housing in a manner responsive to the needs of working and poc people and in cooperation with both government and the privat sector. A new national housing policy ought not let a vibrant an growing community development sector drift out on its own—prc ducing a patchwork of small programs in response to immediate lc cal housing crises. Rather, the energies of community organizatior need to be focused and coordinated by a policy that understand and supports the local non-profit sector.

In Europe and Japan, a regulated non-profit sector produced an now maintains thousands of low- and moderate-income units. Thos countries have used this sector to "build to housing need" by pu ting together vital government, business, labor, and church con munity-based housing organizations. A new housing policy fc America should learn from these examples and create these housin partnerships as a substantial element in its affordable housing prc duction and maintenance program. For such partnerships to be oj timally capable of improving communities, however, they need i be based on a value system consistent with local concerns. In effe tive partnerships each participant needs to come to the table as valued, respected contributor. It is thus important for the federal government to realize that community residents organize not exclusively for new bricks and mortar but also for self-respect, community power, and the opportunity for a better future. They organize to improve whole "communities," not only to produce shelter.

9

Housing for Rural America

Many of the programs identified in this book as central to a new housing policy for America have been implemented by states such as Massachusetts, Connecticut, New Jersey, New York, California, and Florida. Although the latter three states have large rural populations, all these states are principally urban or suburban in character, and most of the political and legislative impetus for the programs cited has come from urban or suburban constituencies. As the Urban and Rural Poverty Committee reports, "The dynamics of housing deprivation in rural communities are often counter to those in urban settings."[1] We therefore believe it necessary to consider whether our policy recommendations adequately address rural needs.

RURAL NEEDS

One 1980 census definition of rural America is that of communities of fewer than 10,000 persons outside of defined urban areas. In 1980, nearly one-third (32.6 percent) of the U.S. population lived in such areas; 31.1 percent of the nation's occupied year-round housing stock is located in these communities. The census reveals that the housing needs of these Americans are great. A disproportionately large number of rural Americans live in substandard housing: 43.7 percent of all substandard units are located in rural communities. More than 2 million units in Farmers Home Administration service areas have

een classified as substandard.[2] However, this classification only de-
otes that a unit lacks complete plumbing or is overcrowded; other
eficiencies abound in rural housing. There are 6.2 million units that
ıck adequate heating systems and 813,000 units that lack complete
itchens, none of which were necessarily counted.[3]

Along with the problem of housing quality is the problem of
ost. Rural housing costs less to purchase, but rural incomes are
ɔwer also. As a result, 26.8 percent of all rural residents live in units
ıat are either substandard or cost-burdened.[4] During the 1970s,
vercrowding in rural housing increased, rising from 269,000 to
93,000 overcrowded units, while, during the same period, over-
ːrowding declined in urbanized America.[5]

Rural homelessness exists too, though it is less apparent than in
ıe cities. Some homelessness goes unnoticed: rural families and in-
ividuals live in public campsites, rest stops, shacks, or trailers that
ːrban building codes would forbid. Other homeless are hidden be-
ind the doors of friends and extended families, still an important
art of the social fabric in many rural areas. These "doubled-up"
ımilies contribute, not to the homelessness statistics, but rather to
ıe overcrowding statistics. Though few good surveys on rural
ɔmelessness exist, one done in California counties found some ru-
ıl counties to have as many as 2,500 homeless persons each.[6] Of
ɔurse, many rural homeless migrate to the cities, compounding the
rban problem.

The shortage of affordable, standard rental housing is a problem
ı rural America, too. Although the 1983 *Annual Housing Survey* re-
ɔrts marginally higher rural than urban rental vacancy rates (6.6
ercent and 5.7 percent respectively), the availability of rural rental
ɔusing is overstated due to the relatively poor quality of many of
ıose units. For example, 10 percent of vacant rural units lacked
ɔmplete plumbing for personal use, as opposed to 3.7 percent in
ıetropolitan areas. Further, in urban environments the lack of com-
lete plumbing for personal use may often mean that facilities are
vailable in a common area. In rural environments, it is more likely
ıat the unit is detached and lacks a complete bathroom. Fully 16
ercent of all vacant, year-round housing units in rural America lack
complete bathroom.[7]

Because so many units lack modern conveniences, it is new home
ɔnstruction, even more than also-needed rehabilitation, that must
e our national housing priority for rural America. A 1986 Congres-
ɔnal Research Service study projects that only 550,000 units will be

built in non-metropolitan areas by 1990, or more than 375,000 units short of the number needed to meet the growing demand.[8]

THE FARMERS HOME ADMINISTRATION

The heart of the federal rural housing program is the Department of Agriculture's Farmers Home Administration (FmHA). Like the fiscally larger HUD programs, the FmHA budget has been dramatically slashed during the last seven years. FmHA budgets have been reduced by nearly 50 percent, from $4.286 billion to $2.243 billion.[9] Of special importance within FmHA is the single-family subsidized mortgage program, the Section 502 program, and the Rural Rental Housing program for low-income renters, the Section 515 program.

The 502 program provides subsidized federal mortgage financing that can be lent at rates as low as 1 percent for a term of 3½ years. The number of such loans fell from 64,264 in 1979 to 25,479 in 1986.[10] The average family income served by the 502 program is estimated to be only about $12,938.[11]

In 1979, the construction of Section 515 units peaked with the production of 38,740 units. Since that time production has trailed off to only 21,252 in 1986.[12] As discussed previously, the need for standard rental units is critical in rural areas, particularly for the very low-income population served by the 515 program. A 1986 survey estimates that the average family served by the 515 program has an annual income of $8,265.[13]

Despite the continuing need, the federal government has walked away from FmHA, just as it has from HUD. The budget cuts that FmHA has endured come at a particularly bad time for rural America; for, whereas many urbanized areas of the nation are enjoying economic growth, rural America, beset by farm foreclosures and oil, gas, and coal production declines, is facing economic hardship not known since the Great Depression.

The FmHA network, localized as it is, is uniquely positioned to be the local arm of a rejuvenated federal partnership with state, local, and private-sector housing providers. It is imperative that an agency so experienced and so accessible to its rural clientele continue to exist. The program that we advocate is national in scope. It supplements many existing HUD and FmHA programs. However, we are aware that not every program that we advocate works as well in rural as in urban areas. Therefore, we see a continuing need for 'mHA programs, in addition to fair rural allocations from our new programs.

MORTGAGE BUYDOWNS AND DOWNPAYMENT ASSISTANCE

As indicated above, there are more than 2 million substandard homes n rural America. To address part of this problem, new single-family housing will be required. For low-income families, the Section 502 homeownership program has been the key to affording new homes. Under Section 502, the federal government lends the entire mortgage needed to purchase the house at rates varying between 2 percent and 9 percent for a 33-year term.

The program is an important one, but for a government so deep in debt that must go to the capital markets to obtain the principal that will be lent, we believe that the 502 program is needlessly expensive and inefficient. Instead, we would propose that borrowers who would otherwise receive 502 loans at rates between 9 percent and 6 percent be served by the national mortgage buydown program.

Although the buydown program is a grant program, as opposed to the lent 502 funds, the funds needed to create equivalent levels of housing affordability require far less government borrowing than the existing 502 program. For example, if the federal government borrows $70,000 for 30 years at 9 percent, the principal and interest paid on the loan during the full term of the loan will total $202,860. A 502 borrower, receiving a $70,000 mortgage for 30 years at 6 percent will pay, during the term of the loan, $151,088 in principal and interest charges. The difference between these two sums, $51,772, is paid by the taxpayers. But a $70,000 mortgage with an interest buydown from 9 percent to 6 percent requires a grant of only $11,200. Thus, the federal expenditure required for an equivalent buydown program is $40,572 less than the current 502 program.

From an annual national mortgage interest-rate buydown program of 110,000 mortgages, rural areas could expect to receive between 25,000 and 30,000 mortgages. In 1986 FmHA only made 25,475 mortgages under the 502 program.

We would advocate that funds saved from not writing 6–9 percent loans be retained by the 502 program for writing additional mortgages below 6 percent for very-low-income homebuyers. A national mortgage interest buydown program would double the size of

rural subsidized single-family mortgage programs (based on 198[
funding levels) without adding any additional funds to the FmH,
budget.

Downpayment assistance programs seem to be more difficult t
implement in rural America. Although young rural families have di
ficulty accruing downpayments, it is less clear that the program
that we advocate would work well in rural areas. Of the two na
tional downpayment assistance programs that we advocate, lease
purchase would seem to work the best, though there are formidabl
obstacles. Lease/purchase, as developed in New Jersey, usually re
quires a municipal government to issue short-term project financin
that will pay for the development of the units. In rural areas, loca
governments may not have this financing capacity, and a state agenc
would have to assume this role instead. Second, during the leas
period an entity is needed to manage the units. Typically a nor
profit local development corporation manages a project, though othe
entities are conceivable. Finding a qualified management entity i
some rural areas may prove difficult. Finally, lease/purchase projec
are usually built as subdivisions. Land on which the subdivision
built is usually provided by a municipal or non-profit entity. Asid
from the questions of land acquisition and buyer interest in living i
small subdivisions is the cost of infrastructure improvements that
subdivision would require, such as road, water, and sewer service

It is unclear whether very much lease/purchase housing coul
be implemented on a scattered-site basis. Acquiring land in nume
ous areas could be difficult and so would managing scattered prop
erties during the lease period. Developing properties a few at a tim
poses other problems concerning the repayment of the short-ter
debt if the lease purchasers do not purchase the property at the en
of the lease period. There are also short- and long-term financin
efficiencies lost with small debt issues. Additional research must b
done to test the feasibility of lease/purchase housing in rural areas

Expanding homeownership opportunities through the propose
National Housing Investment Corporation (NHIC) could also prov
difficult in rural areas. The NHIC's purpose is to make joint dow
payments with home purchasers in order to lower monthly mor
gage payment costs to acceptable underwriting levels. The NHI
would expect a balloon repayment of its loan, with interest, at th
end of six years. For some, loan repayment would be possible fro
increased personal savings resulting from job promotions or a spous
returning to the job market. However, in an economy of job scarci

ıd vagaries of international agricultural and energy prices, rising
mily income is not a sure thing. Alternatively, the NHIC debt could
ɛ repaid by refinancing the home to recapture the market appreci-
ion during the six years of the NHIC loan. However, housing val-
ɛs have actually declined in some rural areas, and it is conceivable
ʌat, unlike most urbanized areas, there may be no appreciation to
·capture for repaying the NHIC.

If a homeowner could not repay an NHIC loan, the homeowner
ould have the option of making the NHIC a permanent partner in
ıe ownership of the home, until such time as the home is sold or
ıanges title. At that time the NHIC would receive both its loan and
portion of the value of the home. Whether families would enter
to NHIC agreements in economies where there was a high risk
ıat the federal government would become a permanent partner in
ıeir home purchase is unclear. The conversion of NHIC loans into
ɛrmanent interests in homes would also slow the relending of NHIC
ınds to the next generation of families.

In summary, many rural areas lack the strong local partners and
ʀong market forces that would enable lease/purchase and NHIC
·ograms to work at optimal levels. Nonetheless there certainly are
·me areas where these programs could successfully function. Di-
ct assistance to home buyers as offered by a national interest buy-
ʃwn program would be valuable to rural families in all areas since
requires neither public partners nor favorable market forces.

ɛNTAL HOUSING

ıe need for standard, affordable rental housing for low- and mod-
ate-income families in rural areas is great and increasing. In re-
·onse to this need, Congress created the Section 515 program in
63. Prior to 1980, the 515 program financed 192,000 low- and mod-
ate-income units costing more than $3.3 billion.[14] As with the HUD
·ction 236 and 221(d)(3) programs, these pre-1980 515 units are in-
ɛasingly subject to prepayment of their mortgages and the conver-
ɔn to market-rate rent. A few thousand 515 units have been con-
rted already; nearly all the 400,000 units in the 515 program will
subject to conversion by the year 2005. Like low-income urban
ıd suburban tenants, current rural tenants need to be protected
rough the issuance of Section 8 Certificates that will enable them
continue living in these units if they are converted. Congress should

also create refinancing or tax incentives to keep this valuable n
tional resource available for low- and moderate-income tenants.

It may be necessary to issue Section 8 Certificates or adopt ne
incentives to retain the old housing stock, but this kind of stop-ga
is not the basis for a new housing policy. Public housing, whic
permanently adds to the available low-income housing stock, h
been successful in rural areas. Rural areas need to receive a fair sha
of a rejuvenated national public housing program.

Rural public housing authorities can be successful managers
projects, but too often HUD policy has been to ignore rural housir
authorities until there is a local crisis and then suspend the authori
for mismanaging a project (a particularly prevalent practice with I
dian Housing Authorities). HUD must be forced by national con
mitment from the Secretary's office to cooperate with rural publ
housing authorities. Procedures and paperwork must also be r
duced or simplified by HUD for rural authorities, who often ha
limited capacity to process paperwork that, while arguably nece
sary in urban settings, is less vital in rural areas.

In addition to a rejuvenated public housing program, rur
America also needs a community-based supply program. This pr
gram, with its front-end construction subsidies, would be financ
by a matching federal and state housing trust fund program. W
envision a program capable of assisting in the construction of 300,0
low- and moderate-income rental units annually. Projects would
developed by state, municipal, non-profit, and, in some circur
stances, employer entities. Because the units would be publicly hel
or owned by corporations specifically created to develop moderat
cost housing, the units would not be subject to the market forc
that have encouraged the owners of Section 515 units to conve
these units to market-rate rentals. Rural areas of the nation wou
participate in the federal/state-financed community-based supp
program. It is likely that 75,000 low- and moderate-income ren
units would be built in rural areas annually.

EMPLOYER-ASSISTED HOUSING

Finally, there is the question of whether employers can be a partn
in addressing rural low- and moderate-income homeownership a
rental needs. Certainly opportunities for employers to provide fina
cial assistance will be fewer in rural areas than in urbanized are

because there are fewer large employers with the financial capacity and sophistication to administer such programs. With rural employer-assisted housing there is also the potential that a major employer in a small community could experience financial difficulty that would result in personnel layoffs. Layoffs at a large employer in a small community are always devastating to the community, but in a community where the employer also owns much of the housing stock the situation could be a replay of our company town history.

We therefore believe that employer-assisted housing should only develop in rural communities when the employer is a large national or international firm, but is a relatively small employer in the particular local labor market. In this way the firm would have the financial and technical capacity to assist the employee, but the community would be somewhat protected should the firm close its rural facility. This principal would hold true for rental housing as well as home-ownership.

In the case of rental housing, an employer could not generally have an employee/employer housing development corporation, as there would be too few employees. Instead, an employer and employees should work with local non-profit organizations to form a local housing development corporation to codevelop and manage the project. With these provisions, rural communities, too, can forge new housing partnerships with employers.

HOUSING FOR RURAL AMERICA

Building a strong federal partnership with the states and various private sectors may be more difficult in rural areas than in urbanized ones, but strong partnerships are no less necessary. We believe that the housing needs of rural Americans have been neglected and that our program reverses that neglect.

10

Recapturing the American Dream: A Call to Action

Shelter is so basic a human need, so central to the well-being of individuals and whole societies, that governments all over the world have accepted some affirmative role in helping people meet their housing needs. Our federal government has accepted such a role for more than a century.[1]

In the 1980s, however, America's housing policies are simply not working: homeownership is declining all across the country, especially among young families and first-time home buyers,[2] homelessness afflicts millions and is increasing rapidly,[3] a growing majority of America's 30 million tenants live in substandard, overcrowded, or cost-burdened apartments,[4] the physical condition of the housing stock is deteriorating,[5] and low-income families face a severe and worsening shortage of affordable housing in every state of the Union.[6]

Recent national housing policies have caused, failed to prevent, ignored, or tolerated these negative trends in the 1980s. They hold no promise of meeting the housing needs of the 1990s. The huge cuts in federal expenditures that have been the dominant feature of national housing policies in the 1980s will not help our fastest-growing population sectors obtain appropriate shelter in the coming decade.

In the 1990s, we will experience large and rapid increases in the number and population percentage of the frail elderly, young families in their prime first-home-buying years, single persons living alone,

ingle-parent, female-headed households, and poor people, living
nostly in central cities.[7] Each of these demographic groupings will
ave housing needs not matched by our present housing stock. Each
vill have lower than average incomes and lower than average sav-
ngs. They will confront a housing market producing ever more costly
welling units—in sizes, locations, and layouts poorly suited to their
fe needs and pocketbooks. Present national policies, amounting to
ear abandonment of a federal role in housing, will do little or noth-
ng to help them.

Present policy has not worked in the 1980s. Continuation of that
olicy will not work in the 1990s. America needs a new national
ousing policy.

A New Housing Policy for America Restated

n preceding chapters, we have suggested a new housing policy for
merica, advancing a largely self-financing, 10-point plan. Let us
riefly summarize the plan here.

To expand homeownership opportunities, especially for young
amilies and first-time home buyers, we advocate a federal down-
ayment assistance loan program, a lease/purchase home buying
rogram, a mortgage interest rate buydown fund, and tax incentives
or employer-assisted homeownership plans. We recommend that
ome of these programs be administered by a new National Housing
nvestment Corporation, an entity authorized to make coinvestment
nortgage loans and develop a shared-equity mortgage instrument
nd secondary mortgage market for these new mortgages to create
 secondary market for such loans. By making a secondary market
n shared equity mortgages, the new corporation would encourage
nore banks and companies to offer such loans, bringing to bear the
ower of major private-sector financial entities to produce and main-
ain affordable homes. The National Housing Investment Corpora-
on would also coventure housing development activities with em-
loyers, labor unions, community groups, and religiously oriented
on-profit organizations—and could do so on a deferred, shared-
ppreciation basis so that these organizations could acquire com-
lete ownership over time. Like the Federal Housing Administra-
on, the Federal National Mortgage Association, and the Govern-
nent National Mortgage Association, this new corporation would be
 self-supporting entity—indeed should earn a modest public-sector

profit once loan repayments begin. We believe the new corporatio
would be powerful enough to do the job it is intended for, lea
enough to do that job efficiently, modern enough to do the job i
joint venture with the private sector, and responsive enough to giv
citizens, local elected officials, and community groups a real role i
the process.

We also advocate federal restoration of tax-free bonding author
ity to the states, now scheduled to terminate in 1988, so that stat
governments can continue to stimulate homeownership in America

To enhance the supply and affordability of rental housing, w
propose a new apartment construction subsidy program funded o
a pay-as-you-go basis via a Federal Housing Trust Fund. This pro
gram would differ dramatically from existing federal rental pro
grams. First, it would not contract for apartments to be built b
investors who will want to withdraw the units from low-income us
after a term of years in order to maximize profit by going to marke
rents, but rather it would coventure the units with community-base
non-profit organizations whose purpose is to maintain the units fo
low-income tenants. Second, our program features a simple and ef
ficient one-time, up-front development or financing subsidy, alread
in effect in several states, rather than continuing rent subsidies. Third
the funding source (a Federal Housing Trust Fund) is a permanent
annually self-replenishing account, dedicated to this one purpose
Fourth, our proposed program is highly leveraged, attaining match
ing funds from the states and local governments and offering thes
governments a real inducement to expand their housing activities i
a targeted fashion. We also suggest reauthorization of existing low
income tax credits, some improvements in those credits and restc
ration of some recently eliminated tax incentives for the private sec
tor to build affordable rental units.

Our proposed policy also helps the frail elderly. Most senior ci
izens today have substantial equity with which to pay for the reha
bilitation of their homes to meet their changing life needs (i.e., t
cope with frailties) if only they could access that equity safely, eas
ily, and inexpensively. We suggest a national home equity access o
reverse mortgage program. For frail elderly and handicapped per
sons of lower income who need specialized facilities or services i
order to stay out of nursing homes, we propose a governmental as
sistance program that, once capitalized, would continue to be funde
from a recapture of taxes paid as a direct result of the initial subsidy
This is doubly cost-effective, as well as compassionate, because

aves the substantial cost of needless nursing home care and re-
uires only startup funding.

The housing production programs mentioned above are also part
f our proposed homelessness prevention effort because the key to
reventing and curing homelessness in America *is* affordable hous-
1g. But we also suggest a targeted crisis intervention program to
elp those facing imminent eviction or foreclosure due to temporary
)ss of income beyond their control.

In our housing production programs, we emphasize the inclu-
ion of shared housing, housing plus services, and purchase/reha-
ilitation/subdivision of larger homes—all programs useful to work-
1g female heads of households, whose numbers have skyrocketed
1 America and are expected to rise rapidly again in the 1990s. We
lso emphasize some single-room-occupancy construction for lower-
1come single persons, a fast-growing group and one that is dispro-
ortionately vulnerable and homeless.

Last, but certainly not least, we submit that the federal govern-
1ent should recommit itself to a decent, expansive public housing
olicy. We should fully fund the upkeep of existing public housing
nits, for we do not want the federal government to be or to become
ur nation's worst slumlord. We should constrain efforts at privati-
ation so that we continue to have an affordable low-income hous-
1g stock for the very poor, and we should fund the construction
nd upkeep of needed new public housing units—at least when and
/here local communities stand ready to welcome and support them.
)ur proposed housing policy includes new construction or substan-
al rehabilitation of 40,000 public housing units annually.

; A NEW HOUSING POLICY ACHIEVABLE?

he processes by which national public policy is adopted are ulti-
1ately, of course, political. To be achievable, therefore, any pro-
osed new housing policy must not only be capable of getting built
1e housing our nation needs today and will need in the 1990s, but
1ust also be consistent with (indeed must contribute to) the Amer-
an political consensus emerging in the late 1980s.

More specifically, an achievable housing policy must have the
)llowing four characteristics. Initially, it must be fair, offering hous-
1g opportunities to all America, rather than appealing to the special
1terests of any one region, social class, or age group. The policy

should advance broadly shared benefits, targeted to need, attained
at broadly borne and affordable costs, based on ability to pay.

Second, a new housing policy must be one that is welcomed,
even shaped, certainly not resisted, by those who will be asked or
required to implement it, including state officials, shelter industries,
local governments, and community groups. These key groups must
be coventurers, not junior or silent partners, in a new national housing policy.

Third, a housing policy for the 1990s must be perceived to be
genuinely new. Incremental tinkering with the failed policies of the
past will not solve the housing problems of the future. Tiny modifications of present policy will not mobilize needed public support.

Finally, a new housing policy for America must be responsive
to several national political imperatives: presidents, presidential candidates, and federal legislators simply will not subordinate their view
of the national interest or sacrifice their electibility in pursuit of a
new housing policy. We can and should ask our leaders to broaden
the American political agenda and to stretch the American political
consensus, but we should do so in terms acceptable, indeed appealing, to political leaders.

Let us apply these four criteria of achievability to the new housing policy for America proposed above.

A Fair Housing Policy

We have endeavored to craft a housing policy for all America, not
just for any one age group or social class or region or type of community. Young families and older Americans are both benefited by
this policy—the young primarily to acquire homeownership, the elderly primarily to retain and rehabilitate the homes they already own.
And this mutuality of benefit is as it should be, for we are a multigenerational society and would be morally diminished and politically destabilized by any policy that pitted young against old.

Similarly, our policy seeks to treat all the social and economic
classes in our country fairly: we would target very considerable resources to the real and pressing housing needs of the poor but refuse to isolate lower-income Americans politically by ignoring the
equally real and legitimate housing needs of working-class people
and young families aspiring to middle-class status. We need a housing policy, not a disguised incomes policy, for America. A compre-

1ensive housing policy, one that is politically attainable and sustain-
1ble in this country, must recognize that homeownership assistance
oans for young middle- and working-class families and policies
stimulating the creation of suitable dwelling units for middle-class
frail elderly persons are complementary to, and compatible with, assistance programs for low- and moderate-income households. It is a
political wasteland, not the moral high ground, to which we have
been led by current policies which give huge tax subsidies to the
housing of the rich, paltry cash subsidies for the rents of a very few
of the very poor, and nothing for the housing needs of most people
in between.

Our policy also offers even-handed benefits for business and labor. In Chapter 1, we estimated that the housing construction to be
stimulated via the proposed policies would generate perhaps $.5 tril-
lion in private-sector economic activity in the 1990s. Those policies
include a counterrecessionary interest-rate buydown fund and strong
supply-side (i.e., less inflationary) economic stimulants, programs
that were called for by the shelter industries during the recession of
the early 1980s and that many are predicting will be much needed
in the 1990s. For workers and trade unionists, the proposed policy
would mean millions of new jobs, most of them good jobs, in a wide
variety of industries, trades, crafts, and professions. Our policies ask
workers to give up none of the wage and safety benefits in existing
federal housing construction laws.

These proposals are also both urban-targeted and rurally responsive. We know that much of America is in real danger of becoming two separate and distinct economies—one suburban, affluent and booming, the other urban and rural, poor and declining.
That is a deplorable, intolerable condition. Our housing policy must
and will encourage substantial, appropriate housing opportunities in
the suburbs and will seek fairly to apportion the societal costs of
low-income housing among all communities. But it must target needed
housing resources and resulting economic development benefits to
the areas of greatest housing need, our cities and rural areas. Targeting resources to need is an essential element of fairness.

No American subpopulation is more in need of housing help
than single women and their children. The policies we propose would
recognize, for the first time, federal responsibility to address the
housing-plus-service needs of these families—providing programs for
housesharing, for the purchase/rehabilitation/conversion of larger
homes, and for child care and related services in housing complexes

reserved for the use of such families. We also emphasize strength
ening anti-discrimination laws and the enforcement of fair housing
statutes. Building appropriate and needed housing units, only to have
access to them denied to minorities and women, is no housing policy for America.

If the benefits of our proposed housing policy are to be broadly
shared, so too are the costs. A fair housing policy, we believe, must
include fair taxation to pay for the housing created. Our proposals
include deriving some of the tax revenues to be spent for housing
programs from taxes paid on newly subsidized units; we advocate,
in other words, a revolving tax recapture program, expending on
housing primarily the tax revenues that would never have come into
the federal Treasury but for the new housing subsidies. We also suggest a Federal Housing Trust Fund to be capitalized by a small tax
on a certain class of mortgage-backed securities, a product that has
already received substantial federal encouragement and whose issuers have unusually great ability to pay the tax.

But most of the revenues needed for our proposed policies are
derived from those people who actually receive the housing benefits. Our various homeownership programs are, basically, loan programs. The young families enabled to purchase an existing home via
a downpayment assistance loan or to occupy a starter home via a
federal coinvestment mortgage are required to pay back the federal
Treasury, with interest, over the years. Our proposed home equity
program by which older Americans can rehabilitate their homes to
cope with frailties or the changing physical needs associated with
aging merely allows senior citizens to use their own money in a safe
and easier manner, it is a self-financing program with several prudent payback features. The shared equity features in some of our
proposed programs, which will allow many lower-income families
to achieve homeownership and many single-parent households to
purchase and convert larger homes, is basically a deferred payback
loan, collateralized by the home itself, which properly utilizes the
future appreciation in value of our housing stock to help people who
need housing now to get it now while ensuring payback to the government. In each case, the people who live in the housing are providing the vast preponderance of the revenues needed to get the
housing built or make it affordable.

Housing user-fees for those who can afford it and progressive
taxation on those who have enjoyed economic benefit from specific

federal housing subsidies to defray housing costs for those who cannot afford fully amortizing user-fees—we think that is broadly borne cost-sharing, a fair revenue plan for a fair housing policy.

A Housing Policy Supported and Shaped by Those Asked to Implement it

Like virtually all other current discussions of federal housing policy, our proposals presuppose that:

- state and local spending on housing will be enhanced in the 1990s;
- a good portion of the administration of new federal programs will fall to (or on) the states, local governments, and community-based non-profit corporations;
- much of the construction, financing, and sale of new housing will continue to be done by the extant shelter industries (home builders, bankers, mortgage bankers, and realtors).

These assumptions seem to imply that the success and achievability of any proposed new housing policy for America will depend, in significant measure, on the support (and support-mobilizing activity) of state and local officials, community activists, and grassroots shelter industry representatives. These people are unlikely to participate in, pay for, or properly implement efforts not consistent with their values, experiences, and interests.

For these reasons, we have sought to design our proposed housing policy so as to be highly consonant with the concerns and capacities of those who will be asked to implement it. The policy is largely derived from state-level initiatives undertaken in the 1980s. These are programs that governors, state legislators, and mayors have already worked with and endorsed through their national organizations.

Downpayment assistance loans, lease/purchase homeownership plans, shared coinvestment or equity mortgages, reverse mortgage programs, homelessness prevention initiatives—all these recommended features of a new national housing policy were invented by the states. State governments have the capacity to administer these programs now. The wide variety of programs contained in our proposed policy allows states to emphasize those problems and those solutions most appropriate to their perceived needs.

While providing substantial flexibility, the proposed policy does direct the attention and activity of state and local officials to some specific problems and some specific solutions to those problems. This policy is not just another block grant in which the federal government throws out a relatively small amount of money and says to the states, in effect: "Here it is. Match it and do whatever you think best with it."

A small joint checking account is not a satisfactory housing policy for America: no amount of rhetoric about "leveraging federal money" or "challenging the states" will make it satisfactory. Some state governments have proved that they are willing to invest substantial amounts of their own tax revenues for housing; others have yet to do much. A federal matching grant program for state housing initiatives could be a valuable tool to encourage state activity. But the real enticement for greater state spending will come from a complete federal housing policy—one that directly promotes homeownership, rental production, rehabilitation of substandard units, and the prevention of homelessness.

That policy must also warrant and enjoy the support of the neighborhood groups, religious organizations, labor unions, and nonprofit housing corporations that have proliferated across America, contributing magnificently to the building of community and to the stability of neighborhoods at the local level. The national housing policy we seek must work with, not against, those who are so willing to work at community-building.

A new National Housing Investment Corporation could be a working partner, an equity partner, a risk-sharing partner, with local non-profit corporations and agencies. It would grant local organizations the funds and technical assistance they require to preserve existing housing units and to develop needed new housing. Whatever else a new national housing policy must do, it must build on and enhance the energies of neighborhood groups and religious organizations and labor unions who want not only to build needed new housing but to preserve that housing for the use of low-income Americans. Our community-based supply program for rental housing seeks to do just that.

And America's housing policy must also be responsive to the shelter industries. Builders, bankers, realtors, home remodelers, and

other sectors of the shelter industry have made crucial, historic contributions to housing the American people. The housing policy
America is searching for must be responsive to the needs of, and
trends in, the shelter industries because the shelter industries will
have a major role in building support for any such policy. Our proposals for an interest-rate buydown fund, a downpayment assistance loan fund, a secondary market for shared equity loans, and a
senior citizens reverse mortgage program are all initiatives on which
we have worked together with major organizations and institutions
in the shelter industries. These programs have already drawn favorable comment from national and grassroots shelter industry leaders.

Drawing upon and working with the ideas and initiatives of state
and local governments, church and union groups, non-profit and
for-profit organizations—we think that is a cooperative housing policy for America.

An Authentically New Housing Policy

There are times in American public life when the most achievable
policy proposals seem to be those that are tiny modifications of previous programs, small incremental changes in existing policies. When
things appear to be going well enough it seems wise to leave well
enough alone, to fix only that which is demonstrably broken. At
such times, public officials can and do practice conflict avoidance
and conflict minimization, processes favoring few and small changes
in policy.

America's housing conditions today, however, are not nearly well
enough. The American people have seen the suffering of the homeless, if only on TV, and want it ended. They know that they (or their
children) cannot buy a home and that they (or their parents) might
need help to live in the one they own. Recent political surveys in
every region of the country show a large percentage of voters to be
concerned about these issues.

These concerns, these problems, will not yield to tired or timid
solutions. To deal with them effectively, even to persuade people
that we mean to deal with them effectively, requires us to think and
act with expansive responsibility. The 1990s will be a period of great
challenge, even crisis, for our national government on many policy

issues, including housing. Such periods are, inevitably and properly, eras of innovation. The times, and our present and future housing needs, call upon us to dream larger dreams, not merely to tinker with existing programs or to offer minor adjustments to major policy failures.

This is important because something very significant, very precious, has been broken and now needs fixing: trust. Federal housing policy in the 1980s has been a string of broken promises. In our time, America has not pursued the national goal of previous federal housing acts (a decent home in a suitable living environment for all Americans); rather our government has repeatedly retreated and receded from that goal.

We believe that only an authentically new housing policy targeted to the needs of the 1990s, a policy at once bold and prudent, is capable of restoring the trust that has been broken. Restoring some of the reduced or rescinded federal funding for housing programs would be useful but, alone, that is certainly not an authentically new housing policy. Federal support for some new national housing demonstration projects might be useful, but that too is not a genuinely new housing policy. Getting the states to spend more money on housing and/or encouraging the development and use of new building technologies—these, too could be useful but these too, alone, do not constitute the bold but prudent new policy we need.

A genuinely new housing policy would be one that recognizes the new diversity of America's families, the fact that America's families are changing and that their housing needs are changing rapidly and will continue changing in the 1990s. It would be a policy that overcomes the various barriers that real families are experiencing in meeting their housing needs. Ozzie and Harriet might have needed only federal mortgage insurance to buy their home; their grandchildren need downpayment assistance to attain homeownership.

The key problem our new housing policy must confront is that America's families are changing dramatically but our housing stock and housing finance systems are not changing fast enough to meet their needs. Thirty years ago, more than half of America's families looked like Ozzie and Harriet (father working outside the home, mother primarily occupied as a homemaker); today, fewer than one in five families fit that traditional pattern. We built tens of millions of large suburban houses to meet the life needs of yesterday's families. The houses we are building now are still larger, still more costly, and still suburban.

That housing won't meet the life needs of most American families now or in the 1990s, and it won't fit the budgets or bank accounts of most of the families who want such housing anyway. Let's look at the facts. America's family sizes and savings rates are shrinking.[8] We now have more single persons living alone and more single-parent families, both about 25 percent of the population, than ever before.[9] The household size of intact families is smaller today than it was a decade ago and will be smaller still a decade hence. Median family income has been stagnant, flat for about 15 years, while median family savings rates have declined precipitously.[10] The number of frail elderly persons has risen substantially and will rise even more dramatically in the 1990s.[11] The number and percentage of poor people has risen too, concentrated mostly in central cities.[12] But house prices are higher than ever and so are downpayment requirements, mortgage interest rates, rents, and the interest rates for loans to rehabilitate units for the frail elderly or to convert larger homes for single-parent families.[13] The houses we have, and the houses we are building, don't meet the family sizes, job locations, life needs, or pocketbooks of an increasing percentage of our people.

The housing needs of all the different kinds of families that have emerged and will be emerging in the 1990s are, obviously, as diverse as the family types themselves. Undifferentiated budget-cutting hasn't helped meet any of these needs, but undifferentiated, untargeted budget restorations or block grants won't optimally meet many of these needs either.

Our proposed new housing policy for America moves to meet the specific barriers our families face in buying, renting, converting, maintaining, and improving their homes. It recognizes that many young families need downpayment assistance loans to achieve homeownership even in non-recessionary periods when mortgage interest rates are only moderately high; that an interest-rate buydown fund might be needed if interest rates or recessionary trends rise; that the future appreciation in the value of American homes can be used to help present generation of young families buy them now; that different but equally cost-effective programs will be needed to help house frail elderly persons and single-parent families; that rental unit construction subsidies *are* homelessness prevention programs, but that many hidden homeless families need emergency assistance and services, as well as affordable housing to avoid eviction into the streets.

The policies we recommend are relatively new but they are not

untried. Each of them has worked at the state level or in other countries. And they are largely self-financing.

Meeting real and diverse needs by targeting sufficient resources
to overcome the specific housing barriers families are facing, and
doing so at costs and in ways that seem to make sense—we think
that is an authentically new housing policy for America.

A Policy Responsive to National Political Imperatives

To govern is to choose, to decide which problems to emphasize and
which policies best address those problems. The need for such choice
is constant because no society can pursue all its goals, with all its
vigor, all at once. Now, as always, America faces hard choices about
where and how to allocate finite resources.

The process of making these choices requires political leaders to
assess both the needs of the nation and the electoral and institutional consequences of alternative policies. In that process, the political imperatives are constant: winning elections; winning interest
group support for policy proposals; winning congressional votes. The
new housing policy for America proposed in this book seeks to be
responsive to these imperatives.

Our 1988 presidential and congressional candidates know what
the polls are showing: American voters are deeply concerned about
at least two housing issues—the inability of young people to achieve
homeownership and the plight of the homeless.[14] The policy proposals advanced in this book deal extensively with these issues. The
proposals made are also likely to appeal to the large number of voters concerned with senior citizen issues (because of the home equity
and frail elderly housing recommendations), women's issues (because of the single-parent housing proposals), civil rights (because
of the fair housing law improvements suggested), and labor issues
(because of the job-creating character of these proposals). Tens of
thousands of Americans in churches, community-based organizations, tenant groups, and labor unions are working for better housing and waiting for a new national housing policy worth supporting.
These people vote and volunteer in campaigns. And, we think, plenty
of small business owners—not just in the shelter industries—will
support parties and candidates offering realistic economic growth
through a pro-housing platform. No policy can appeal to everyone,

of course, but we think political leaders *can* successfully take these proposals to their constituencies.

There is already emerging in Congress some strong interest and strong leadership toward developing a new housing policy for America. The Senate Housing Subcommittee Chairman has announced his intention to seek a bipartisan landmark housing bill in 1988–1989,[15] a timetable apparently also favored in the House. In consequence, scores of interest groups, think tanks, and scholars are producing such a flurry of reports, plans, symposiums, conferences, and coalitions as housing advocates have not seen in a decade.[16] Major interest groups and advocacy organizations that have not really talked with each other for years are getting together and working together. Congressional votes on major policy initiatives are often a product of external group pressure and internal readiness for change. Both of these conditions are mounting. We know already that some members of Congress, and some major interest groups, favor some parts of our plan.

THE CONSEQUENCES OF FAILING TO ACHIEVE A NEW HOUSING POLICY FOR AMERICA

If our national government is unable to adopt a new, more expansive housing policy soon, profoundly negative consequences are likely to be visited upon millions of American families, on the American economy, and on many American communities. Acceptance of lowered homeownership levels, inattention to the needs of the frail elderly, continued failure to prevent homelessness, malign neglect of both urban and rural housing requirements, cuts in needed housing construction programs for the poor, weak anti-discrimination laws weakly enforced—these characteristics of our present policy don't just hurt individuals and families. They hurt our economy; they truncate our middle class; they reduce equality of opportunity; they sap the vibrancy of our efforts to revitalize cities or restore farm communities; they create new ghettos (mostly for the aged) while reinforcing a culture of poverty in the too many older ghettos and slums. A national governmental decision to continue these policies, or a non-decision (which has the same effect), will accelerate these hurtful trends and diminish the quality of life, the moral stature, and perhaps the social peace of the nation.

Consequences of Diminished Homeownership Levels

If the millions of young families who have been priced out of the housing market in the 1980s, and the millions more who are coming of first-home-buying age in the 1990s, cannot be helped to attain homeownership, a substantial truncation of the American middle class is likely to result—a phenomenon of considerable and troublesome significance. If our government will not help, the opportunity gap between those whose parents can help and those whose parents cannot will widen dramatically—moving America toward a "patrimony society."[17] Housing equity is a major tool for, as well as a symbol of, achieving and maintaining middle-class status. A continued diminution in homeownership means diminished opportunity for families to pay the costs of college education for their kids, the costs of health care and retirement for themselves, the costs of caring for their elderly parents. Lower homeownership levels affect a downward spiral of opportunity with probable detrimental impact on our economy and societal structure. The result is unlikely to be a better-educated, healthier, more prosperous, politically stable America.

What we are saying is that, for millions of young families, a lost opportunity to attain homeownership could mean the failure to achieve or maintain middle-class status. Homeownership and the equity reserve that builds up in an appreciating home is now as important as, or even more important than, second incomes as a basic tool Americans are using to acquire and maintain middle-class status. Home equity is increasingly the only fixed financial asset most people have that rises in value as fast as the costs of major health care, college education costs, nursing home care for frail elderly parents, or retirement expenses.

Let us look closely at the financial situation confronting an "average American family" today. Median family income, in constant dollars, has been flat for a decade. In constant 1982 dollars it was $27,421 in 1975 and $27,735 in 1985.[18] With all the increase in two-wage-earner families, the median family income in America rose by only 1.5 percent over 10 years. Personal savings from 1976 to 1986 fell from 9.2 percent to 3.9 percent of disposable income.[19] In 1986, the "average" American family (with the median income and the median savings rate) was able to put in the bank the munificent sum of $940 a year.[20]

But what has happened to the costs of the things they are savng for? College costs rose 111 percent in public colleges and 161 percent in private colleges between 1975 and 1985.[21] If they only saved $940 a year for 20 years (or its inflated equivalent), that would not put one child through the average private college or two children through a public university. Health care emergencies? The daily cost of a hospital room leaped 223 percent from 1975 to 1985, up from $75.49 to $242.23.[22] A year's family savings won't buy four days in a hospital bed today. Unusual medical bills? Health care outlays per capita in the United States jumped 198 percent from 1975 to 1985, increasing from $340 to $1,013.[23] Or suppose our average American family needs to help Mom and Dad pay for nursing home care. Between 1975 and 1985, nursing home expenses skyrocketed at rates that vary from 146 percent to 248 percent, depending on the nature of care.[24] With nursing home beds now costing an average of $58 to $68 a day,[25] a year's worth of our average family's annual savings will pay for six months or less for one parent in a nursing home.

It's been happening for at least a decade: median family income is essentially stuck (around $27,635, the 10-year average)[26] and personal savings are generally declining (to a mean of 6.9 percent of disposable income),[27] while the major life expenses for which people want or need to save keep going up at double-digit rates. For the average American family, absent home equity, the savings curve tends never to cross the major expense curve. It is homespun economics, of course, but it is faithful to the facts. In the 1980s, without home equity, the average American family has been unable to save enough, and has been hard pressed to borrow enough, to meet the rising costs of major life expenses.

But let us add only one factor: home equity. The median price of a new home rose 89 percent from 1977 to 1986 (from $48,800 to $92,000);[28] the median price of existing homes escalated 87 percent (from $42,900 to $80,000).[29] Homeownership brought a return, an appreciation, of 40 percent in constant dollars, over the 1977–1986 period. Families purchasing the average American home in 1975 *would* have the financial base, the ability to accrue or borrow the money, to meet the emergency expenses all of them (all of us) are likely to face some day. Home equity has provided the cash or credit resources needed to pay for the major life choices most Americans want and expect (and often need) to make.

The impact of declining homeownership levels today percolates not only across our economy (see Chapter 1) but across the genera-

tions. The generational impact diminishes social mobility. Rober
Kuttner of the *New Republic* summarized this impact insightfully;

> One large group of young people can still readily afford their first house
> those who are helped by their parents. The people who collected a rea
> estate windfall in the 1960s and 1970s have a huge amount of wealth stashed
> in their homes today. And increasingly those people, now in their 50s and
> 60s, are using some of that unexpected wealth to help their own children to
> become homeowners. This form of socialism-in-one-family is fine for younger
> families whose parents own real estate. But the people whose parents did
> not own homes are doubly set back. They are less likely to have the cushion
> of family wealth to help overcome the high barriers to their own homeown-
> ership; and as rental costs keep rising relative to income, their parents may
> instead become dependent on them.
>
> It is true, as a gross generalization, that the generation now approach-
> ing retirement got a much better economic deal than the baby boom gener-
> ation. They bought houses cheap and cashed them in dear. They started
> out when expectations were low, and enjoyed 30 years of rising real in-
> comes. They paid far less into Social Security, compared with what they're
> getting out, than the ratio future retirees will enjoy. But since wealth trans-
> fers between generations occur mainly within families, the children of the
> economic haves are far better able to compensate for the generational rip-
> off than the children of have-nots. In this respect, the ticket of entry to a
> "starter house" has become less a matter of self-reliance, and more a matter
> of patrimony.
>
> According to the Chicago Title Insurance Company, the percentage of
> first-time homebuyers who report getting financial help from relatives jumped
> from 8.7 percent in 1978 to over 30 percent in 1979 and 1980, and has settled
> back to below 20 percent as mortgage rates have declined. But these statis-
> tics are notoriously unreliable. That question on the mortgage application
> form—"Is any part of the downpayment borrowed?"—must rank up there
> with the job application question "Have you ever seen a psychiatrist?" as
> one of the most common invitations for lying in modern life."[30]

If our political leaders cannot or will not adopt a better national
housing policy, enhancing homeownership, America's future seems
likely to have a somewhat smaller middle class composed mostly of
those whose parents have already made it, and a somewhat larger
worker class, dispossessed of the American dream and disadvantaged in their efforts to educate their children, nurture aged parents,
or meet their major life expenses.

The absence of a better housing policy, then, will probably contribute to a diminution in equality of opportunity and an increase in

social class rigidification. As shown in Chapter 1, it will also mean fewer jobs, less economic growth, and lower tax revenues than would a more proactive housing policy. Homeownership is and has been the American dream: a housing policy faithful to that dream would be good for American families, economy, and society. The continued absence of such a policy, on the other hand, will hurt America in the 1990s and beyond.

Urban Consequences of Failing to Achieve a New Housing Policy

In the 1980s, as shown in Chapter 1, there were more poor people in America, with less money, seeking fewer apartments at sharply rising rents. In the 1990s, there will be still more poor families, increasingly concentrated in central cities. A continuation of present policy (cuts in new construction and rental assistance for low-income housing coupled with no emergency homeless prevention program) and of current housing trends (most new construction in suburbs, loss of lower-income urban rental stock to gentrification and abandonment) will make the present crisis even worse. The Neighborhood Reinvestment Corporation found, in 1987, that continuation of present policy will lead to a homeless and hidden homeless population of 18 million people by 2003.[31] This is not an assessment that can make anyone sanguine about American societal peace in the 1990s or the twenty-first century or about the future of our urban areas.

Continuation of present housing policy will negatively impact both our cities and our class structure. America's older cities declined (and parts of them burned) in the 1960s, then stood poised between renaissance and further decline in the 1970s, and now are experiencing, simultaneously, large-scale commercial revitalization of some areas and rapid retrogression of other neighborhoods. Absent a new, urban-targeted housing policy, these cities may become glittering Babylons of business culture downtown but they will have far too many deteriorating and even slum conditions in the urban neighborhoods where most city residents actually live.

There is, then, some news to report about urban policy in the United States. But the news is mixed, at best. The good news is that there is an emerging debate on social policies that could improve the lives of urban people—on welfare reform, educational reform, and programs to combat illiteracy. The bad news is that this debate does not yet extend to rebuilding our urban neighborhoods. The worst news of all is that these new policies that are designed to help urban people will not work unless they are joined with a more complete urban policy that assists both city people and the cities they live in.

Learning in city schools is unlikely to improve much if the world just outside the schoolyard fence—the world urban kids come from and return to—is one of deteriorated housing, empty stores, and joblessness. Spending a little more on urban schools while cutting programs for urban housing, jobs, and economic development is not much of a strategy. Putting new dollars into job-training programs for welfare mothers will not work unless we help create better jobs and neighborhoods. And trying to help urban people while letting the cities decline is no urban policy for America.

The centrality of housing improvement, and the local economic development that improved housing constitutes, to the future of America's cities can be seen in recent research that shows that children form expectations early in life of what their future niche will be in the world. For some, expectations are broad and expansive, fed by a sense of opportunity. For other children, especially those from lower-class backgrounds, the scope of opportunity has contracted, and the pictures they hang in their heads are drear and static. All children, but especially youngsters from poor backgrounds, need visible signs of hope and improvement.

John Ogbu, a social anthropologist at the University of California, has pointed out that educational reforms misfire when they are not connected to real changes in the "opportunity structure" of minority students. Ogbu stresses that theories of child-rearing and education have failed to take into account "the most obvious and common-sense aspect of education, namely, that education is directly related to typical adult roles in the contemporary post-school world."[32] The educational process alone does not create a better future. It is the hope for a better future that creates educational motivation and skills. Minority groups, Ogbu reminds us, have reality-based "job ceilings" that define ambition and limit the desire to compete and achieve beyond a certain level. Educational reforms, in other words, will have little impact without visible changes in the economic environment and the structure of ambition.

Welfare and educational reforms are important, but they will not get the job done. In the absence of a genuine urban policy, these proposals reflect a curious inversion of the neutron bomb approach to warfare. While the neutron bomb would destroy human life but reserve property, these proposals would save urban people as the cities crumbled and died.

In truth, these reforms suggest an old and very traditional approach to urban life in America. John Adams once wrote that the real genius of America was that it "transformed people," converting immigrants into dignified and industrious citizens. The uncited model for these proposals would seem to be the immigrant saga, where foreigners settled in densely populated urban ghettoes, worked hard, and transformed their lives in successful pursuit of the American dream. They were, to borrow Mario Puzo's apt phrase, "the fortunate pilgrims," who as the reward for their mettle and commitment were able to escape the cities' squalor.

Cities have often been relegated to a dark corner of our national psyche. From Jefferson's warnings about the "scum" and corruption of the cities,[33] to the mass suburban migration in the twentieth century, the city has been the one place that most Americans were quick to leave behind. Our "solutions" to urban problems have generally been individualistic, not communitarian. Indeed, much of our suburban experience has been undercut by the chaotic individualism that spawned it, and by the urban problems that came as unwanted stowaways.

Hence, it is little surprise that the emerging agenda focuses on saving urban people, while neighborhoods and cities are being ignored. Under the Reagan Administration the proposed budget of every community development program with communitarian goals has ended in zero. Cuts in UDAG, CDBG, and HODAG have stifled many urban areas, and have slowed the momentum toward improvement in others.[34] Unfortunately, the "liberal" position has been merely fewer cuts.

The current spate of reform proposals presumes that, like the immigrants before them, urban people can move to take advantage of new jobs in an expanding economy. President Reagan has suggested, in this regard, that one solution to urban problems is the natural flow of population adapting to regional changes in the job market.[35] But labor mobility is less of a reality than in the past, and many people do not want to move.

At a time when the American family is under enormous pressure, we do not want to foster a new class of urban nomads. Too many areas of our country that have jobs now lack adequate housing for lower-income urban migrants. In addition, most of the new jobs being created are relatively low-paying positions, and are not exactly the stuff out of which major population shifts are made

Clearly, we need a new and creative urban policy, and the cen
terpiece of the urban policy must be housing and the neighborhood
economic development that derives from housing construction and
rehabilitation. We need to renew, not reduce, those federal pro
grams that have helped bring some economic growth and visibl
improvement to American cities. We have to implement a thought
ful and innovative housing agenda that can generate new homes
new jobs, and new hope in our urban areas.

A continuation of present national housing policy, on the othe
hand, will mean a continuation if not exacerbation of urban decline

Other Consequences of Failing to Achieve a New Housing Policy

Continued inattention to the housing needs of elderly people in gen
eral and the frail elderly in particular—a hallmark of current policy—
will mean an increase in home accidents and injuries, some numbe
of them fatal, and an increase in the incidence of premature, need
less institutionalization. We will pay more for health and nursin
home care and lose the company and community-enhancing partic
ipation of many senior citizens.

It is happening now. It will happen with much greater fre
quency at much greater expense in the 1990s, because there will b
so many more "old elderly" in our population in that decade an
the costs of health care and nursing home care will rise. It does no
have to be that way: it would surely be cheaper, wiser, and mor
compassionate to help senior citizens remain in the community (vi
home equity and housing rehabilitation loan programs). But the con
tinuation of present policy will have the effect of causing avoidabl
hurt to some senior citizens and of driving others from our midst.

Continued inattention to the housing needs of single-parent, fe
male-headed households, in combination with the feminization o
poverty, will consign more children to bad living environments
mostly deteriorating apartments. It doesn't have to be that way: w
could provide their mothers (the vast majority of them working) wit
long-term deferred-payback loans to purchase larger homes an
convert or rehabilitate them to several smaller units, the rental in
come from which would facilitate loan repayment; we could encour
age homesharing and housing with child care. But continuation o
current policy will have the effect of causing or tolerating avoidabl

urt to a generation of children in an America where 60 percent of
ie kids born today can expect to live in a one-parent family before
iey reach 18.

Continued inattention to the housing needs of rural America, to
ie weakness of our fair housing laws and the weakness of their
nforcement, continued inattention to the stagnation and decline in
ie physical condition of our housing stock and to the need for pub-
c housing construction—all these will have the same effect, causing
r tolerating avoidable harm to millions of American families. It does
ot have to be that way. We could instead adopt a new housing
olicy for America.

CALL TO ACTION

i the end, any book about public policy is about the future, about
ternative futures. So it is with this book, which seeks to encourage
id to chart a better housing future for the American people.

Bringing such a future into being, in a representative democ-
cy, is a responsibility and opportunity widely shared. But the
merican people require no new political primer to achieve it, for
ery peaceful democratic political process can and ought to be bent
the task. We know well enough how to create and evaluate can-
dacies and coalitions, how to vote and to write letters and make
ione calls and visit leaders, and how to hold those leaders ac-
untable. We can do, here and now, personally and together, all
at it would take to make a better housing future, if only that is
hat we decide to do.

To decide to influence our destiny in that way, it might be well
remind ourselves, in the words of John Schaar, that "the future
not a result of choices among alternative paths offered by the
esent, but a place that is created—created first in mind and will,
eated next in activity.

"The future is not some place we are going to, but one we are
eating. The paths are not found, but made, and the activity of
aking them changes both the makers and the destination."[36]

We think this activity, creating a better housing future for Amer-
i, a fit task for our readers and ourselves, a great and worthy pur-
ise to which we and our nation are called, an achievable dream.

Appendix: Selected National Housing Organizations

American Association of Retired Persons
1909 K Street, NW
Washington, D.C. 20044

National Coalition for the Homeless
1620 I Street, NW
Washington, D.C. 20005

National Housing Conference
1126 16th Street, NW
Washington, D.C. 20036

National Housing Institute
439 Main Street
Orange, N.J. 07050

National Housing Law Project
1950 Addison Street
Berkeley, Calif. 94704

National Low Income Housing Coalition
1012 14th Street, NW
Washington, D.C. 20005

Planners Network
1901 Q Street, NW
Washington, D.C. 20036

COMMUNITY DEVELOPMENT CORPORATIONS

Center for Community Change
1000 Wisconsin Avenue
Washington, D.C. 20007

Community Information Exchange
1120 G Street, NW, Suite 900
Washington, D.C. 20005

Development Training Institute
2315 Hollins Street
Baltimore, Md. 21223

Enterprise Foundation
505 American City Building
Columbia, Md. 21044

Institute for Community Economics
151 Montaque City Road
Greenfield, Mass. 01301

Local Initiatives Support Corporation
666 Third Avenue
New York, N.Y. 10017

Neighborhood Reinvestment Corporation
1850 K Street, NW, Suite 400
Washington, D.C. 20036

Pickman and Associates
11 DuPont Circle, NW, Suite 700
Washington, D.C. 20036

Pratt Institute for Community Development
379 DeKalb Avenue
Brooklyn, N.Y. 11205

COMMUNITY REINVESTMENT

Center for Community Change
1000 Wisconsin Avenue
Washington, D.C. 20007

National Training and Information Center
954 West Washington Boulevard
Chicago, Ill. 60607

DISCRIMINATION

National Committee Against Discrimination in Housing
733 15th Street, NW, Suite 1026
Washington, D.C. 20005

National Housing Law Project
1950 Addison Street
Berkeley, Calif. 94704

ELDERLY HOUSING

American Association of Homes for the Aging
1129 20th Street, NW, Suite 400
Washington, D.C. 20036

American Association of Retired Persons
1909 K Street, NW
Washington, D.C. 20044

EQUITY LOAN FUNDS

Enterprise Foundation
505 American City Building
Columbia, Md. 21044

Institute for Community Economics
151 Montaque City Road
Greenfield, Mass. 01301

Local Initiatives Support Corporation
666 Third Avenue
New York, N.Y. 10017

McAuley Institute
1320 Fenwick Lane, Suite 600
Silver Spring, Md. 20006

National Corporation for Housing Partnerships
1225 Eye Street, NW
Washington, D.C. 20005

National Reinvestment Corporation
1850 K Street, NW, Suite 400
Washington, D.C. 20036

National Trust for Historic Preservation
1785 Massachusetts Avenue, NW
Washington, D.C. 20036

HOME OWNERSHIP

Council of State Housing Agencies
444 North Capitol Street, NW, Suite 118
Washington, D.C. 20001

Mortgage Bankers Association of America
1125 Fifteenth Street, NW
Washington, D.C. 20005

National Association of Home Builders
15th and M Streets, NW
Washington, D.C. 20005

National Association of Realtors
777 14th Street, NW
Washington, D.C. 20005

Neighborhood Reinvestment Corporation
1850 K Street, NW, Suite 400
Washington, D.C. 20036

HOMELESSNESS

American Institute of Architects
735 New York Avenue, NW
Washington, D.C. 20006

National Coalition for the Homeless
1620 I Street, NW
Washington, D.C. 20005

HOUSING TRUST FUNDS

David Paul Rosen and Associates
1 Taurus Avenue
Oakland, Calif. 94611

Housing Trust Fund Project
10 Shepard Street
San Pedro, Calif. 90731

LABOR AND HOUSING

AFL-CIO Housing Investment Fund
15 Fifteenth Street, NW, Suite 736
Washington, D.C. 20005

LAND TRUSTS

Institute for Community Economics
1 Montaque City Road
Greenfield, Mass. 01301

LEGISLATION

Council of State Community Affairs Agencies
4 North Capitol Street, NW, Suite 251
Washington, D.C. 20001

Council of State Housing Agencies
4 North Capitol Street, NW, Suite 118
Washington, D.C. 20001

Housing and Development Reporter
2300 M Street, NW, Suite 100
Washington, D.C. 20037

National Association of Housing and Redevelopment Officials
1320 18th Street
Washington, D.C. 20036

National Center for Policy Alternatives
2000 Florida Avenue, NW
Washington, D.C. 20009

National Housing Conference
1126 16th Street, NW
Washington, D.C. 20036

LOW-INCOME TAX CREDITS

Council of State Housing Agencies
444 North Capitol Street, NW, Suite 118
Washington, D.C. 20001

National Low Income Housing Coalition
1012 14th Street, NW
Washington, D.C. 20005

MUTUAL HOUSING

National Association of Housing Cooperatives
2501 M Street, NW, Suite 451
Washington, D.C. 20037

National Mutual Housing Network
1012 14th Street, NW, Suite 1006
Washington, D.C. 20005

Neighborhood Reinvestment Corporation
1850 K Street, NW, Suite 400
Washington, D.C. 20036

JBLIC HOUSING

ɔuncil of Large Public Housing Authorities
9 C Street, NE
ashington, D.C. 20002

ıtional Association of Housing and Redevelopment Officials
20 18th Street
ashington, D.C. 20036

ıtional Low Income Housing Coalition
12 14th Street, NW
ashington, D.C. 20005

lesis Corporation
25 Thomas Jefferson Place
ashington, D.C. 20037

LIGIOUS ORGANIZATIONS AND HOUSING

bitat for Humanity
bitat and Church Streets
ɪericus, Ga. 31709

Auley Institute
:0 Fenwick Lane, Suite 600
ver Spring, Md. 20006

RAL HOUSING

ɪusing Assistance Council
,5 Vermont Avenue, Suite 606
shington, D.C. 20005

tional Rural Housing Coalition
1 S Street, NW, Suite 500
shington, D.C. 20009

IANTS

:ional Housing Institute
Main Street
ɪnge, N.J. 07050

URBAN HOMESTEADING

Association of Community Organizations for Reform Now
401 Howard Avenue
New Orleans, La. 70130

Urban Homesteading Assistance Board
1047 Amsterdam Avenue
New York, N.Y. 10025

WOMEN AND HOUSING

Housing Opportunities for Women
1400 I Street, NW, Suite 520
Washington, D.C. 20005

National Congress of Neighborhood Women
249 Manhattan Avenue
Brooklyn, N.Y. 11211

Women's Institute for Housing and Economic Development
179 South Street
Boston, Mass. 02110

ZONING

National Association of Home Builders
15th and M Streets, NW
Washington, D.C. 20005

National Housing Law Project
1950 Addison Street
Berkeley, Calif. 94704

Pratt Institute for Community Development
379 DeKalb Avenue
Brooklyn, N.Y. 11205

Notes

1. James Brown and John Yinger, *Home Ownership and Housing Affordability in the United States, 1963–1985* (Cambridge, Mass.: Joint Center for Housing Studies of MIT and Harvard, 1986), p. 6 ff; National Council of State Housing Agencies (NCSHA), *Delivering the American Dream* (Washington, D.C.: The Council, 1987), pp. 12–13; Raymond L. Flynn, *A Housing Agenda for America* (Des Moines: National League of Cities, 1987), p. 3. See also National Association of Home Builders (NAHB), *Low- and Moderate-Income Housing: Progress, Problems, and Prospects* (Washington, D.C.: The Association, 1986), p. 23 ff; National Governors' Association (NGA), *Decent and Affordable Housing for All* (Washington, D.C.: The Association, 1986), pp. 3–4; William C. Apgar, Jr., "The Declining Supply of Low Cost Rental Housing," testimony presented to the U.S. Senate Subcommittee on Housing and Urban Affairs, Washington, D.C., June 5, 1987, pp. 5–8.

2. National Coalition for the Homeless, *Homelessness in America* (Washington, D.C.: The Coalition, 1986), p. 2 ff; Nora Richter Greer, *The Search for Shelter* (Washington, D.C.: American Institute of Architects, 1986), p. 11 ff; Jon Erickson and Charles Wilhelm, eds., *Housing the Homeless* (New Brunswick, N.J.: Center for Urban Policy Research of Rutgers, 1986), pp. 127–164.

3. Iredia Irby, "Attaining the Housing Goal?" unpublished paper, Division of Housing and Demographic Analysis, Office of Economic Affairs, U.S. Department of Housing and Urban Development, Washington, D.C., July 1986, table 2-1.

4. [Nancy Andrews], *The Challenge of Affordable Housing: A Perspective for the 1980s* (New York: Ford Foundation, 1986), pp. 3–14; Richard W. Peach,

An Assessment of the Housing Situation (Washington, D.C.: Mortgage Banke
Association of America, 1987); William C. Apgar, Jr., *The Housing Haves ar*
the Housing Have-Nots: The Growing Disparity (Washington, D.C.: RAM D
gest, 1985), p. 10; Margery Austin Turner, *Housing Needs to the Year 20*
(Washington, D.C.: National Association of Housing and Redevelopmer
Officials, 1986); National Low Income Housing Information Service, "Rent.
Housing Crisis Deepens for Low Income Renters," news release, Washing
ton, D.C., March 3, 1986, pp. 1–5. See also NGA, *Decent and Affordable Hou.*
ing, p. 5, and Apgar, "Declining Supply," pp. 9–20.

　　5. Peach, *Assessment of the Housing Situation*, pp. 3–4.

　　6. NGA, *Decent and Affordable Housing*, p. i; [Andrews], *Challenge (*
Affordable Housing," pp. 23–24 and 26–27; NAHB, *Low- and Moderate-Incom*
Housing, pp. 41–43; NCHSA, *Delivering the American Dream*, pp. 19–20; au
thors' analysis of federal budgetary actions, 1981–1987.

　　7. See, for example, Turner, *Housing Needs*, pp. 12–17; Marjorie Tiver
and Barbara Ryther, *State Initiatives in Elderly Housing: What's New, What'*
Tried and True (Washington, D.C.: Council of State Housing Agencies and
National Association of State Units on Aging, 1986); Sandra Newman and
Raymond J. Struyk, *Housing and Supportive Services: Federal Policy for the Frar*
Elderly and Chronically Mentally Ill (Cambridge, Mass.: MIT Press, 1987, esp
pp. 4 and 6.

　　8. Turner, *Housing Needs*. See also Eugenie Ladner Birch, ed., *The Un*
sheltered Woman (New Brunswick, N.J.: Center for Urban Policy Research o*
Rutgers, 1985), p. 30 ff.

　　9. Turner, *Housing Needs*. See also U.S. Department of Commerce, Bureau of the *Current Population Reports: Estimates of the Population of the Unitea*
States by Age, Sex, and Race (Washington, D.C.: The Bureau), ser. P-25, vol.
917, 952, and 1000.

　　10. Turner, *Housing Needs*, and [Andrews], *Challenge of Affordable Hous-*
ing, p. 14.

　　11. William C. Apgar, Jr., "Remarks," speech given to the Council of
State Community Affairs Agencies, Housing Conference, Washington, D.C.,
May 3, 1987; Brown and Yinger, *Home Ownership*, p. 9; National Association
of Home Builders (NAHB), *Policy Statement* (Washington, D.C.: The Association, 1981); Conference Board, *Housing* (New York: The Board, 1982), economic road maps, nos. 1918–1919, p. 1.

　　12. "The Nation's Housing: An Affordability Crisis," *New York Times*,
March 16, 1986, p. E-5.

　　13. James R. Healey and David Landis, "Housing Hitch: Big Down
Payments," *USA Today*, April 20, 1987, p. E-1; material on interest rates
supplied to the authors by the Mortgage Bankers Association of America
and the U.S. Veterans Administration, July 1987.

　　14. Information supplied to the authors by the National Association of
Home Builders, July 1987.

15. Apgar, "Declining Supply" and Apgar, *The Housing Haves and Have-*ots.

16. Authors' analyses of federal budgetary actions, 1981–1987.

17. Hanes W. Christian et al., *Home Ownership: Celebrating the American* *ream*, prepared by Economics Department, U.S. League of Savings Asso-ations (Chicago: The Department, 1984), p. 146.

18. Cited in National Association of Home Builders (NAHB), National ssociation of Realtors, and Mortgage Bankers Association of America, *Toward* *National Housing Policy* (Washington, D.C.: The Associations, 1987), p. 3.

19. Brown and Yinger, *Home Ownership*, p. 6 ff. See also Central Jersey uilders Association, *CJBA News* (Plainsboro, N.J.), September 1987, p. 16

20. Brown and Yinger, *Home Ownership*, pp. 1–5.

21. Letter from Tom Marder, Mortgage Bankers Association of Amer-a, to the authors, July 7, 1987.

22. Healey and Landis, "Housing Hitch," p. E-1.

23. See Susan Garland and John Reilly, "Home Ownership: The Amer-an Dream Fading Out of Reach" and "Soaring Prices Cut Many People ut of Housing Market," *Newark Star Ledger,* February 22 and 23, 1987. See so David C. Schwartz, "Toward a New Housing Policy for America," key-ote address to the American Affordable Housing Conference, Rutgers Uni-ersity, New Brunswick, N.J., November 14–15, 1986.

24. U.S. Department of Commerce, Bureau of the Census, *Number and* *edian Income (in 1985 Dollars) of Families and Persons: Selected Years, 1960–* *85* (Washington, D.C.: The Bureau, 1986).

25. Central Jersey Builders Association, *CJBA News,* September 1987, p. ff.

26. Cited in Democratic Policy Commission, *New Choices in a Changing* *merica* (Washington, D.C.: Democratic National Committee, 1986, p. 10, d Schwartz, "Toward a New Housing Policy."

27. Cited in Schwartz, "Toward a New Housing Policy"; also in "Na-n's Housing," *New York Times.*

28. Brown and Yinger, *Home Ownership.*

29. Information supplied to the authors by the National Association of ome Builders, July 1987.

30. Brown and Yinger, *Home Ownership.*

31. NAHB, *Low- and Moderate-Income Housing,* p. 23 ff.

32. Ibid.

33. Ibid.

34. Ibid.

35. Christopher Boyd, "Housing Gap Widens Between Haves, Have-ots," *Home News* (New Brunswick, N.J.), February 8, 1987, p. RE-13.

36. Apgar, "Remarks."

37. See, for example, Garland and Reilly, "Home Ownership."

38. This study was facilitated by the Mortgage Bankers Association of America. A description of survey methods (e.g. sampling, item wording) is available from the authors.

39. Brown and Yinger, *Home Ownership*, pp. 7–9.

40. Ibid., pp. 10–30.

41. Ibid. See also Apgar, "Declining Supply"; Apgar, *Housing Haves an Have Nots*; [Andrews], *Challenge of Affordable Housing*; Apgar, "Remarks," p. 4.

42. Sandra Oliveth Martin, "Housing, 1987," *Planning*, January 1987 p. 16. Information on this subject suggesting these levels of probably ren increases was made available to the authors by the National Apartment As sociation, July 1987.

43. Actually conditions in rental housing, on a multiplicity of moder indicators of physical inadequacy, declined between 1974 and 1983. This i discussed in greater detail later in Chapter 1.

44. [Andrews], *Challenge of Affordable Housing*, p. 11.

45. Brown and Yinger, *Home Ownership*, pp. 30 and 12.

46. On this point, see Apgar, "Remarks," p. 4; Apgar, "Declining Sup ply," p. 18 ff, p. 19 to a Joint Center Research Update, March 28, 1987 [Andrews], *Challenge of Affordable Housing*, p. 11, provides useful data or this subject as well.

47. U.S. Department of Housing and Urban Development (HUD), *An nual Surveys* (Washington, D.C.: The Department, selected years.

48. See Brown and Yinger, *Home Ownership*, p. 26; NGA, *Decent an Affordable Housing*, p. 5; Apgar, "Declining Supply," p. 3 ff; Apgar, "Re marks," p. 4.

49. See [Andrews], *Challenge of Affordable Housing*; Irby, "Attaining th Housing Goal?" p. 2; Peach, *Assessment of the Housing Situation*, pp. 2–4.

50. Brown and Yinger, *Home Ownership*, p. 27 ff.

51. See [Andrews], *Challenge of Affordable Housing*, NGA, *Decent and Af fordable Housing*, p. 5; Apgar, "Declining Supply," p. 9 ff.

52. Apgar, "Declining Supply" and "Remarks."

53. NGA, *Decent and Affordable Housing*, p. 5.

54. NAHB, *Low- and Moderate-Income Housing*, p. 15 ff.

55. Information provided to the authors, July 1987.

56. "Nation's Housing," *New York Times*, p. 5.

57. William C. Apgar, Jr., *Recent Trends in Housing Quality and Afforda bility: A Reassessment* (Cambridge, Mass.: Joint Center for Housing Studie of MIT and Harvard University, 1985), p. 5.

58. Proprietary survey made available to the authors, July 1987.

59. Apgar, "Remarks," p. 4.

60. Discussions of single-room-occupancy units (SROs), and their im portance in preventing homelessness can be found in Greer, *Search for She ter*, p. 37 ff, and in Erickson and Wilhelm, eds., *Housing the Homeless*, pp 190–252.

61. See [Andrews], *Challenge of Affordable Housing*, p. 10; Irby, "Attaining the Housing Goal?" p. 11 ff; Peach, *Assessment of the Housing Situation*, p. 9–16.

62. [Andrews], *Challenge of Affordable Housing*, p. 5.

63. National Low Income Housing News Service, "Rental Housing Crisis Deepens," pp. 1–5.

64. Report available from the League. For 1987 data, see National League of Cities, *A Time to Build Up: A Survey of Cities About Housing Policy* (Washington, D.C.: The League, 1987).

65. Report available from the U.S. Conference of Mayors.

66. Discussed in Turner, *Housing Needs*, p. 14 ff and bibliography.

67. Phillip L. Clay, *At Risk of Loss: The Endangered Future of Low-Income Rental Housing Resources* (Washington, D.C.: Neighborhood Reinvestment Corporation, [1987]).

68. Department of Housing and Urban Development (HUD), Office of Policy Development and Research, *A Report to the Secretary on the Homeless and Emergency Shelters* (Washington, D.C.: The Department, 1984).

69. S. Anna Kondratas, "A Strategy for Helping America's Homeless," in Erickson and Wilhelm, eds., *Housing the Homeless*, pp. 144–149; National Coalition for the Homeless, *Homelessness in America*, p. 2.

70. Ibid., p. 149.

71. Survey methodology available on request.

72. Cited in National Coalition for the Homeless, *Homelessness in America*, p. 3.

73. Report available from the U.S. Conference of Mayors.

74. Partnership for the Homeless, *National Growth in Homelessness, Winter 1987* (New York: The Partnership, 1987).

75. National League of Cities, *Time to Build Up*, p. 111.

76. Mario Cuomo, *1933–1983—Never Again: A Report to the National Governor's Association Task Force on the Homeless* (Washington, D.C.: National Governors Association, 1983).

77. See, for example, House Committee on Government Operations, *The Federal Response to the Homeless Crisis*, H.R. Report no. 99-47, 99th Congress, 1st sess., 1985.

78. Cited in National Coalition for the Homeless, *Homelessness in America*, p. 3.

79. Report available from the U.S. Conference of Mayors.

80. Partnership for the Homeless, *National Growth in Homelessness*, p. 6.

81. Cited in National Coalition for the Homeless, *Homelessness in America*, p. 6.

82. Report available from the U.S. Conference of Mayors.

83. Partnership for the Homeless, *National Growth in Homelessness*, esp. p. 30.

84. Mitch Snyder, Community for Creative Non-Violence, statement to the National Conference of State Legislatures, Indianapolis, July 1987.

85. National Coalition for the Homeless, *Homelessness in America.*

86. Cited in ibid.

87. Ibid.

88. Partnership for the Homeless, *National Growth in Homelessness,* pp 9 and 15.

89. "Nation's Housing," *New York Times,* p. 5.

90. Cited in National Coalition for the Homeless, *Homelessness in America,* p. 6.

91. Cited in Greer, *Search for Shelter,* p. 14.

92. Report available from U.S. Conference of Mayors.

93. NAHB, *Policy Statement* (1981), p. 1 ff.

94. See HUD, *Annual Housing Surveys,* selected years. See also Irby, "Attaining the Housing Goal?" and Peach, *Assessment of the Housing Situation.*

95. President's Commission on Housing, *Report* (Washington, D.C.: U.S. Government Printing Office, 1982); General Accounting Office, *Rental Housing: Potential Reduction in the Privately Owned and Federally Assisted Inventory,* Resources, Community and Economic Development Series 26113 (Washington, D.C.: GAO, June 1986), p. 28.

96. Brown and Yinger, *Home Ownership,* esp. pp. 6–7.

97. U.S. Census Bureau, *Number and Median Income of Families and Persons.*

98. U.S. Department of Commerce, Bureau of Economic Analysis, *Disposition of Personal Income, 1929–1968* (Washington, D.C.: The Department, 1987).

99. Turner, *Housing Needs,* p. 12 ff; Tiven and Ryther, *State Initiatives,* p. ix; Newman and Struyk, *Housing and Support Services,* passim and bibliography.

100. Turner, *Housing Needs,* p. 15.

101. See Raymond J. Struyk and Harold M. Katsura, *Aging at Home* (Washington, D.C.: Urban Institute, 1985); Newman and Struyk, *Housing and Support Services;* David C. Schwartz, "Housing America's Elderly: A State-Level Policy Perspective," *Policy Studies Journal* 13, no. 1 (September 1984); Tiven and Ryther, *State Initiatives.*

102. Tiven and Ryther, *State Initiatives,* pp. ix, 1–2, and 41.

103. See, for example, H.R.-4, "The Housing and Community Development Act of 1987," sec. 317.

104. Schwartz, "Housing America's Elderly," p. 161 and passim. See also Tiven and Ryther, *State Initiatives.*

105. For an excellent discussion of this issue, see Rachel G. Bratt, "Housing for Low Income People: A Preliminary Comparison of Existing and Potential Supply Strategies," *Journal of Urban Affairs* 7, no. 3 (Summer): 1 ff.

106. Information provided to the authors by the American Apartment Association and the National Association of Home Builders, both July 1987.

107. Grace Milgram and Robert Bury, *Existing Housing Resources vs. Need,* ongressional Research Service Report no. 87-81E (Washington, D.C.: CRS, brary of Congress, 1987), p. 4 ff.

108. Ibid., p. 10 ff.

109. Ibid., p. 17 ff.

110. Birch, *Unsheltered Women.* See Turner, *Housing Needs,* p. 12 ff; Peach, *ssessment of the Housing Situation,* p. 14 ff and HUD, *Annual Housing Surys,* selected years.

111. Ibid.

112. [Andrews], *Challenge of Affordable Housing;* Turner, *Housing Needs.*

113. James W. Hughes and George Sternlieb, *The Dynamics of America's ousing* (New Brunswick, N.J.: Center for Urban Policy Research of Rutgers, ₁87).

114. Robert Ball, "Employment Created by Construction Expendi-res," *Monthly Labor Review,* December 1981, pp. 38–44.

115. See discussion of this subject in Chapter 3 below.

116. Material made available to the authors by the National Association Home Builders, July 1987.

117. See, for example, Edwin S. Mills, "Dividing Up the Investment e: Have We Overinvested in Housing?" in Federal Reserve Bank of Phil-delphia, *Business Review,* March/April 1987, pp. 13–23.

118. Ibid., pp. 20 ff.

119. NGA, *Decent and Affordable Housing,* p. i; [Andrews], *Challenge of fordable Housing,* pp. 23–24 and 26–27; NAHB, *Low- and Moderate-Income ousing,* pp. 41–43; NCHSA *Delivering the American Dream,* pp. 19–209; au-ors' analysis of federal budgetary actions, 1981–1987; U.S. Census Bureau, umber and Median Income of Families and Persons.

120. Deborah C. Eisenstadt and Peter Ciroux, "Benefits of Low Income ousing," *Taxation for Accountants* 30 (January 1987): 22.

121. Information provided to the authors by the American Apartment ssociation and the National Association of Home Builders, July 1987.

122. Teresa Riordan, "Housekeeping at HUD," *Common Cause,* March/ pril 1987, pp. 30–31.

123. James W. Brown, remarks delivered to the National Housing Con-rence, Washington, D.C., March 1987.

124. Proprietary surveys made available to the authors, July 1987.

125. Joseph Guggenheim, Robert Maffin, and others, remarks deliv-ed to the Housing Taskforce, National Conference of State Legislators, 'ashington, D.C., February 1987.

126. For two different analyses on two different versions of the sale of ublic housing, see Howard Bray, "The FHA: Selling Off a Dream," *Across e Board* (New York: Conference Board, June 1986), pp. 8–14, and Peter reier, "Public Housing for Sale," *New Republic,* August 4, 1986, pp. 1–3.

127. Dreier, "Public Housing for Sale," pp. 1–3.

128. Summary of a study by Abt Associates of Massachusetts in re-

marks by Robert Maffin of the National Association of Housing and Redevelopment Officials to the Housing Taskforce of the National Association of State Legislatures, February 1987.

129. The discussion of vouchers in this section is drawn largely from the following sources: U.S. Department of Housing and Urban Development (HUD), *The President's National Urban Policy Report* (Washington, D.C.: HUD, 1986), pp. 25–27; E. Jay Howenstine, *Housing Vouchers: A Comparative International Analysis* (New Brunswick, N.J.: Center for Urban Policy Research of Rutgers, 1986); "Freedom of Choice," *Time Magazine*, February 1987, p. 23; U.S. Department of Housing and Urban Development (HUD), *The HUD Region II Newsletter* (New York), June 1987.

130. The discussion of the President's proposed 1988 budget derives largely from the authors' analysis of the basic budget documents submitted. See also Housing Assistance Council, Inc. (HAC), *Abandonment: An Analysis of the Administration's Proposed Fiscal 1988 FmHA, HUD, and Indian Housing Budgets* (Washington, D.C.: The Council, 1987); Mortgage Bankers Association of America, *MBA Media Fact Sheet*, January 7 and April 29, 1987 (available from the Association); "Industry Sees Dim Future for Young Home Buyers," *Courier News* (Bridgewater, N.J.), January 8, 1987, p. A-11.

CHAPTER 2

1. Drawn from the authors' secondary analysis of the following sources: Council of State Community Affairs Agencies (COSCAA), *State Housing Initiatives: A Compendium* (Washington, D.C.: The Council, 1986); Council of State Community Affairs Agencies (COSCAA), *The States and Housing: Responding to the Challenge* (Washington, D.C.: The Council, 1987); Council of State Housing Agencies (CHSA), *Housing Initiatives of State Housing Finance Agencies* (Washington, D.C.: The Council, 1987); Council of State Housing Agencies (CHSA), *Production Activities of State Housing Finance Agencies: 1985 and Cumulative* (Washington, D.C.: The Council, 1986); National Association of Home Builders (NAHB), *Low- and Moderate-Income Housing: Progress, Problems and Prospects* (Washington, D.C.: The Association, 1986), pp. 77–94. See also Michael A. Stegman and J. David Holden, "States, Localities Respond to Federal Housing Cutbacks," *Journal of State Government* (May/June 1987): 110–116; Mary K. Nenno, "States Respond to Changing Housing Needs," *Journal of State Government* 60, no. 3 (May/June 1987): 122–127; Randy Welch, "Responding to the Housing Crisis," *State Legislatures* 13, no. 10 (November 1987): 20–25; David C. Schwartz, "Demanding a National Housing Policy," *State Legislatures* 13, no. 10 (November 1987): 34.

2. This is, undoubtedly, an underestimate of the number of new state programs adopted in the 1980s. It is based largely on the authors' secondary analysis of COSCAA, *State Housing Initiatives*; CHSA, *Housing Initiatives*; Marjorie Tiven and Barbara Ryther, *State Initiatives in Elderly Housing: What*

ew, What's Tried and True (Washington, D.C.: Council of State Housing gencies and National Association of State Units on Aging, 1986).

3. Ibid. See especially COSCAA, *State Housing Initiatives*, pp. 1–9, and OSCAA, *States and Housing*, vols. 2 and 4.

4. Authors' secondary analysis of COSCAA, *State Housing Initiatives*; OSCAA, *States and Housing*; CHSA, *Housing Initiatives*; CSHA, *Production ctivities*; NAHB, *Low- and Moderate-Income Housing*; Stegman and Holden, 3tates, Localities"; Nenno, "States Respond"; Welch, "Responding to the ousing Crisis"; and Schwartz, "Demanding a National Housing Policy."

5. See especially COSCAA, *State Housing Initiatives*, esp. pp. 1–9, and OSCAA, *States and Housing*. Some partnerships were identified through ie authors' secondary analysis of COSCAA, *State Housing Initiatives*; OSCAA, *States and Housing*; CHSA, *Housing Initiatives*; CSHA, *Production ctivities*; NAHB, *Low- and Moderate-Income Housing*; Stegman and Holden, 3tates, Localities"; Nenno, "States Respond"; Welch, "Responding to the ousing Crisis"; and Schwartz, "Demanding a National Housing Policy."

6. Ibid.

7. Ibid.

8. Ibid.

9. Authors' secondary analysis of COSCAA, *State Housing Initiatives*; HSA, *Housing Initiatives*; CHSA, *Production Activities*; and Tiven and Ry-ier, *State Initiatives*.

10. State of Connecticut, Department of Housing, *Housing Programs* Iartford: State of Connecticut, 1986), p. 14.

11. New Jersey Housing and Mortgage Finance Agency (NJHMFA), nnual Report (Trenton: The Agency, 1986).

12. CHSA, *Housing Initiatives*, p. 12.

13. Ibid., p. 16. See also NAHB, *Low- and Moderate-Income Housing*, p. 94.

14. Descriptive and interpretive material made available to the authors y California State Senate Housing Staff, July 1987. See also "California Uses hared Appreciation Loans to Assist New Homebuyers," Federal Home Loan Iortgage Corporation, *Community Finance Forum* (Washington, D.C.), July)87.

15. Authors' secondary analysis of COSCAA, *State Housing Initiatives*; HSA, *Housing Initiatives*; CHSA, *Production Activities*; and Tiven and Ry-ier, *State Initiatives*.

16. Ibid.

17. COSCAA, *State Housing Initiatives*.

18. See, for example, CHSA, *Housing Initiatives*, p. 77.

19. Authors' secondary analysis of COSCAA, *State Housing Initiatives*; HSA, *Housing Initiatives*; CHSA, *Production Activities*; and Tiven and Ry-ier, *State Initiatives*.

20. Ibid.

CHAPTER 3

1. Council of State Community Affairs Agencies (COSCAA), *State Housing Initiatives: A Compendium* (Washington, D.C.: The Council, 1986).
2. Ibid.
3. Interview with Thomas Gleason, Director, Massachusetts Housing Finance Agency, Home Ownership Opportunity Program, Boston, August 28, 1987.
4. Letter from Tom Marder, Mortgage Bankers Association of America, Washington, D.C., to the authors, July 7, 1987.
5. Letter from Anthony E. Pizzutillo, New Jersey Builders Association, Woodbridge, N.J., to the authors, September 9, 1984.
6. Daniel J. O'Connell, "What Is a Point Really Worth?" *Mortgage Banker* no. 6 (March 1981): 31–34.
7. U.S. Department of Commerce, Bureau of Economic Analysis, *Disposition of Personal Income, 1929–1986* (Washington, D.C.: The Department, 1987).
8. U.S. Department of Commerce, Bureau of the Census, *Number and Median Income (in 1985 dollars) of Families and Persons, and Poverty Status, by Race: Selected Years, 1960–1985* (Washington, D.C.: The Bureau, 1986).
9. Letter from John Lee, New Jersey Office of Legislative Services, to Assemblyman David C. Schwartz, Trenton, N.J., June 15, 1987.
10. State of Connecticut, Department of Housing, "Downpayment Assistance Program," unpublished memorandum, Hartford, May 1987.
11. Home Share Equity, Inc., *Equity Participation* (Hampton, N.J.: Home Share Equity, 1986).
12. Albert Graf, Counselor, German Federal Republic, Washington, D.C. January 29, 1987.
13. Conference Board, *Corporate Response to Employees' Housing Needs* (New York: The Board. 1975).
14. Thomas J. Lucek, "As Housing Costs Mount, New York Companies Move Away," *New York Times*, March 3, 1987, p. B-1.
15. Hagen Marketing Research, Inc., A Study of Employee Relocation Policies Among Major U.S. Corporations. (White Plains, N.Y.: Merrill Lynch Relocation Management, 1986).
16. Bradford W. O'Hearn, "Housing Taxes Companies," *New York Newsday*, February 21, 1987.
17. Ibid.
18. Martin Douglas, "Accounting Firm Plans to Leave Manhattan," *New York Times*, June 19, 1987, p. B-1.
19. Interview with Rosalyn Hoffman, Placement Interviewer, New Jersey State Employment Service, New Jersey Department of Labor, New Brunswick, N.J., August 18, 1987.
20. Regina B. Armstrong, *Analysis of Regional Projections* (New York: Regional Plan Association, 1985).

21. Robert Lindsey, "Executives Blame California Housing Costs for Dip in Migration," *New York Times*, December 31, 1981, p. A-8.

22. Ibid.

23. Myron DuBain, *Corporate Housing Action Guide* (San Francisco: Bay Area Council, 1983).

24. Letter from Dan Hauser, California State Assemblyman, Sacramento, Calif., to Assemblyman David C. Schwartz, May 15, 1987.

25. Linda Gorou, "Boston's a Nice Place to Work In . . . but Who Can Afford to Move Here?" *Boston Globe*, March 18, 1986, p. 25.

26. Ibid.

27. "Boston Hospitals Lure Doctors with Housing," *New York Times*, September 5, 1987, p. 27.

28. Ibid.

29. Citizens Housing and Planning Association, Inc., *Tenancy and Costs in Public Housing: Policies, Attitudes, and Case Studies* (Boston: The Association, 1986).

30. Council of Large Public Housing Authorities (CLPHA), *Public Housing Today* (Boston: The Council, 1986).

31. U.S. Department of Housing and Urban Development, *Participation and Benefits in the Urban Section 8 Program* (Washington, D.C.: The Department, January 1981).

32. Phillip L. Clay, *At Risk of Loss: The Endangered Future of Low-Income Rental Housing Resources* (Washington, D.C.: Neighborhood Reinvestment Corporation, [1987]).

33. Ibid.

34. CLPHA, *Public Housing Today*.

35. Ibid.

36. Clay, *At Risk of Loss.*

37. CLPHA, *Public Housing Today*.

38. Housing Assistance Council, Inc. (HAC), *Abandonment: An Analysis of the Administration's Proposed Fiscal 1988 FmHA, HUD, and Indian Housing Budgets* (Washington, D.C.: The Council, 1987).

39. Interview with Steve Hornburg, Analyst for Housing and Transportation, U.S. Senate Budget Committee, Washington, D.C., November 10, 1987.

40. CLPHA, *Public Housing Today*.

41. John Simon, remarks at the American Affordable Housing Conference, Workshop on Public Housing, Rutgers University, New Brunswick, N.J., November 14–15, 1986.

42. CLPHA, *Public Housing Today*.

43. Interview with John Simon, Chairman, National Housing Conference, New York, April 8, 1987.

44. CLPHA, *Public Housing Today*.

45. The Council of State Housing Agencies (CSHA), *Production Activities of State Housing Finance Agencies 1985 and Cumulative* (Washington, D.C.: The Council, 1987).

46. State of Massachusetts, *EOCD Resource Guide* (Boston: Executive Office of Community Development, 1987).

47. Council of State Community Affairs Agencies (COSCAA), *The States and Housing: Responding to the Challenge—Building State Housing Capacity* (Washington, D.C.: The Council, 1987).

48. Massachusetts, *EOCD Resource Guide*.

49. Council of State Community Affairs Agencies (COSCAA), *The States and Housing: Responding to the Challenge—Meeting Special Housing Needs* (Washington, D.C.: The Council, 1987).

50. COSCAA, *State Housing Initiatives*.

51. Ibid.

52. American Homestead Mortgage Corporation, *The IRMA Program* (St. Laurel, N.J.: 1986).

53. U.S. Department of Housing and Urban Development, *Programs of HUD, 1985/1986* (Washington, D.C.: The Department, April 1986).

54. General Accounting Office, *Analysis of Options for Aiding the Home-building and Forest Products Industries,* GAO/CED-82-121 (Washington, D.C.: The Office, 1982).

55. U.S. Department of Labor, *Employment and Earnings,* March 1977.

56. N. R. Kleinfield, "The Ripple Effects of Housing," *Mortgage Banking* 43, no. 13 (September 1983): 10–21.

57. Hornburg interview.

58. Ibid.

59. Ibid.

60. Thus, to develop 70,000 units of low-income housing annually (30,000 202 units for the elderly and 40,000 public housing units) will require new federal capital outlays of $4 billion per year. In addition, each renting family will require some rent subsidy support. This will entail an additional annual expenditure of approximately $250 million dollars for each 70,000 units constructed. This is the price of properly sheltering those who have no place else to turn for decent, safe, and affordable housing. This is an expenditure that this nation, whose annual HUD budget has declined by more than $20 billion dollars since 1981, should be willing to support.

61. Academy for State and Local Government, *Tax Exempts and Tax Reform: Assessing the Consequences for the Tax Reform Act of 1986* (Washington, D.C.: The Academy, 1987).

62. CSHA, *Production Activities.*

63. Ibid.

64. Joseph Guggenheim, *Tax Credits for Low Income Housing* (Washington, D.C.: Simon Publications, 1986).

CHAPTER 4

1. David Paul Rosen, "Public Capital: Investing in America's Public Trust," draft by David Paul Rosen and Associates, 451 Taurus Avenue, Oakland, Calif., 1986, p. 38.

2. Ibid., p. 144.

3. "Revenue Sources for Housing Trust Funds," *News from the Housing Trust Fund Project* (San Pedro, Calif.), October 1986, p. 5.

4. James Pickman et al., *Producing Lower Income Housing: Local Initiatives* (Washington, D.C.: Bureau of National Affairs, 1986), p. 234.

5. "Technical Notes," *News from the Housing Trust Fund Project*, p. 7.

6. Rosen, "Public Capital," p. 71.

7. "Technical Notes," *News from the Housing Trust Fund Project*, p. 2.

8. Interview with Rick Cohen, Executive Director, Jersey City Redevelopment Agency, Jersey City, N.J., July 1987.

9. Philip Tegeler, "Developer Payments and Down Town Trust Funds," *Clearinghouse Review* 18, pt. 2 (November 1984): 679–696.

10. *Burlington County NAACP v. Township of Mount Laurel* (Mount Laurel II), 92 NJ 456, A2d 390 (1983).

11. Ibid.

12. New Jersey, *Revised Statutes*, Fair Housing Act of 1985, P.L. 1975, L. 291; L. 1985, L. 222.

13. J. Albert Mastro, "Mount Laurel II and Municipal Home Rule," *New Jersey Municipalities*, May 1984, p. 7.

14. U.S. Department of Housing and Urban Development, Office of Policy Development and Research, *Allowing Accessory Apartments* (Washington, D.C.: The Department, October 1983), p. 5.

15. California Department of Housing and Community Development, Division of Housing Policy Development, *Second Units* (Sacramento, Calif.: The Department, March 1987).

16. Urban Housing Partnerships, "Opportunities and Challenges for CLTs," *Community Economics*, Fall 1986.

17. Rachel Bratt, "Community-Based Housing: Potential for a New Strategy," unpublished paper, 1985, p. 22.

18. Development Training Institute, Proceedings of the Urban Partnership Conference, Baltimore, December 1987.

19. City of Boston, *Breaking Ground: A Report on Boston Hearing Policy and Performance* (Boston: The City, April 1987), p. 16.

20. David Kirkpatrick, Mary Ann Dillon, and Susan Block, "Local Trends in Nonprofit Housing Production," *Economic Development and Law Center Report*, Winter 1986, p. 14.

21. Ibid.

22. Local Initiatives Support Corporation (LISC), *Annual Report* (New York: The Corporation, 1985).

23. Pickman et al., *Producing Lower Income Housing,* p. 74.

24. Enterprise Foundation, *Annual Report* (Columbia, Md.: The Foundation, 1986).

25. Bratt, "Housing for Low Income People."

26. Center for Community Change, "National Citizen's Project Monitoring Community Development" (Washington, D.C.: The Center, 1980–1985).

27. Ibid.

28. James Cook, "Priming the Urban Pump," *Forbes,* March 23, 1987, pp. 62–63.

29. Neighborhood Reinvestment Corporation, *Annual Report* (Washington, D.C.: The Corporation, 1985).

30. Ibid.

CHAPTER 5

1. Sandra Newman and James Reschovsky, "Federal Policy and the Mobility of Older Home Owners," *Journal of Policy Analysis* 6 (Spring 1987): 403–405.

2. Marjorie Tiven and Barbara Ryther, *State Initiatives in Elderly Housing: What's New, What's Tried and True* (Washington, D.C.: Council of State Housing Agencies and National Association of State Units on Aging, 1986), p. ix.

3. Newman and Reschovsky, "Federal Policy."

4. David C. Schwartz, opening remarks at the conference "Toward a New Housing Policy for America," Rutgers University, New Brunswick, N.J., November 11–12, 1986.

5. See Judith Ann Hancock, ed., *Housing the Elderly* (New Brunswick, N.J.: Rutgers University Press, 1987), pp. xiv–xxii.

6. Cited by James Burke, President, American Homestead Mortgage Corporation, at the conference Toward a New Housing Policy for America, Rutgers University, New Brunswick, N.J., November 11–12, 1986.

7. Newman and Reschovsky, "Federal Policy," p. 404. See also Edward Steinfeld, "The Place of Old Age: The Meaning of Housing for Older People," in James Duncan, ed., *Housing and Identity* (Holmes and Meier, 1982).

8. Robert Kuttner, "The Patrimony Society," *New Republic,* May 11, 1987, pp. 18–21.

9. Raymond J. Struyk, "Housing-Related Needs of Elderly Americans and Possible Federal Responses," *Journal of Housing for the Elderly,* Winter 1984/1985, p. 8.

10. Newman and Reschovsky, "Federal Policy," p. 405.

11. David C. Schwartz, "Housing America's Elderly: A State-Level Policy Perspective," *Policy Studies Journal* 13, no. 1 (September 1984): 157.

12. Ibid.

13. Tiven and Ryther, *State Initiatives*, p. 19.

14. Ibid., pp. 19–20.

15. Ibid., p. 19.

16. See Schwartz, "Housing America's Elderly," p. 162; Tiven and Ryther, *State Initiatives*, p. 22. See also J. Kevin Eckert and Mary Ittman Murrey, "Alternative Housing Modes," in Hancock, ed., *Housing the Elderly*, pp. 57–80.

17. Tiven and Ryther, *State Initiatives*, pp. 24–26.

18. Ibid., pp. 4–6; Schwartz, "Housing America's Elderly," p. 168; Hancock, ed., *Housing the Elderly*, pp. 125 and 231.

19. See the essays by Vincent J. Trichilo and Michael Hoeflich in Hancock, ed., *Housing the Elderly*, pp. 121–134; also Tiven and Ryther, *State Initiatives*, pp. 1–4.

20. Schwartz, "Housing America's Elderly."

21. Tiven and Ryther, *State Initiatives*, pp. 7–8.

22. Linda Daily, "Housing Options for the Elderly," in Hancock, ed., *Housing the Elderly*, p. 234.

23. Tiven and Ryther, *State Initiatives*, pp. 9–11. On accessory apartments, see Martin Gellen, *Accessory Apartments and Single Family Housing* (New Brunswick, N.J.: Rutgers University Press, 1985).

24. Tiven and Ryther, *State Initiatives*, pp. 27–34.

CHAPTER 6

1. Jon Erickson and Charles Wilhelm, eds., *Housing the Homeless* (New Brunswick, N.J.: Center for Urban Policy Research for Rutgers, 1986), pp. xxii and xxiii.

2. National Coalition for the Homeless, *Homelessness in America* (Washington, D.C.: The Coalition, 1986), p. 3; U.S. Conference of Mayors, *Status Report: Emergency Food, Shelter, and Energy Programs in Twenty Cities* (Washington, D.C.: The Conference, 1987), pp. 1–2; Partnership for the Homeless, *National Growth in Homelessness, Winter 1987* (New York: The Partnership, 1987), p. 6.

3. Cited in National Coalition for the Homeless, *Homelessness in America*, p. 9.

4. Materials supplied to the authors by the National Center for Policy Alternatives, November 1987.

5. Ellen L. Bassuk, "The Homelessness Problem," in Erickson and Wilhelm, eds., *Housing the Homeless*, p. 255.

6. Richard P. Nathan et al., *The Consequences of Cuts: The Effects of the Reagan Domestic Program on State and Local Governments* (Princeton, N.J.: Princeton Urban and Regional Research Center, 1983).

7. But see Donna Wilson Kirchheimer, "Social Programs for Homeless Families: Subnational Expansion Despite Federal Retrenchment," paper de-

livered to the annual meetings of the American Political Science Association, Chicago, 1987.

8. Erickson and Wilhelm, eds., *Housing the Homeless*, p. xv.

9. Nora Richter Greer, *The Search for Shelter* (Washington, D.C.: American Institute of Architects, 1986). See also Bassuk, "Homelessness Problem," and Philip Kasinitz, "Gentrification and Homelessness: The Single Room Occupant and the Inner City Revival," in Erickson and Wilhelm, eds., *Housing the Homeless*, pp. 241–252.

10. See National Coalition for the Homeless, *Homelessness in America*, pp. 5–6; Partnership for the Homeless, *National Growth in Homelessness*, esp. p. 9.

11. National Coalition for the Homeless, *Homelessness in America*, pp. 7 ff; Partnership for the Homeless, *National Growth in Homelessness*, esp. p. 7.

12. H. Richard Lamb, "Deinstitutionalization and the Homeless Mentally Ill," in Erickson and Wilhelm, eds., *Housing the Homeless*, pp. 262–278. See also Greer, *Search for Shelter*, and National Coalition for the Homeless, *Homelessness in America*, pp. 8–9.

13. Ibid.

14. Ibid.

15. Ibid.

16. Peter H. Ross et al., "The Urban Homeless: Estimating the Composition and Size," *Science* 235 (March 13, 1987): 1336.

17. National Coalition for the Homeless, *Homelessness in America*, p. 6; Partnership for the Homeless, *National Growth in Homelessness*, esp. p. 30.

18. Ibid. See also Greer, *Search for Shelter*.

19. Mario Cuomo, *1933/1983—Never Again: A Report to the National Governors Association Task Force on the Homeless* (Washington, D.C.: National Governors Association, 1983).

20. Greer, *Search for Shelter*, p. 14.

21. Ibid.

22. For a discussion of the political consequences of this change, see Julie Kosterlitz, "They're Everywhere," *National Journal*, February 28, 1987, pp. 492 ff.

23. New Jersey Department of Community Affairs, Homelessness Prevention Program, *Preventing Homelessness in New Jersey: Fact Sheet, Fiscal Year 1987* (Trenton: New Jersey Department of Community Affairs, 1987), and interviews with program staff.

24. Information in this section is taken from telephone interviews with and letters from staff of the Pennsylvania Housing Finance Agency, July 1987, and from letters and printouts provided by the Homelessness Project of the Community Information Exchange, Washington, D.C., July 1987.

25. Information in this section was provided by the Maryland Department of Housing and Community Development, July 1987.

26. ACTION-Housing, *Addressing the Problems of the Homeless in Pitts-*

urgh and Allegheny County: A Comprehensive Plan (Pittsburgh: Action Hous-
ng, June 1985), pp. 20–22.

27. Information provided by the Homelessness Project, Community In-
ormation Exchange, Washington, D.C., July 1987.

28. Ibid.

29. National Coalition for the Homeless, *Homelessness in America.*

30. Greer, *Search for Shelter,* pp. 42–46.

31. Ibid., passim.

32. Ibid.

CHAPTER 7

1. *Toward a New Housing Policy for America,* conference proceedings of
ne American Affordable Housing Conference, Workshop on Women and
Housing, Rutgers University, New Brunswick, N.J., November 14–15, 1986.

2. Eugenie Ladner Birch, ed., *The Unsheltered Woman: Woman and Housing
t the Eighties* (New Brunswick, N.J.: Center for Urban Policy Research of
utgers, 1985), p. 34.

3. Eugenie Ladner Birch, speech delivered to the American Affordable
Housing Conference, Workshop on Women and Housing, Rutgers Univer-
ty, New Brunswick, N.J., November 14–15, 1986.

4. Birch, ed., *Unsheltered Woman,* p. 41.

5. New Jersey Department of Community Affairs, *Housing the Single-
arent Family: A Resource and Action Handbook* (Trenton: The Department,
March 1987), p. 3.

6. Birch, ed., *Unsheltered Woman,* p. 40.

7. Ibid., p. 32.

8. National Low Income Housing Coalition, *Triple Jeopardy: A Report
t Low Income Women and Their Housing Problems* (Washington, D.C.: The
oalition, 1981.

9. Sandra J. Newman and Ann B. Schnare, "Housing: The Gap in the
Welfare System," *Journal of State Government* 60, no. 3 (May/June 1987): 118.

10. R. W. Maruns et al., *Measuring Restrictive Rental Practices Affecting
amilies with Children: A National Survey* (Washington, D.C.: U.S. Depart-
ent of Housing and Urban Development, 1980), p. 27.

11. Jill Nelson, "No Kids or Dogs Allowed," *City Limits,* April 1985, p.
2.

12. Emily Alman, speech delivered to the American Affordable Hous-
g Conference, Workshop on Women and Housing, Rutgers University,
ew Brunswick, N.J., November 14–15, 1986.

13. Jacqueline Leavitt, "Shelter Plus Issue for Single Parents," *Women
d Environments* 6 (November/April 1984): 16.

14. Birch, ed., *Unsheltered Woman,* p. 34.

15. Ibid.

16. U.S. Department of Housing and Urban Development, *Report o* *Homeless Shelters* (Washington, D.C.: The Department, May 1984).

17. Marjorie Hope and James Soung, *The Faces of Homelessness* (Lexing ton, Mass.: Lexington Books, 1986).

18. Women's Institute for Housing and Economic Development, Inc. *A Manual on Transitional Housing* (Boston: The Institute, June 1986).

19. Ibid., p. 34.

20. Interview with Jackie Glock, Director, Jersey City YWCA, Augus 1987.

21. Memo on California Bill SB-1527, California Senate Housing an Urban Affairs Committee, Sacramento.

22. Women's Institute for Housing and Economic Development, *Man ual on Transitional Housing.*

23. Leavitt, "Shelter Plus," p. 16.

24. Troy West, speech delivered to the American Affordable Housin Conference, Workshop on Women and Housing, Rutgers University, Ne Brunswick, N.J., November 14–15, 1986.

CHAPTER 8

1. Gale Cincotta, testimony presented to the U.S. House of Represen tatives Housing and Development Subcommittee on Banking, Finance, an Urban Affairs, Washington, D.C., March 12, 1985.

2. Center for Community Change, *The Community Reinvestment Act: Citizen's Action Guide* (Washington, D.C.: The Center, March 1981).

3. Ibid.

4. Calvin Bradford, *A Tool for Community Capital: Home Mortgage Di closure Act* (Minneapolis: Hubert H. Humphrey Institute).

5. *ACORN Newsletter*, Summer 1986, p. 1.

6. Marc A. Weiss, "The Role of Community-Based Organizations an Finance Institutions in Negotiated Development," paper presented at th Lincoln Institute of Land Policy, Cambridge, Mass., 1986.

7. Clare Ansberry, "Banks with Interstate Ambitions Are Challenge by Law Requiring Commitment to Local Level," *Wall Street Journal*, June 2 1986, p. 64.

8. ACORN Legislative Report, March 11, 1987, ACORN National Le islative Office, Washington, D.C.

9. *ACORN Newsletter*, Summer 1986, p. 1.

10. James Pickman et al., *Producing Lower Income Housing: Local Initi tives* (Washington, D.C.: Bureau of National Affairs, 1986), p. 356.

11. Rachel Bratt, "Community Based Housing Programs: Overview A sessment and Agenda for the Future," *Journal of Planning, Education, an Research* 5, no. 3 (Spring 1986): 165.

12. Conference proceedings of the Conference on Housing and Lo

ncome Community Development, Workshop on Tenant Management, Washington, D.C., December 9–11, 1986.

13. Bratt, "Community Based Housing Programs."

14. *Economic Justice for All: Catholic Social Teaching and the U.S. Economy,* bishops' letter on the economy, 1986.

15. *Toward a New Housing Policy for America,* conference proceedings of the American Affordable Housing Conference, Workshop on Housing and Religious Institutions, Rutgers University, New Brunswick, N.J., November 14–15, 1986.

16. Community Information Exchange, data base, Washington, D.C.

17. New York State Catholic Conference, "Housing," *Legislative Agenda, 1987* (Albany, The Conference, 1987).

18. Habitat for Humanity, *Annual Report, 1986* (Americus, Ga.: Habitat, 1986).

19. Community Information Exchange, data base.

20. McAuley Institute, *1986 Annual Report* (Silver Spring, Md.: The Institute, 1986).

21. Community Information Exchange, data base.

22. Sherrie Hannan, "Boston Unions Build Affordable Housing," in Chicago Rehab Network, *Network Builder Newsletter* 14 (August/September 1987): 1.

23. Community Information Exchange, data base.

24. AFL-CIO Housing Investment Trust, *Third Quarter Report, 1987* (Washington, D.C.: The Trust, 1987).

25. AFL-CIO Industrial Union Department, *Labor and Investments* 3, no. 9 (November 1983): 1.

26. Ibid.

27. "New York AFL-CIO Backs In-Statae Investment Plans," in AFL-CIO Industrial Union Department, *Labor and Investments* 5, no. 4 (May 1985): 1.

28. Rick Watson, "Investing Pension Funds in Home Mortgages: The Connecticut Experience," in Council of State Governments, *Innovations.*

29. Community Information Exchange, Data Base.

30. Neighborhood Reinvestment.

31. Ibid.

32. Mutual Housing Association of Baltimore, "Alameda Place," *Annual Report* (Baltimore: The Association, June 23, 1987).

CHAPTER 9

1. Urban and Rural Poverty Committee, "The Challenge of Affordable Housing: A Perspective for the 80's," discussion papers, June 1986.

2. Housing Assistance Council, Inc. (HAC), *Taking Stock: Rural People and Poverty from 1970–1983* (Washington, D.C.: The Council, 1984).

3. Housing Assistance Council, Inc. (HAC), *Rural Housing and Poverty Monitor* (Washington, D.C.: The Council, 1987).

4. Iredia Irby, "Attaining the Housing Goal?" unpublished paper, Division of Housing and Demographic Analysis, Office of Economic Affairs, U.S. Department of Housing and Urban Development, Washington, D.C., July 1986.

5. HAC, *Rural Housing and Poverty Monitor.*

6. Ibid.

7. Ibid.

8. Ibid.

9. Housing Assistance Council, Inc. (HAC), *Abandonment: An Analysis of the Administration's Proposed Fiscal 1988 FmHA, HUD, and Indian Housing Budgets* (Washington, D.C.: The Council, 1987).

10. Ibid.

11. Housing Assistance Council (HAC), *The FmHA Housing Program in Year 1986: Rural Housing Opportunities at Risk* (Washington, D.C.: The Council, 1987).

12. HAC, *Abandonment.*

13. HAC, *FmHA Housing Program in Year 1986.*

14. Susan Peck, *Statement of the California Coalition for Rural Housing Project Before the [California State] Senate Subcommittee on Housing and Urban Affairs* (Sacramento, Calif.: Housing Assistance Council, June 5, 1987).

CHAPTER 10

1. Some would date federal involvement in housing policy to the Homestead Acts of the last century. See David C. Schwartz, "Toward a New Housing Policy for America," keynote address to the American Affordable Housing Conference, Rutgers University, New Brunswick, N.J., November 14–15, 1986.

2. See, especially, H. James Brown and John Yinger, *Home Ownership and Housing Affordability in the United States, 1963–1985* (Cambridge, Mass.: Joint Center for Housing Studies of MIT and Harvard, 1986), pp. 6 ff. See also National Council of State Housing Agencies (NCSHA), *Delivering the American Dream* (Washington, D.C.: The Council, 1987); Raymond L. Flynn, *A Housing Agenda for America* (Des Moines: National League of Cities, 1987); National Association of Home Builders (NAHB), *Low- and Moderate-Income Housing: Progress, Problems, and Prospects* (Washington, D.C.: The Association, 1986); National Governors' Association (NGA), *Decent and Affordable Housing for All* (Washington, D.C.: The Association, 1986); William C. Apgar, Jr., "The Declining Supply of Low Cost Rental Housing," testimony presented to the U.S. Senate Subcommittee on Housing and Urban Affairs, Washington, D.C., June 5, 1987.

3. See, especially, National Coalition for the Homeless, *Homelessness*

n America (Washington, D.C.: The Coalition, 1986), p. 2 ff. See also Nora Richter Greer, *The Search for Shelter* (Washington, D.C.: American Institute of Architects, 1986), and Jon Erickson and Charles Wilhelm, eds., *Housing the Homeless* (New Brunswick, N.J.: Center for Urban Policy Research at Rutgers, 1986).

4. Iredia Irby, "Attaining the Housing Goal?" unpublished paper, Division of Housing and Demographic Analysis, Office of Economic Affairs, U.S. Department of Housing and Urban Development, Washington, D.C., 1986, table 2-1.

5. See, especially, Richard W. Peach, *An Assessment of the Housing Situation* (Washington, D.C.: Mortgage Bankers Association of America, 1987), esp. pp. 3–4.

6. National Low Income Housing Information Service, "Rental Housing Crisis Deepens for Low Income Renters," news release, Washington, D.C., March 3, 1986, pp. 1–5.

7. Margery Austin Turner, *Housing Needs to the Year 2000* (Washington, D.C.: National Association of Housing and Redevelopment Officials, 1986), esp. p. 12.

8. Conference Board, *Housing* (New York: Conference Board, 1982), Economic Road Maps nos. 1918–1919, p. 1.

9. Turner, *Housing Needs,* esp. p. 12.

10. U.S. Department of Commerce Bureau of the Census, *Number and Median Income (in 1985 Dollars) of Families and Persons: Selected Years, 1960–1985* (Washington, D.C.: The Bureau, 1986). See also U.S. Department of Commerce, Bureau of Economic Analysis, *Disposition of Personal Income, 1929–1986* (Washington, D.C.: The Department, 1987).

11. Turner, *Housing Needs,* p. 12.

12. Ibid.; [Nancy Andrews], *The Challenge of Affordable Housing: A Perspective for the 1980s* (New York: Ford Foundation, 1986), p. 14.

13. Brown and Yinger, *Home Ownership,* pp. 1–5; letter from Tom Marder, Mortgage Bankers Association of America, to the authors, July 7, 1987; James R. Healey and David Landis, "Housing Hitch: Big Down Payments," *USA Today,* April 20, 1987, p. E-1.

14. Proprietary polling data made available to the authors by various national organizations and political campaigns, July–November 1987.

15. U.S. Senator Alan Cranston, remarks to the National Housing Conference, Washington, D.C., March 1987.

16. Given the informal character of many of these meetings, and the lack of time series data on conference and symposia, it is not possible to document this assertion in strict, qualitative terms. Virtually all contemporary housing advocates, however, know this to be true.

17. Robert Kuttner, "The Patrimony Society," *New Republic,* May 11, 1987, pp. 18–21.

18. U.S. Census Bureau, *Number and Median Income of Families and Persons.*

19. Turner, *Housing Needs,* esp. p. 12.

20. Derived by applying the data in Brown and Yinger, *Home Owner ship,* p. 6 ff, to that in Turner, *Housing Needs,* p. 12.

21. W. Vance Grant and Thomas D. Snyder, *Digest of Education Statis tics, 1985–1986* (Washington, D.C.: U.S. Government Printing Office, 1986) See also Jean Evangelawf, "College Charges to Students Rising 6 Percen This Fall," *Chronicle of Higher Education,* August 6, 1987, pp. 23–30.

22. Health Insurance Association of America, *Annual Room Surve* (Washington, D.C.: The Association, 1987).

23. Helen Lazenby, Katharine R. Levit, and Daniel R. Waldo, "Na tional Health Expenditures, 1985," in U.S. Department of Health and Hu man Services, *Health Care Financing Notes,* no. 6 (September 1986).

24. National Center for Health Statistics, "Nursing Home Characteris tics," in U.S. Department of Health and Human Services, *NCHS Advanced Data,* no. 131 (March 27, 1987). See also no. 135 (May 14, 1987) and compare to National Center for Health Statistics, "Utilization Patterns and Financial Characteristics of Nursing Homes in the United States: 1977 National Nurs ing Home Survey," in U.S. Department of Health and Human Services, *NCHS Advanced Data,* ser. 13, no. 53 (1981).

25. Ibid.

26. Turner, *Housing Needs,* esp. p. 12.

27. U.S. Census Bureau, *Number and Median Income of Families and Per sons.*

28. Information provided the authors by the National Association of Home Builders, July 1987.

29. Ibid.

30. Kuttner, "Patrimony Society."

31. Phillip L. Clay, *At Risk of Loss: The Endangered Future of Low-Income Rental Housing Resources* (Washington, D.C.: Neighborhood Reinvestment Corporation, [1987]).

32. John Ogbu, *Minority Education and Caste* (New York: Academic Press, 1978).

33. John P. Foley, ed., *The Jeffersonian Cyclopedia* (New York and Lon don: Funk & Wagnalls, 1900), vol. 1, pp. 143, 209.

34. Harold Wolman, "The Reagan Urban Policy and Its Impacts," *Ur ban Affairs Quarterly* 21 (March 1986): 311–335.

35. P. Gavigan, "Motels Used in Shortage of Migrant Housing," *Journal of Environmental Health* 48 (November 3, 1985): 143.

36. John Schaar, as quoted in *Peace: The Alternative,* pamphlet published by Sidney Philip Gilbert, 1985.

About the Authors

David C. Schwartz is Professor of Political Science at Rutgers University; a member of the New Jersey General Assembly; Chairman of the Board, National Housing Institute; Member of the Board, National Housing Conference; and Vice-Chair, National Conference of State Legislature's Housing Task Force. His writings on housing issues have been most recently published in the *Journal of Housing*, the *New York Times*, and the *Christian Science Monitor*. He is the author of landmark housing legislation in New Jersey and model legislation on homelessness prevention. Schwartz's work on housing and human resource policies has resulted in awards from the U.S. Department of Labor, the National Association of Social Workers, and the New Jersey Council on Urban Economic Development.

Richard C. Ferlauto is a community organizer and legislative analyst, concentrating on housing and community economic development issues. A graduate of Georgetown University, Ferlauto has been staff and consultant to numerous community-based organizations across the nation, has served in leadership positions in several states for Citizen Action (a national issue-oriented grassroots political organization), and now works as staff to the New Jersey State Assembly. He is co-author of forthcoming articles in the *Journal of Housing* and of a forthcoming book on urban housing partnerships.

Daniel N. Hoffman is presently a consultant on housing and urban economic development with The Atlantic Group in New Jersey. A

323

graduate of Rutgers University and the Humphrey Institute of Pub
lic Affairs at the University of Minnesota, Hoffman has drafted ma
jor housing legislation in New Jersey and has developed housing
programs for the Sioux Indian Tribes of Minnesota and for the City
of Plainfield, New Jersey. Hoffman is also co-author of several forth
coming articles and books on housing issues.

Index